The Loire

THE LOIRE

Vivian Rowe

Robert B. Luce, Inc.
Washington — New York

Contents

Illustrations

ENDPAPERS

The château du Moulin near Lassay-sur-Croisne, in the very heart of the Sologne, is a happy combination of brick and stone, with moats of running water fed by the river Croisne

---

LINE DRAWINGS IN TEXT

drawn by F. P. Boudignon

MAPS

Drawn by W. H. Bromage

All black and white photographs are by courtesy of the Commissariat Général au Tourisme, as are the line drawings, the colour photograph on the dust jacket and its smaller reproduction in the book. The remainder of the colour photographs are by the author.

Foreword

The ideal travel book should meet four basic requirements:

it should be the result of the author's irresistible urge to write it;
it should reflect the author's considerable personal knowledge of the area it describes;
it should, less visibly, demonstrate the author's search for meticulous accuracy, his appreciation of the arts in general, his basic grasp of architecture, his good knowledge of the language of the country, its history and its literature, and his ability to guide his readers in a practical way to the places and buildings he describes;
it should bear the evidence of well-considered selection.

With this in mind, is it not presumptuous for any author to write a travel book? 'Yes.' Has not the reader a right to know why the author thinks himself competent to write one? 'Yes.' I could not claim to have written an 'ideal' book but in what follows I explain my presumption and my belief that it should at least be a well-informed one.

My travel writing began in the years between the wars with the *Continental Daily Mail* in Paris, for which I wrote numerous articles on France. Useful knowledge thus gained has been added to ever since, both during the twelve years I spent in France, and in repeated visits since the war. After my return from service, work for the French Government Tourist Office in London added to and brought up to date my knowledge of France.

Each month with that Office I wrote *The Traveller in France,* which was then a modest miscellany of travel facts and general articles. I reviewed, under a pseudonym, travel books for a London magazine. Also during that period, and after, I wrote travel books myself. Of these, by far the most difficult to write was *Châteaux of the Loire,*

(1954) mainly from the great excess of material. It brought me more pleasurable correspondence from readers in Europe and America than all the rest of my books put together, and I grieved when it went finally out of print in 1964.

It was also a relief, for it had dated. It covered only from Saumur to Sully, ignoring Anjou, the Sologne and the upper reaches of the river. *Son et lumière* had still been in its relative infancy. The single map was of little practical use.

Above all, I was already itching to write a successor to the astonishing work of G. Touchard-Lafosse who, in the 1850s covered the whole 600 miles of the Loire on foot, on horseback and by diligence. This tough Napoleonic soldier, who must have been in his 60s at the time, painstaking, indefatigable, deserves more than the bare mention of his name by Louis Barron thirty years later, whose own book so clearly owes so much to his predecessor. Neither bring much help to today's traveller.

More recent books have concentrated less on the river and its tributaries than on a few well documented, well restored, now famous châteaux. They were not so in earlier times. As comparatively recently as 1882, Henry James (*A little tour in France*) quoted of Amboise that 'it was dirty, very, very dirty, but very curious'.

Tens of thousands now visit the great châteaux where dozens did in those days, whilst less important ones are still seldom visited. I have tried to restore a balance and to do justice also to those smaller châteaux some of which are inferior to only a few of the famous ones in architecture and historical interest.

Experience as a reviewer emphasized the need to undertake one's own historical research and the value of good maps. In *The Loire* the maps are intended as guides to a particular district, giving a rough idea only of the situation of any particular building. I have assumed that every motorist in France is likely to have the Michelin motoring map (1:200,000, approx. three and one sixth miles per inch) of the area. By the use of map references in the index and a grid method explained in the introduction to it, the most difficult places to find can be quickly and accurately located on the Michelin map.

The book covers the Loire from mouth to source in considerable detail, but is still only a selection. The reader will have opportunity enough to make his own discoveries. It does not claim to be a complete guide. It is, on the contrary, one person's most carefully considered choice. I can hope it will interest everybody; I cannot hope that it will satisfy all.

Bon voyage!

The assistance of many people was sought in the preparation of this book and was, in every case, most willingly and usefully given. It would be invidious to place in any but alphabetical order the names of those to whom I am most particularly obliged:

Monsieur Georges Anderla, of the Commissariat Général au Tourisme, Paris

Monsieur André Bizouillier, of the Préfecture at Angers

Mr John East, of the French Government Tourist Office in London

Monsieur Michel Guérin, of the Office de Tourisme at La Baule

Monsieur Daniel Guillon-Verne, of Nantes

Monsieur S. Heurtaux of the Direction de l'Equipement, Electricité de France

Monsieur Paul-Jacques Levêque, of the Préfecture at Tours

Monsieur Michel Nottale, of Le Havre

and

Mr Robert Wilson, without whom a large part of these journeys could not have been made so pleasurably and so efficiently

My thanks are due also to Miss Ethel Mannin, through whose book *The Country of the Sea* I first learned of Robert Browning's connection with Le Croisic.

Introduction

Extent of the river – Contrast between upper and lower parts – Woods and forests – Tributaries, and tributaries of tributaries – Navigation – Towns – History – The coming of the Renaissance – Wines – Food – The Climate – Son et Lumière – Les fantômes des châteaux.

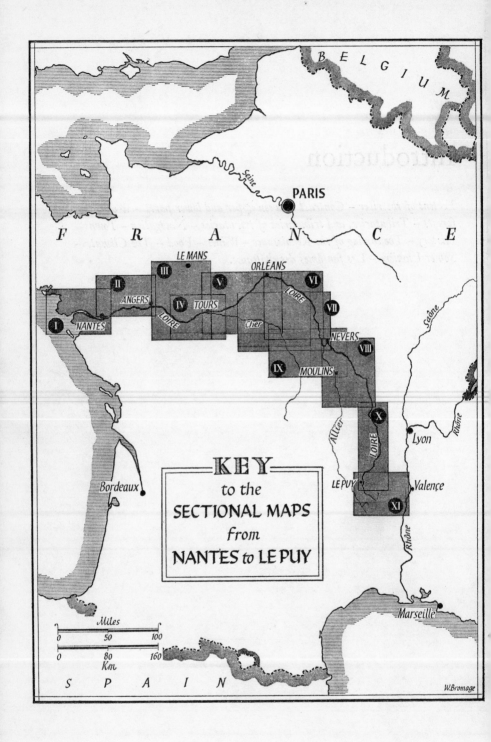

KEY
to the
SECTIONAL MAPS
from
NANTES to LE PUY

Miles
0   50   100

0   80   160
Km

W. Bromage

Introduction

The river Loire is the fourth longest in Western Europe and the longest in France. There is no one figure universally accepted for its total length. Just from my own books of reference I was faced with five different measurements from five different authorities, the lowest of which was 610 miles and the highest 1020 kilometres, 634 miles. A mean figure between the two, 622 miles must be as near the truth as anyone would need.

It rises in the little-known Vivarais mountains, west of the river Rhône, at a point about 30 miles from Valence. It is almost 100 miles from this point to another where the sands of La Camargue are lapped by the Mediterranean. A straight line from source to estuary, itself just 100 miles south of Dinard and marking the southern edge of the Breton peninsula, would cover no more than 360 miles in a north-westerly direction. The other 260 miles of its length are accounted for by the great bends of the lower part and the shallower windings of the upper.

The two halves seem almost to be different rivers. The upper part, which starts off with every apparent intention of reaching the Mediterranean, is turned by the base of a mountain (*Suc-de-Bauzan*) and from a south-flowing direction changes to a north-western one. It finds its twisting way through featureless mountains, said to include the coldest slopes in France, to within a few miles of Le Puy-en-Velay, the one place of supreme interest on the upper part of the river. Then it goes north-east, close to Saint-Etienne, and there begins the long succession of the narrow Gorges of the Loire. These are not dramatic as the Gorges du Tarn are, and are unlikely to produce in anyone the feeling of claustrophobia induced by the tall rock cliffs through which a steel grey tarn has cut its narrow cleft, dark and sunless. After the gorges, the Loire flows northwards to Digoin, losing speed now with every mile, and then north-west as far as the vineyards of Sancerre. Here begins the vast, slow bend which stretches as far as Blois, but long before getting there, Nevers marks the separation between the upper part, the fast mountain river, and the lower part, the broad and lazy waterway, now too shallow over much of its length to take more than a canoe.

Along the stretch between Nevers, which in style belongs to Auvergne, and Orléans, which is characteristic of what most people think of as The Loire Valley, the river itself is typical of neither the upper nor the lower reaches. The mountains are not far away and cold winds blow off them, but the river is broader and slower, and the land more fertile already. Then, at Orléans, the lower river begins. The light blue sky, dotted with small, white and fleecy clouds, begins to be an almost constant feature. The clouds are like the white sails of small yachts, engaged in a perpetual regatta between sunrise and sunset.

The upper part of the river has some kind of beauty of its own; an alien beauty of unfrequented high pastures, green in winter and spring, often burnt up in the high summer. It begins as rills joining together, and swells quickly. It turns and runs through and by little lakes. The mountains themselves are unimposing, without the towers and pinnacles of the Alpine *aiguilles*; little enough distinguishes one from the other. The villages are unimposing, grey stone houses turning an almost blind face upon the world – an unfriendly and suspicious face. It is a poor country this, perhaps the poorest in France, and those who dwell in it have little enough to make them cheerful.

Between the bleak pastures are many miles of river valley which by comparison are a part of Paradise. Some of these valleys, with castles surmounting a rocky peak above a village, are like 18th century pictures, with romantic settings and the contrast of the stern castle and the sunlit river. Once you are past the gorges and approach Moulins and the Bourbonnais, Nature's wealth begins to be poured out upon the countryside, and from there onwards the river, stately and slow, moves between an ever-increasingly green and fertile land.

The beauty of the lower part of the river does not lend itself easily to excited description. The broad and placid river is a turquoise necklace edged with emeralds, but the beauty of it all is not entirely visual. To my mind the highest-ranking attribute of the Loire is its thrice-blessed peacefulness. The visual attraction of the countryside it runs through in its lower part depends greatly upon forests. These are seldom conifer forests, but hardwood, grown and regenerated still according to the principles laid down by Colbert three centuries ago. Finer far for its specimen trees than the famous forest of Fontainebleau, for example, is the forest of Tronçais in the Sologne. It is still only a few years ago that the last of the beech trees planted in Colbert's day was cut down. In this forest you may see the whole life of oak and beech in the living examples of trees of all ages, from seedling to the giants approaching the end of their 225-year cycle. Endless other and smaller forests decorate the landscape of the Loire, almost to its mouth.

Vine-clad slopes are a feature from estuary to Orléans, and orchards, and fields of vegetables, and meadows, make up a constantly changing pattern. The broad river itself alternates between silver and the light blue of the sky it reflects. Only occasionally do the hills run down to the river bank, but where they do they provide viewpoints of wide landscapes running up to other hills on the farther side, of lush islands in mid-stream, and of a countryside seemingly eternally peaceful. This last word comes back to me over and over and over again as aided by colour photographs I recall the detail of the changing landscape of all the lower half of the river. The great and blessed peace of that vast stretch of countryside from Brittany, through Maine and Anjou and Touraine, through the Orléanais or Berry to the Nivernais, and onwards through the empty mountains to the river's source, is something so extraordinary in what is now primarily an industrial country that it literally has to be experienced to be believed.

This countryside is not unique to the Loire alone. The winding tributaries have their full share of a land

> *Où les prés sont toujours tapissés de verdure,*
> *Les vignes de raisins,*
> *Et les petits oiseaux gazouillants au murmure*
> *Des ruisseaux cristallins*

as Robert Garnier, a poet of the Renaissance, described. (Where the meadows are ever clad in green,/the vines adorned with grapes/and the little birds chirp to the murmuring/of crystalline streams.) The Loire is an open river for most of its way, not hemmed in by steep slopes or even by trees, so that it can be seen from great distances. Many of the tributaries are far more secret, having cut a way deep through the earth and become almost covered in by trees. These dark passages are full of little noises as frogs leap, as fish come up to breathe or snap up a fly on the surface, and the birds rustle their way through bushes. Some reaches are truly remote, and here the sight of a flashing kingfisher or of a pearl-grey heron standing vigilant in mid-stream upon one leg, may well reward the quiet watcher.

Many of these tributaries are big rivers in their own right, and feed themselves by their own tributaries, which in their turn have long tributaries. For example, the Gartempe flows 113 miles into the Creuse; the Creuse itself flows 159 miles into the Vienne; the Vienne runs 226 miles before it enters the Loire. Other major rivers feeding the Loire are the Allier (256 miles), the Cher (219 miles), the Indre (166 miles), the Loir – very confusing, *le Loir* and *la Loire* – runs 194 miles to join the Sarthe (178 miles), which runs into the Maine (only 6 miles long), which also in that short space receives the waters of the Mayenne (122 miles).

These tributaries have determined the geography and to a great extent the history of the whole Loire valley. The vast quantities of silt brought by the daughter-rivers into the mother-river have ended by putting an end to navigation on by far the greatest part of the Loire, and by depriving it of its once proud position of one of the three leading waterways of France.

Trade had long been declining upon the river, up which, before the turn of the millennium, the Vikings had been able to sail to lay siege to Tours, but in 1844 a valiant new attempt was made to restore commercial navigation. The steamboat, it was believed, was the answer to the problem. One after another no fewer than four companies were formed to carry passengers and goods by river from Orléans to Nantes. There was bitter competition, and overstressed boilers blew up, ships got stuck on sandbanks, and black clouds of smoke from soft coal disfigured the landscape and dirtied passengers.

There was some improvement when one company launched the *Inexplosibles*, fitted with safety devices guaranteed to prevent boilers exploding. These were rivalled by the *Etincelle*, the largest, fastest and most luxurious river steamer ever to sail these waters. The end was near, so soon after the beginning. In 1846 the new railway from Paris to Orléans was opened and not long after new lines directly competing with river navigation were opened. After a thousand years, the upper Loire was deprived of nearly all commercial traffic. It may well be that this prevented the industrial and commercial development of the entire region, which perhaps was a great mercy.

Despite two atomic power stations, quarrying developments such as the great Trélazé slate quarries and some local industry around the larger towns, the Loire and its affluents have remained unspoiled and the villages and towns and cities are so pleasing in themselves that there can be few parts of the world in which the work of man has enhanced rather than marred the work of Nature to the same extent . . . the new Saint-Nazaire, Nantes, Angers, Saumur, Amboise, Blois, Orléans, Sancerre, Le Puy-en-Velay and Le Monastier, on or very near the Loire itself are full of interest and each has its own particular charm.

The towns have character, and charm, but it is the villages which are such a constant delight. Usually they are old, but without being museum pieces, sleepy but alive and cheerful up as far as the *Massif Central*. Many have a few medieval and Renaissance houses, often huddling together for mutual support. Nearly all have a castle of some kind in, or alongside, or above the houses. Some have a curious mixture of roofing materials, with sun-faded red tiles alternating with the typical blue-grey of the local slate. The larger buildings are likely to be built of the local tufa which, according to the *Oxford English Dictionary* is 'a generic name for porous stones, formed of pulverulent matter consolidated and often stratified'. From the architectural point of view it is a stone naturally white, easy to work, which hardens and whitens with time. This gives the châteaux and other large buildings of the Loire a shining air of cleanliness which is most attractive.

Of Touraine La Fontaine wrote in *Le Voyage de Limousin* that along the rivers 'there are smiling slopes on either side, fine dwellings and well-planted parks, and the whole countryside abounds in green meadows, vineyards and woods: indeed, there is such diversity that, at first sight, it might seem another world'. That was written almost exactly three hundred years ago: it remains almost as true today as it was then.

Already by then Touraine had ceased to be of historical importance and had on the whole little to show of the new style of architecture which Louis XIV favoured. Touraine belonged essentially to the Renaissance and the 'fine dwellings' which La Fontaine admired were nearly all examples of that extraordinary efflorescence of architectural genius to which there are few parallels.

Over much of the region watered by the Loire and its affluents, history and architecture walk hand in hand. The simplest possible outline of the various component parts of the whole region, and then swift coverage of the main developments in France after all the region had become French, may help to explain much that concerns the main body of the book.

At the mouth, history begins with Brittany. Of the people who erected the megaliths, almost nothing at all is known. They were superseded by Gallic tribes some time in the 6th century B.C. The Romans came in the year 56 B.C. and brought their own civilization to part of the country, but four centuries later they were swept away by barbarian invasions and Brittany became a land of warring, savage tribes. In the 5th and 6th centuries the already Christianized Celts, driven out of Great Britain, crossed from Cornwall to found Little Britain, or Brittany. It remained independent in the form mainly of isolated communities until Charlemagne brought it under his rule. In 826, Louis the Pious, last remaining son of Charlemagne, made Nominoë of Vannes first duke of Brittany. The latter threw off the Frankish yoke and founded a dynasty of independent Breton dukes. In 919 came the first Norman invasion; the war against the Normans went on for twenty years. It led to the building of fortresses all over the country. After the last Normans were driven out in 939, these castles enabled local nobility to defy the authority of the dukes of Brittany for some four centuries.

The first stage of Brittany's history ends therefore with a land rife with disorders, and poverty-stricken. The Hundred Years War which began in 1337 made certain that there would be no reprieve for Brittany until it became part of France in 1491. A war of succession (with which Froissart's *Chronicles* are much concerned) broke out in 1431 at the death of Duke Jean III. The claims of his niece, Jeanne de Penthièvre, married to Charles de Blois were supported by the French. Those of her brother, Jean de Montfort, were backed by the English. And those castles were all re-furnished and brought up to date once again as civil war swept the land. In the end the House of Montfort won; the dukes finally united Brittany and paid only lip service to their feudal lords, the kings of France. In 1488 the last duke of Brittany died, leaving his daughter Anne as sole heiress. In 1491 she married Charles VIII of France, whilst still remaining duchess of Brittany, to which she returned on his death. However, next year Louis XII, having repudiated his first wife, made Anne queen of France for the second time, and practically though not yet officially, Brittany became a permanent part of France. This was finally and legally the case only in 1532, when Anne's daughter (Claude de France), wife of François d'Angoulême, who became François I, ceded her duchy to France.

For a long period the history of Brittany is mingled with that of France. In 1789 the Bretons welcomed the Revolution, but the laws against the Church and the priests, and the mass levies for the Army, brought not only the royalist Breton nobility but all their followers as well into active opposition. This was the *Chouannerie*, which faded out after the failure of a British-aided royalist landing at Quiberon in 1795. There was a last outburst as late as 1804 when Cadoudal, the last Chouan leader, went to Paris with a mad scheme of capturing Napoleon, then First Consul. He was caught and executed.

There is to this day a fierce under-current of Breton nationalism which may well come to the fore if this naturally poor country continues to be the Cinderella of the French provinces.

Anjou has a simpler history. Foulques I, in the 9th century, drove the Normans out of Anjou and took, or was given, the title of count. He founded a dynasty which included Foulques-Nerra, Black Fulk, third Foulques to be duke. This extraordinary man who lived from 971 to 1040, spent his life fighting the counts of Blois. His territory was separated by the latters' territory, and to reach it the counts of Blois expected him either to pay or to fight. Foulques much preferred the latter and succeeded, by building an incredible number of *donjons* and fortresses, in keeping the way open for his troops. This whole series of fortresses could be reached by an easy day's march from the nearest one. In 1060 the male line became extinct and the little realm passed by marriage to the Gâtinais family. One of this clan, Geoffrey of Anjou, used the province as a base from which to attack Normandy, the greater part of which passed under his control. He assumed the title of duke (nobody particularly cared to argue with him about it), married the daughter of Henry I of England, and through her his son became king of England as Henry II. Anjou thus became a possession of the kings of England. The luckless John of England lost it to the French in 1205. Bestowed upon his son Philip by Louis VIII, it passed to the former's brother Charles, founder of the House of Anjou which gave a dynasty of kings to Naples and Sicily. In 1360, Anjou was made a duchy. Louis, the first duke, inherited the throne of Sicily, and thereafter Anjou was an apanage of this kingdom. Poor René of Anjou ('Good King René') became king of Sicily in 1417 but was never able to take possession of the kingdom of Naples to which he became entitled in 1434. His unhappy daughter was married to Henry VI of England, and he himself, taking his misfortunes with a most philosophical cheerfulness, remembered he was also count of Provence, settled in Aix-en-Provence and gave his life to the improvement of agriculture and the writing of Provençal poetry. The Angevin dynasty of Naples was permanently overthrown under René II, and Anjou was firmly annexed to the throne of France under Louis XI in 1484.

The history of the counts of Blois is not unlike that of the counts of Anjou. The town was the capital of a tiny quasi-state which in early days owed little allegiance to French kings. The outstanding count of early days was Thibault I, better known as Thibault the Trickster, opponent of Foulques Nerra of Anjou, and able to keep his end up against the better warrior more by cunning than by force. It was he who built the first fortress at Blois, the better to be able to resist the attacks of his bitter enemy. Stephen, grandson of William the Conqueror, was count of Blois before he became king of England. As count, he seems to have left little mark. In 1397, the county passed to the House of Orléans. For a quarter of a century from 1440, Charles of Orléans lived in the castle and entertained all the poets of his day. Louis XII was the last of the counts, and was born in his own capital. When he came to the throne (1498) the county became part of France.

Touraine was early a part of France, after having been seized by Foulques Nerra, and through the Plantagenets became a fief of the English Crown. However, it was made over to the French Crown as early as 1242.

Orléans and the Orléanais have had no political history other than that of France since 613. For the rest, we are concerned with the history of France as a whole.

From the long history of France as a State, facts particularly pertinent to the Loire can be recalled to the reader's mind without adding unduly to length.

Joan of Arc had seen her dauphin crowned and anointed as king of France, and not just of Bourges, in 1429. The French monarchy was established and sixty relatively peaceful years followed. Charles VIII found that in acquiring Brittany for France (his sole consideration in his marriage) he had acquired a wife of character, common sense and all the typically bourgeois qualities, in Anne of Brittany. The order she helped bring to financial affairs, the support she unfailingly brought him, and the unexciting but real domestic happiness, both made him a powerful king and enabled him to indulge in dreams of conquest of foreign lands. With an army of 30,000 men, with Swiss foot-guards and Scottish archers and the rest mainly cavalry, he crossed into Italy, freed Pisa and marched triumphantly into Florence. 'A King,' the Italians found, 'conspicuous for his ugly face and misshapen figure,' but a fierce and able fighter. To oust him from Italy took such a combination of forces (Venice, Spain, the Pope, Milan and the Emperor) that though he had to abandon his positions he returned almost in triumph. With him he brought Italian artists. He had conquered by force of arms; the Italian Renaissance conquered him.

After centuries of war, a spiritually starved France swallowed with ravenous hunger all that the Italian artists had to offer. In peaceful Touraine above all the New Wave of art found its natural home. The Italians first began to build, to paint, to carve in the manner to which they were accustomed under Italian skies, but very soon the delicate colours, the gentler skies of Touraine influenced them and an even newer New Art was born along the banks of the Loire and its tributaries. Then the French proved brilliantly gifted and lively pupils, creating in a few years an indigenous style, owing much to their Italian masters, but none the less essentially French and not Italian. Buildings, statues, decorations, gardens sprang up overnight in a blaze of glory. Then two women created modern masterpieces, Katherine Briçonnet at Chenonceaux, Philippa Lesbahy at Azay-le-Rideau, throwing away the long, draughty corridors, the outside staircases, the inter-communicating rooms of the old fortresses and fortified palaces, and turning the noble house into a home.

High Gothic had prepared the way for the Renaissance and distant signs of the arrival of a new phase of civilization were already to be observed, but the break between the old and the new was to prove a clean one. Not only domestic architecture underwent a complete change: churches too turned a new face upon the world. In this something was lost: the faith and piety which built the great Gothic cathedrals and animated Gothic ecclesiastical carvings were absent from the Renaissance. Post-Gothic churches are often very lovely, but they do not have the atmosphere of places of prayer to the same extent.

Not that the Renaissance lacked fine statuary and carvings; on the contrary it excelled in wealth of new ideas and new designs and magnificent execution. This was the major art offering of its time. It flowered, it died, and the world may never look upon its like again.

The other facet of the Renaissance was the use of words. Like Elizabethan English, the French language was used as it had never been before and enriched with new words and new thoughts. Suddenly France was full of poets, who sang with rhythm and melody. They were the apostles of the new paganism, the re-born hedonism of the Greeks. Admittedly, some of them put psalms into French verse for the Protestants, but it was done to earn a little money rather than from any religious conviction. For here we come to the reverse side of the Renaissance, the ugly side.

Clément Marot emerged from the bawdy houses of Paris to write his rhymed version of the psalms. A delighted Calvin had them set to music. The Court and the people sang them day in, day out, at all times. As far as the Court and the people were concerned, this was as far as their Christian behaviour ever went. Yet they were ready at any time to set forth to slaughter their fellow Christians, the Catholics. The Catholics were equally ready to slaughter the Protestants. The dispassionate observer will find nothing at all to choose between them in cruelty and intolerance.

François I, Henri II, were at least men of action. Thereafter the monarchy fell to depths of degradation without parallel in France. Vile and twisted, the kings paraded their unnatural desires, cared nothing for the responsibilities of their position, lived only for themselves and were mourned only by their mother, Catherine de Médicis.

The greatness of Touraine began with one woman and ended with another. One chill day in the Spring of 1429, Joan of Arc arrived at Chinon; that day saw the first step towards the establishment of a real, single kingdom of France. In 1589, on the eve of Epiphany, Catherine de Médicis, her heart broken by her viper's brood, bade farewell to this life. Joan, dedicated hearer of saintly voices, Joan who, through them, communed with God, was the last great figure of the Gothic age. Catherine, now Catholic, now Protestant, now half-way between the two, lived out her life in a perpetual atmosphere of falsehood, yet was more sinned against than sinning. With her, the Renaissance died, and a great decline set in as new kings visited their Loire palaces and châteaux less and less frequently, and Versailles became an irresistible magnet to the great and the would-be great.

The lights went out in the châteaux. Now they are more visited than ever before. Some are still lived in by noble owners, others have passed into the hands of the wealthy (and no praise can be too high for the way they have poured out their fortunes to maintain these châteaux in perfect condition), many have passed to local authorities or to the State. In all, I would say that French civilization is not anywhere in any way more magnificently demonstrated than by the present state of these marvellous buildings. In this at least France can teach the whole wide world a lesson and, alas, put my own country to shame.

To return to a more comprehensive view of the Loire, one pleasant feature accompanies the river almost from its mouth to Le Puy-en-Velay, in the *Massif Central*: there is a local wine practically everywhere, and mostly excellent wine. I agree that the Loire wines are not the equal of the better Bordeaux and Burgundies: they are not the same price, either. Even then, Pouilly-Fumé, Sancerre and Quincy, Chinon and Bourgueil are very good wines that need no apology if offered even to the most esteemed wine lovers. However, the bulk of the many wines of the Loire are best drunk young, are inexpensive and of fine flavour. The number and variety of them will come as a surprise to all who have never made the journey between sea and *Massif Central* in its entirety.

Generally speaking the wines are of two grades: A.C., appellation contrôlée, and V.D.Q.S., vin délimité de qualité supérieure. The first indicates that the regional name the wine bears can only be applied to wines grown and made in a clearly defined and limited area. This is very strictly adhered to, and the consumer can be certain that no fortifying with North African or Spanish wines, or wine from Languedoc, has taken place. The second indicates that the wine is from a limited area and has been selected as being of superior quality amongst the wines grown there. In general, these V.D.Q.S. wines are not of as high a standing as the A.C. wines.

First, upstream from the sea, come the Muscadet A.C. wines, from the Loire-Maritime and Maine-et-Loire *départements*, thin, dry wines best with shellfish and *hors-d'oeuvres* but very pleasant drinking at all times. The traveller unfamiliar with the French countryside may be surprised to find that, even in good and quite expensive restaurants, the French themselves are more and more confining their wine drinking at table to a single kind. As most of the Loire wines are whites this may well cause some traditionalists to raise their eyebrows in horror-struck surprise. This is the country of Rabelais, and the motto of the abbey of Thelema is almost universally accepted, 'do as you please'. After all, if wine growers in the Bordeaux area drink their own Sauternes with mutton, who are we to hesitate to drink a Muscadet through a meal?

Upstream from the Muscadets, there are pleasant little white, red and rosé wines grown near Ancenis (Coteaux d'Ancenis). Higher up still in Maine-et-Loire there is the quite rich red wine of Champigny, the wines of Saumur (the best in this area), which include sparkling wines of good quality and flavour, the Coulée de Serrant whites which are very good, the Coteaux de l'Aubance which are as good as the Saumur, and the Coteaux du Layon, particularly rich in taste, which I personally greatly appreciate from time to time but not for daily drinking. Finally, the wines of Savennières are also very good, but the widely sold Coteaux de la Loire do not, to my palate, have the same distinction as some of the others.

On the north side of the river two particularly interesting wines are grown, the fine yellow wine of Jasnières, either very dry or a little sweeter and fuller flavoured, and the fruity Coteaux du Loir, red, white and rosé.

Indre-et-Loire, next upstream, is the *département* of the best of the Loire red wines, usually bottled in their third year. These are the wines of Chinon, on one side of the river, and of Bourgueil and Saint-Nicholas-de-Bourgueil on the northern bank. Some quite expert wine lovers claim that they cannot detect the difference between them, others that Chinon wines have a flavour of violets and the Bourgueil wines of raspberries! My own palate refutes the latter and disagrees with the former claim. If you are in the country and drinking both kinds fairly frequently there should be no difficulty in distinguishing the slightly more vigorous Bourgueil from the more delicate Chinon. Indre-et-Loire includes Vouvray, which makes still and sparkling wines of very good quality. Less exciting are the Coteaux de Touraine wines (white, red and rosé) but still very pleasant and inexpensive.

The Coteaux de Touraine vineyards stretch out into the next *département*, Loir-et-Cher, where Montrichard grows the best of them. Some quite agreeable V.D.Q.S. wines are grown near Chambord and at Cour-Cheverny.

V.D.Q.S. wines are grown again in the next *département*, Loiret.

These are the vins de l'Orléanais. The Gris Meunier grape gives reds and rosés; Auvernat Blanc and Auvernat Gris provide the whites. These are not very good wines. The whites sometimes remind one that Orléans wine vinegar is famous.

Then, with the *département du Cher*, we enter the region of A.C. wines again. White Sancerre has become a fad in France of late years: many Frenchmen think it the best white wine in France at a modest price. I think the best of the Sancerre wines is the one sold as Château de Sancerre. This is a fresh and delightful wine made from the Sauvignon grape. Personally I think the dry and mellow Quincy (also from the Sauvignon grape) just has an edge on it, being just that little finer, lighter and drier. Reuilly has a similar wine, but with a much stronger bouquet. It is a good wine, but it definitely lacks the delicacy of the others. Then, for quite inexpensive but pleasant drinking, there are the white, red and rosé wines of the Coteaux du Sancerrois, the white, red and *gris* wines of the Coteaux de Châteaumeillant, and the white, red and rosé wines of the Coteaux du Cher and Coteaux de l'Arnon.

There are no really good wines in the *département de l'Indre*, but there are light whites and reds sold as vins de l'Indre, of which the whites are the better.

Then, in the *département de la Nièvre*, approaching Burgundy, we come to perhaps the very best Loire wine of all, Pouilly-Fumé.

It is made from the Sauvignon grape, on the east side of the river, the opposite side to Sancerre and Quincy, and its delicious flavour has characteristics both of Loire wines and the fine whites of Burgundy. It is also known as Blanc fumé de Pouilly. Some wine loving friends describe this as a great wine, but this may be placing it a little above its station. Certainly it is a most delightful wine, but to me it cannot be a great one as it lacks that subtle quality of the great wines, the ability to improve with age over many years.

Not to be confused with it is the dry, white Pouilly-sur-Loire, an altogether coarser wine made from the Chasselas grape. It is perfectly drinkable, but quite ordinary compared with its Sauvignon-based companion. Local wines which are well worth tasting, though they are all unpretentious, are the white wines of Tannay and the full reds Riousse, Sagoule, La Charité and Cosne.

And at the end, from the *Massif Central,* come wines which I respect but do not greatly admire, the V.D.Q.S. of Saint-Pourçain-sur-Sioule. These are mainly red, but there are some rosés, whites and *gris*. They have been the object of a really magnificent effort by wine-growers over the last ten years or so to improve and maintain their quality. Some people love them; to me they are altogether too acid. This is a sad note on which to end this short and admittedly incomplete survey of the wines of the Loire. The next local wine you will meet will be beyond the source of the river, though not very much – the still and the sparkling white wine of Saint-Péray on the Rhône.

Does the choice of food match the choice of wines? Emphatically, yes! Right up into the *Massif Central* the choice is wide, the material excellent, the preparation careful and not too rich. Specialities are not all that frequent, but it matters the less as the *spécialité de la maison* throughout France usually entails long preparation and an amount of prior notice varying from a few hours to a day or more. This rich countryside virtually self-sufficient in food, may be said to specialize in the growing of vegetables and fruit, in the raising of poultry and in the preparation of river fish. The last I cannot too strongly recommend: baked pike and stuffed carp, as prepared along the Loire, are delicacies fit for the most exigent taste.

Nantes is famous for its ducks and its pork. North of the river, towards Le Mans, is the land of poultry. In Maine-et-Loire one can more easily than elsewhere taste stuffed bream (*brême farcie*), baked tench (*tanche au four*) and sorrel-flavoured chad (*alose à l'oseille*), all of which are delicious and best of companions for the Loire's dry white wines.

As you move up towards Orléans and the Sologne, carp from the endless pools comes up on the menu, and venison cutlets and other dishes during the hunting season when the excess of wild deer is reduced and game in general is plentiful.

Good, locally grown meat is universal and of good quality. The pork is particularly to be recommended, being more lean and delicate in flavour than in some countries. Tours, of course, has its famous speciality of potted pork (*rillettes*). For a region with such high food standards in other respects, local cheeses are perhaps not in the variety one would expect. There are goat's milk cheeses everywhere. From near Château-Gontier, north of the river, comes the true Port-Salut, made in the Port du Salut abbey, and a rival, Port-Salut de La Trappe, from a Trappist monastery. Some Brie is made locally, and there is a Bleu de Touraine. All the Norman cheeses are available, and indeed cheeses from all over France are to be found in the shops.

With by now a very wide experience of eating in France, I would incline to agree with that great professional *gastronome*, Curnonsky, that this region 'is to gastronomy as Racine is to literature'. Even more important for most people with little money to spare for the great gastronomical specialities, it is a region where one eats excellently well everywhere, in every kind of restaurant, from the simplest and cheapest to the dearest. And the restaurants are unpretentious, agreeable and welcoming, even if very few of them have a Michelin star. Indeed, this lack of snob value makes them the more endearing.

The weather, like the weather everywhere else, is unpredictable but none the less reasonably good. Naturally, on so long a river, there is no single climate. Again, we can make a division at the *Massif Central*; from Nevers onwards we are in the mountains and in the Midi. Violent rainstorms are possible, cold nights and blazing hot days to be expected, and icy roads in winter. The exposed slopes of the Vivarais mountains are both extremely cold and extremely hot. For the rest, to take Touraine as an average Loire climate, the mean rainfall is under twenty-six inches per annum and is spread over 160 days. Spring comes early, sometimes beginning at the end of February. Out come the snowdrops and the violets, and almond and apricot trees blossom. Frosts return sometimes as late as April, and there can be heavy storms in May and June, all of which do much harm. This, however, is not general. The harvest is in by the end of July, just before the very trying days of *les grandes chaleurs*, the great heat wave. The temperature rises to 85° F in the shade; the grass in August and September dries up everywhere, except in the *prés*, the water-meadows. Streams cease to run. The Loire itself becomes so shallow that the wide river can almost be crossed on foot. The dairy farmers grumble, but the owners of vineyards rub their hands with joy, for the hotter it is, the richer will be the vintage. In the local phrase, 'a hot September makes the wine'.

It would not be right to close this introduction without some reference to that non-gastronomic *spécialité du pays*, the *son-et-lumière*. It was born here, at Chambord, and in the course of relatively few years has proliferated throughout the region. Some of the châteaux give English-language versions at certain times, but for those with any knowledge of French it is a joy to listen to the French versions. Opportunities to listen to French so beautifully and clearly spoken are all too rare.

The value of the performances varies widely. This is very appositely put in the Val de Loire booklet issued by the French Government Tourist Office:

At Chambord, in 1952, a new kind of entertainment was born, *son-et-lumière*, a combination of sound and light effects. The experiment was successful beyond all expectation. The example set was followed, first in France itself, then in other countries, with varying degrees of success. With *son-et-lumière* as with music, there are performers, and there are virtuosi. The latter use all the means their mastery of technique provides to give additional lustre to that very technique. The former do not seek any higher objective than to broadcast in a night-enshrouded landscape a duet of architecture and history, for the sole purpose of contenting the audience. In ideal circumstances those who attend, spellbound by the night, should find themselves rediscovering some of the wonderment of childhood and be penetrated by a new poetic truth arising from the fusion in a single experience of music, and light, and words.*

In *Châteaux of the Loire* which I wrote some fifteen years ago, I quoted a poem by André Theuriet, written half a century before the first *son-et-lumière* which seems most appropriate. So here it is again, followed by my free translation:

* This paraphrase from the French Edition is not the version which appears in the English edition of the booklet.

c

Les Fantômes des Châteaux

C'est vous qu'on voit errer, ô splendides maîtresses,
Vous qui, dans vos tombeaux, sommeillez tout le jour,
Diane, Marguerite, ô Reines, ô Duchesses,
Fantômes des vieux temps et de la vieille cour.
Vous revenez la nuit; vos amants, vos poétes,
Marchent á vos côtés, fiers, souriants et beaux;
Contant de gais propos, chantant des odelettes
Les couples enlacés glissent sous les bouleaux.

Phantoms of the Chateaux

O splendid Paramours, who roam by dark
And in the day stay hidden in your tombs,
Diana, Margaret, Duchesses, Queens,
Dim ghosts of bygone days and royal Courts,
The night is yours: gallants and poets walk,
Smiling and handsome, proudly at your side.
With chatter gay and simple song, enlaced,
Beneath the birches, phantom couples glide.

Now, through the magic of *son-et-lumière*, these unseen phantoms have found again their human voices, and in the strange and changing lights which both distort and etherealize the architectural details of old châteaux, re-enact the scenes of love and hate, of courage and of treachery, of gaiety and of sorrow, which make up the confused pattern of man's history.

Chapter One

The Estuary, North Side. The River from the Estuary to Nantes, North Side

Mindin – The ferry to Saint-Nazaire – Paimboeuf – Donges – Saint-Nazaire – Saint-Marc – Sainte-Marguerite – Pornichet – La Baule-les-Pins – La Baule – Château de Careil – Le Pouliguen – Batz-sur-Mer–Le Croisic – La Turballe – Piriac – Pointe du Castelli – Ile Dumet – Guérande – Moulin du Diable – The Salterns – Pontchâteau, Montoir-de-Bretagne, Saint-Joachim – La Grande Brière – La Chapelle-des-Marais–Missilac – Château de la Bretesche – Saint-Gildas-des-Bois – Lancé – Château de Carheil – Blain – Savenay

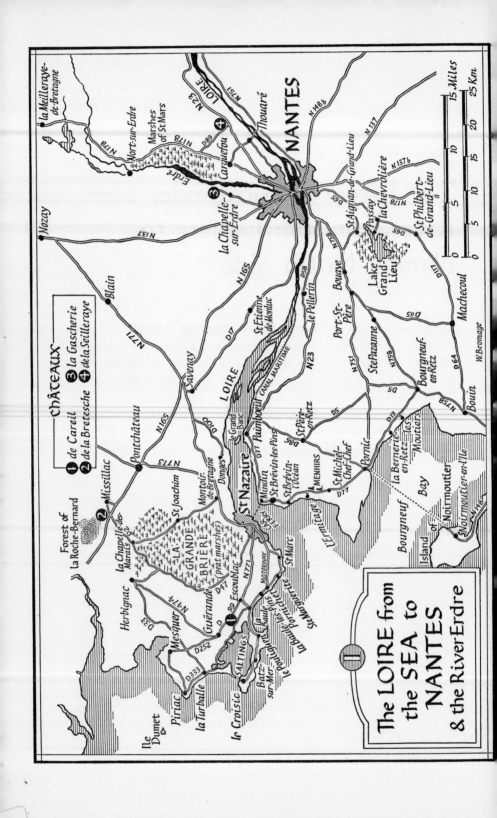

The LOIRE from the SEA to NANTES & the River Erdre

CHÂTEAUX

① de Careil
② de la Bretesche
③ la Gascherie
④ de la Seilleraye

The Estuary, North Side. The River from the Estuary to Nantes, North Side

On the map, Mindin seemed the ideal place to begin a journey up the Loire. This proved to be a sound deduction and, except in one small detail, Mindin could not be bettered as a starting-point for this long, varied and mostly very beautiful exploration of a substantial section of France.

Mindin itself is no more than the extreme northern limit of a long-drawn-out seaside resort, all sand dunes and pine trees, which begins three or four miles to the south as a slightly pretentious village built round a casino and known as Saint-Brévin-l'Océan and continues northwards as Saint-Brévin-les-Pins. Mindin marks the point where the coast, the *Côte de Jade* meets the southern bank of the river Loire. From it there is a car-carrying ferry to Saint-Nazaire on the northern bank.

A friendly sailor with a sense of humour and a dead-pan expression asked me if I realized that the path the ferry boat takes is the line of demarcation between the river Loire and the sea. I replied that the thought had not occurred to me. He pointed to the starboard side. 'Fresh water there,' and, pointing to the port side, 'salt water there.' I nodded my head, and he went on, without any trace of a smile, 'If you like, I'll get you a bucket and a cord, and you can test it for yourself.' This time I caught a little gleam of amusement in his eye. Why, I asked him, should I doubt his word? A momentary twist of his mouth which, I imagine, is the nearest he ever gets to a smile, a

nod of the head, and my sailor was off on whatever duties he may
have during the twenty-minute crossing. I went well forward and
watched the landscape upstream changing slowly as the ferry boat
cut across the estuary.

We now stood well enough out for Paimboeuf, 7 miles away on the
south bank, to come into sight and the big sand bank (*Le Grand-
Banc*) which from mid-stream cuts diagonally towards the little
town. These two together explain much of the history of the lower
reaches of the great river and explain why it is not, as the lower
Seine is, a waterway of major industrial importance.

The bank is only one of many, and by no means the most considerable, which obstruct the Loire between the sea and the once
considerable port of Nantes. This unfortunate river receives each
year a vast tonnage of sediment from its own sandy or muddy tributaries; in their turn they receive silt from a network of little rivers
and streams which make a fantastic hairline tracery on the map.
Much of the Loire sediment thus reaches it at third or fourth hand.
Gradually this silt has built up into a chain of islands the full length
of the Loire from the point it leaves the mountains of the centre.
What was once the great waterway of France now sees hardly any
traffic upstream from Angers, and very little below it.

Year by year the size of ships increased, and year by year the waters
of the Loire became more and more shallow. When, at last, few
ocean-going vessels drew as little water as the deepest channel to
Nantes provided, Paimboeuf grew prosperous. There were docks
at which the ships could unload their cargoes, which were straight-
away re-loaded on to boats small enough to be able with ease to
navigate the Loire to Nantes. Despite this attempt to keep the port
of Nantes busy, it declined still further, and in order to sustain it the
French Government, in 1891, was persuaded to make a ship canal
between Nantes and little Paimboeuf. It saved Nantes as a port, but it
nearly killed Paimboeuf. New quays were built along the banks of
the canal, but as few ships now came into its harbour, that became
and has remained silted up, and only the canal keeps it alive.

On the north bank, facing Paimboeuf, the new town of Donges
shines in the sunlight. In feudal days it was the centre of the entire
area. It decayed. Even before the last war, no trace remained of its

once fearsome castle. In 1943, the little town was virtually destroyed from the air. Now it is again an important place in its own right, from a vast new array of oil refineries. And looking at it again, it seemed to me that if one imagined the flat and desolate shore of Donges without them, how dull and depressing it would be. Perhaps one should look at the foreshore from mid-stream and no nearer; certainly from there these strange constructions make a fascinating pattern – the doodlings of a Leonardo da Vinci interpreted in shining steel and aluminium – and we do wrong to dismiss them because they are industrial and modern.

Straight ahead is another post-war town, Saint-Nazaire which, to the British in particular, holds stirring and tragic memories of World War II – more than any other place which figures in this book. To Americans, its association is more with World War I than with the later one, as it is for Canadians. In 1915 Canadian forces disembarked here; on 26 June 1917, the first of the American forces. The latter was commemorated by a memorial but that, with so much else of Saint-Nazaire, disappeared during World War II and has not been replaced. Then another war came, and when the German armies broke through and no large scale stand could any longer be maintained, 6,000 British troops were embarked at Saint-Nazaire on the disaster ship *Lancastria*. Dive-bombed out of existence, the *Lancastria* sank, and 3,000 British lives were lost; 17 June 1940, goes down in naval history as the day of the greatest loss of life from any single ship in a wartime engagement. As one looks towards Saint-Nazaire, the site of this disaster is to be seen where the estuary widens into the sea. The blue waters look too peaceful for this horror story.

Never were the cross-currents of history which flow between France and England better exemplified than by this one spot. If it recalls the black tragedy of the *Lancastria*, it recalls also the splendid story of enterprise and courage which followed. Saint-Nazaire, occupied by the Germans five days after the *Lancastria* disaster, quickly became a place of paramount importance to the German navy. A bomb-proof submarine base was begun almost as soon as the port was occupied by them, and eventually grew to have fourteen bays with accommodation for three or four submarines in each, which could be reached through a covered, bomb-proof lock. The still-new entry lock, completed only in 1935, allowed for ships drawing 40 feet of water to pass into the Loire at high water. This meant that the 35,000-ton German battleships could use it as a graving dock for repairs, a facility which existed nowhere else on the Channel or Atlantic coasts of German-occupied Europe.

At one o'clock in the morning of 28 March 1942, an ancient British destroyer, *Campbeltown*, and a little flotilla of smaller ships carrying a commando unit, arrived at Saint-Nazaire during the course of a diversionary British air raid. Surprise was complete. *Campbeltown* was in the approach channel and nearing the lock gates before the Germans realized what was happening. It was already too late for them to prevent her ramming the outer gate of the principal lock. Men of the commando unit rampaged through the dock area on their mission of destruction.

It was impossible to take the men off again under the curtain of German fire. The men set out to fight their way out of the town and there was heavy and murderous street fighting. A few found their way back to England by devious routes; it was a miracle that any at all succeeded. Then, just as the Germans felt certain they had mastered the British attack, a time-fuse operated in *Campbeltown*, and the stalwart old ship blew up in Wagnerian tumult and thunder, carrying a German inspection party on board with it. The formidable explosion threw two ships which were under repair in the lock against the inner gates, causing great damage. The commando unit had already severely damaged the lock mechanism and pumps, and the explosion now wrecked the hinges of the outer gate and water came cascading in. The next day time-bombs planted by the commandos blocked the western entrance to the port. The Germans were convinced that more British had landed, and racing through the town in near-panic looking for them caused the death of sixteen civilians and the wounding of many more.

The ferry lands cars and passengers almost where this epic story had its principal scene, but before taking to dry land, there are two more moments of history to recall.

As far as can be traced, you land on the very spot from which a bearded young man, proclaiming himself a student from the Scotch

College in Paris (in those days there was no nonsense about using 'Scots' or 'Scottish' when you meant 'Scotch') clambered into a rowing boat and with a handful of friends was rowed out to a fast brig, *La Doutelle*. She had been hired at Nantes by a Scotch gentleman living there, and had come down river to pick up her passengers, whose absence from France was likely to cause immediate investigation. There was just the chance that Authority might have caught up with the brig between Nantes and the sea, whereas at Saint-Nazaire the ship, already in mid-stream, hoisted sail, caught the wind, and winged her way to sea and to adventure.

There were seven gentlemen in all who clambered aboard, as well as Mr Walsh, who had hired the vessel. The young man with the beard was not a student at the Scotch College, nor was a beard his normal wear, but a disguise; the other gentlemen treated him with a certain deference as they stood on deck and watched the coast of France. Landfall for *La Doutelle* was Eriska, in the Hebrides, and the date of it 2 August 1745. It can hardly be necessary to add that the young man with the temporary beard was Charles Edward Louis Philip Casimir Stewart, known to us all as The Young Pretender, or The Young Cavalier or, as his supporters affectionately called him, Bonnie Prince Charlie. Here, then, exactly where one now lands from the Mindin ferry, began one of the most romantic journeys in all recorded history.

A last glance back upstream to wonder what John Knox made of his first sight of France as the French man-of-war, on which he was a prisoner, made its way up the river towards Nantes, where Knox was to become a galley-slave of a very unusual kind. How he got there makes a strange story. Cardinal Beaton, primate of Scotland, ordered the arrest of a well-known preacher of the Reformed Faith, George Wishart. He was arrested and carried to the cardinal's castle at Saint Andrews. Here Wishart was burnt at the stake, with the cardinal looking on. Then Beaton was assassinated in his own castle, which his enemies proceeded to hold. It became too dangerous for Knox, already known for his inclination towards Reform, to be at large, and he took refuge with Beaton's assassins in the castle of Saint Andrews. Although he had nothing to do with the assassination, he did say of it that it was 'a godly fact'. However, the safety of the castle proved quite illusory. Beaton, twice ambassador to France, and bishop of Foix, was to be avenged. French galleys raided the castle, broke down the defence, and took away as prisoners all the most prominent of the besieged party, and Knox's first view of France was the land either side of the estuary of the Loire.

Which way should one turn on landing? It is largely a question of time. If time presses, Nantes is less than 40 miles by the main road, but to take it means missing a small area of great interest. If a little time can be spared, take the motor road to La Baule for about 3 miles, then turn left on to the very pretty coastal road (D 292) and through the little resorts: Saint-Marc, all cliffs, and Sainte-Marguerite, all sand dunes. A mile or two on, and one gets the first complete views of the great bay of La Baule. To call its 4-mile curve of sand the 'finest bathing beach in Europe' may or may not be correct – who knows every bathing beach in Europe? – but it is undeniably a very splendid one.

Before reaching La Baule, the road passes through Pornichet. It was here that wealthy bourgeois of Nantes and Saint-Nazaire began building themselves seaside villas, towards the end of the 19th century. The more adventurous migrated farther westwards and built amidst the pines of the unknown La Baule. It was not until after World War I that developers moved in on a big scale, and La Baule-les-Pins, between Pornichet and La Baule, was created from the drawing-board. A new kind of resort came into being. The Casino and the satellites of the Casino are on the front, the shopping streets lead inland from it to the town centre. For the rest, its 9,000 villas are hidden away in the trees.

Just north of La Baule, on the western side, is the first of the many châteaux with which this book is concerned. It is the château de Careil, which, from the 14th century, has stood guard over the once valuable salt-pans. Of the 14th century, there remains a long outer wall, with fortifications. The inner courtyard is mainly of the 16th century. Between the two, one can imagine the story of architectural development from the fortress, lived in for safety, and the house, lived in for pleasure. This is the measure of the revolution in thought which we call the Renaissance. The château de Careil is not only the first château to be visited, it is the first example of the New Thought of which there are so many others on the up-river journey. It is not, in itself, an important example; the inside of Careil is much finer than the outside. It belongs in the category of *Demeures Historiques*, those ancient and often historic buildings still lived in by their owners. It gives that lived-in feeling which elsewhere the imagination has to supply. Some of the beautifully preserved timberwork is at least partly of the 14th century; fireplaces and ceilings are rich and varied. From 15 June to the end of the summer, on Wednesdays and Saturdays, it can be visited by candlelight.

Beyond the western end of La Baule is Le Pouliguen, separated from it by a canal, through which, at high tide, sea-water passes into the salt marshes which here turn the coastal strip into a peninsula. Compared with La Baule, it is a little vulgar and certainly very much less expensive. The little port serves a double purpose: fishing boats come in with baskets of crabs and lobsters and unload them on the noisy quay, and twice a day, little sailing-boats of all kinds, like a flock of birds, go flying out to sea in the morning breeze and come flying back again in the evening one.

There is a coastal road as well as a direct one to the next little port, Batz-sur-Mer. The former passes by the sea-cave of the korrigans, a reminder that this is still very much a part of Brittany. The korrigans, in its Celtic folklore, are the pigwidgeons or leprechauns, or hobgoblins, with which most Celtic lands seem always to have been infested.

Batz faces two ways: inland, on the saltings; and seawards. The tiny seaport is not a very good one, being subject to the effects of a dangerous tidal undertow, but little lobster boats come and go and give it a certain animation. The town itself is very Breton, with solid granite houses covered by slated roofs, and a solid granite church with an exceptionally long history. It began, possibly in the 6th century, as a sanctuary dedicated to Saints Cyricus and Julitta (long since expunged from the calendar of saints as apocryphal). The building fell into disrepair and was abandoned when, in the 9th century, Benedictine monks from Landévennec rebuilt it. In the 13th century the Benedictines built a new and presumably much bigger church dedicated to Saint Guénolé, whose name in its

English form is Winwaloe, after whom Landewednac on the Lizard peninsula and Gunwalloe (also in Cornwall) were named. The nave of the church was entirely rebuilt about 1460 and the remarkable campanile about a century later. From its 260 feet-high top platform one gets perhaps the best view of the coast and the flat hinterland. The saltings, in an untidy pattern of rough rectangles, stretch away inland. The indentations of the rocky coast and the islands and islets out to sea can be observed in detail and I have been told that on a day of good visibility Belle-Ile and the Quiberon peninsula, though 25 to 30 miles away, are quite clearly seen.

Le Croisic is almost a continuation of Batz-sur-Mer and, being also on a very narrow part of the peninsula, faces equally to sea and to saltings. The port is both better and bigger than Batz, and has something of the same air as Honfleur, for 17th century houses line the quays. The basins, separated by natural islets, and the vast, exuberant, noisy and smelly fish market are most picturesque. And that is more than can be said of the statue of Hervé Rielle.

A French fleet, under Admiral Tourville, had been prepared by Louis XIV to carry the exiled James II with considerable French forces to a landing in England, from which a restoration could be expected. Instead Tourville's forty-four ships were caught by a much superior Anglo-Dutch fleet. The French fleet was beaten and dispersed. Twelve large line-of-battle ships took refuge in the shallow roadstead of La Hougue, on the Cotentin peninsula, and were destroyed by boats from the English squadron under Admiral Rooke. Twenty-two other ships under Admiral Damfréville were able to break off the engagement and sail for the safety of Saint-Malo. Night came, and it was a dark one. The tide was ebbing. The English were searching for them. The admiral concluded that it was now too late to find shelter and was prepared to give order for the ships to run themselves aground rather than fall to the English, when Hervé Rielle was brought to him. He persuaded the admiral that he, a common sailor, could bring the ships safely into Saint-Malo, in the dark and with an unfavourable tide, between the shore and the offshore reefs, where the English would not dare to follow them. He gave such a good account of his knowledge of these seas that the admiral thought the effort worth the risk. And so it proved;

at dawn, the ships were already under the protection of the guns of the forts of Saint-Malo.

It was 200 years and more before Hervé Rielle got his statue in his native town, and James II never did get his throne back, and the affair would not today be worth mentioning if it had not had an unexpected sequel. It gave rise to what is certainly the worst poem Robert Browning ever wrote, one which would be an odds-on favourite in the stakes for the worst poem ever written by a top-rank poet. One or two examples make the point:

> And just as Hervé Riel hollas
> 'anchor!' – sure as fate
> Up the English come – too late!

Damfréville is full of his praises, and tells him:

> You must name your own reward.
> 'Faith, our sun was near eclipse!'
> Demand whate'er you will,
> France remains your debtor still.
> Ask to heart's content, and have!
> or my name's not Damfréville.

All Hervé asked for was to go ashore and greet his wife, *la belle Aurore*. To Robert Browning's disgust, Hervé was granted exactly what he asked for, and nothing else at all. He should, the poet felt, have become a national hero, but never did.

> Go to Paris, rank on rank
> Search the heroes flung pell-mell
> On the Louvre, face and flank!
> You shall look long enough ere you
> come to Hervé Riel.

Curiously enough though to this day you may search long enough not only on the Louvre but anywhere else in France other than Le Croisic and never find it, Madame Hervé Riel is commemorated by a number of restaurants and *hostelleries* under the name of *La Belle Aurore*. Browning seems determined to have found swans amongst the geese of Le Croisic, for in his *Two Poets of Croisic* he wrote of Paul Desforges Maillard and of René Gentilhomme, two very undistinguished poets whose works have not lived, even in France. Indeed, Le Croisic was ever the birthplace of good men, but not of great ones.

There is a certain satisfaction to be derived from this story of a great poet by the less gifted of us who are never satisfied with the standards of their own work. 'At least,' we can say to ourselves, 'it's no worse than Browning's poem on Hervé Riel, for which he got 100 guineas!'

To visit the two last places on this coast which come within our scope, one needs to take D92 to La Turballe, rather too full of the smell of sardine canneries to linger in. It then becomes D99, a most picturesque coastal road as far as Piriac.

Piriac has all the charm that La Turballe lacks. It is old, with historical records going back to the 12th century. The grey granite houses with their slate roofs look ageless, though most are in fact 17th century. The church is graceful, with a strangely shaped but delightful spire, vaguely reminiscent of Eastern Europe. The little port is quite charming, and the rocks around wrought by the sea into fantastic and sometimes ridiculous shapes.

Out on the rocks one realizes that the micro-climate of the bay of La Baule begins to lose its effect at Le Croisic, and at Piriac can be felt no more. It is colder here, out of the sun, and much windier. Indeed, at the near-by Pointe du Castelli, where the sea has played its most dramatic tricks with the rocky cliffs, it seems as if one had entered a different land altogether. For here it is that the fierce, rebellious tides of autumn beat with all the force they have accumulated in the course of their 3,000-mile journey across the Atlantic, for we have turned a right angle from the south-facing, sunny bay of La Baule to a point where the next parish westwards is in America.

About $4\frac{1}{2}$ miles north-west of Piriac is the strange Ile Dumet (until quite recently it was always written 'du Met'), measuring $1\frac{1}{2}$ miles round. It is possible to reach it by motor-launch from Piriac, at the cost of its hire and the risk of being unhappy in a heavy swell.

It was, in 1936, the subject of a curious piece of calculation by Professor Alphonse Berget. He discovered that if you wished to divide the world in two by a great circle around its maximum circumference so as to include in one half as much land as possible and in the other half as much water as possible, Dumet would be the world's continental pole.

Has this discovery any significance? If so, whatever it is does not spring instantaneously to mind, but it seems possible that it has a bearing on a very odd feature of the little island: it is cloud-free for many more days in the year than the coast 5 miles away, and that in its turn ensures it a degree of natural warmth well in excess of that of the neighbouring land. Has its polar situation any effect on cloud? Is the warmth not derived from some quirk of the Gulf Stream rather than from sunshine? Until there has been a full scientific investigation into this micro-micro-climate no answer can be given, and meanwhile this oddity gives the island a greater interest.

About a century and a quarter ago, G. Touchard-Lafosse wrote:

> On the highest part of the island the ruins of the ancient Fort Ré occupy a circle about 150 feet across; this variation on the usual citadel was bombarded and destroyed by the English at some period not specified by Breton historians. In 1803, the islet was manned for a year, and then abandoned. Though but a short distance from the coast, meteorological conditions are quite different on it: constant temperatures are favourable to vegetation at all times of year. No sandy wastes here, none of those salt-marsh rushes whose presence betokens a sterile soil, but fresh grassland, patterned with clover, and ornamented with daisies and violets and buttercups. To this one must add that there is not a single tree. Cattle put out to fatten on this islet soon acquire remarkable strength and energy; a freshwater spring, surrounded by walls, is available for them to slake their thirst. Horses sent to the island soon acquire great energy, but also turn almost wild. Animals are the only inhabitants of the island, unless one counts black-headed and black-backed gulls who land on it in great clouds, and often nest on it.

What has happened since 1880; when it is last recorded as pasturing a small flock of sheep? Today a few miserably meagre rabbits live off thick, hairy-leaved plants liberally sprinkled with quantities of dried seaweed blown up by the wind. The gulls are still there, and nesting freely. Two or three things may make it worth putting up with the eternal swell on the journey there and back: the marvellous view of the mainland forming the arc of a vast circle, most impressive of all at sunset, from Le Croisic up to Quiberon; the riches it can provide by way of crustaceans and shellfish; the satisfaction of having visited an island known to so few.

At Le Croisic you are no more than 30 miles from your landing-point at Saint-Nazaire, using the longer coastal roads: by the more direct main roads the distance is only 20 miles. From Le Croisic to Piriac is another 15 or so. If we turn inland at Piriac two further totally different worlds can be traversed in a distance not much greater.

From Piriac, one should turn back along the road to La Turballe, and on emerging from the latter, bear left on D99. A surprise is soon in store for the driver – for once, in this flat land, the road rises significantly and at the approaches to a hamlet called Clis gives a general view of the saltings as far as Le Croisic and Batz-sur-Mer. The spires of both churches stand out clear against the sea. After a further rise in the road, and 4 miles after leaving La Turballe, Guérande is before one, a tiny, tiny walled town of the Middle Ages, which may not have kept much of its domestic architecture but has preserved – perhaps better than any other circular, fortified townlet – its essential character as a 'foster-child of silence and slow time'.

The quietness of the streets of this pleasing little town is certainly a blessing after the ear-splitting traffic noises of even quite small provincial towns; the relative silence is almost unnerving to those who have come here from Paris or other great cities. And I doubt if anybody beyond the age of childhood ever runs in this timeless place.

The timeless place, I have called it, and that is what it is. Around it are the new ramparts, completed as recently as 1468, built on the foundations of older ones which themselves superseded others of greater circumference of which all trace has now been lost. Apparently in the early Middle Ages Guérande had a population of some 10,000, but this suddenly declined to not much more than 6,000 and made the old town too big for its walls to be easily manned.

A farm on La Grande Brière, the big peat-marsh on the north side of the Loire estuary.

Clisson and its castle (first built in 1223). To the left is one of its two hump-backed bridges.

The castle at Nantes began as a Gallo–Roman fortification. The present building, late Gothic and Renaissance, is mostly occupied by museums.

The Guardroom of the beautifully preserved castle of Le Plessis-Bourré, dating from the 15th century. An example of the first steps leading to the use of the castle as a residence as well as a fortification.

The population has hardly varied since. Recent figures are 6100 in 1851, 6749 in 1877, 6164 in 1939 and 6688 in 1965 – a most amazing consistency. Thanks to it, it is a very homogeneous townlet and even if most of the buildings are, individually, lacking in interest, as a whole it is most pleasing.

Of its earliest history little is known. There is no record of its early Celtic days, nor even of the Latins who met with such fierce opposition in Brittany, but its situation on a plateau no more than 150 feet high but which, none the less, commanded views over the surrounding plain, out to sea and over the mouth of the Loire, can hardly have escaped the favourable attention of the Roman generals of the time.

In the year 850, Guérande comes out of legend into history. It would have been, at that time, either on the sea or very near it. Nominoé, first king of a more or less united Brittany, fell out with Actard, bishop of Nantes, and appointed Gilard in his place. Five years later Actard was forgiven and was reappointed to the See of Nantes, whereupon the disappointed Gilard accepted a share of the diocese and became bishop of Guérande. He was the first bishop, and he was the last. The See of La Mée (as the new diocese was called) was reunited with the truncated diocese of Nantes. Several bishops' palaces on the same site as the one Gilard built for himself must have gone up over the centuries, for the final one was pulled down only in 1680.

Having made history by being perhaps the only town in the world to have had but a single bishop, Guérande thereafter was seldom out of the news for long. The Normans besieged it in 919 and 952, but were repulsed on both occasions and came back no more. Later all the quarrels between rival dukes of Brittany, with France and England backing first the one and then the other, but always in opposition to each other, cost Guérande dear. The original church of Saint Aubin was burnt, with a great loss of life amongst the inhabitants who had taken refuge in it, the old fort was torn down. Eventually Jean de Montfort retained possession of the town. Peace came a first time, in 1365, when Jean, now accepted as duke of Brittany, swore to wage war no more on Jeanne the Lame, widow of the rival claimant, Charles de Blois. In 1373, it was besieged

D

by the great warrior, Duguesclin, on behalf of Charles V, taken
and occupied. When that other valiant warrior, Olivier de Clisson
tried to do the same thing for the other side in 1379, he failed.
And doubtless the inhabitants cried out 'a plague on both your
houses'. The peace of 1365 was concluded at the altar of Saint
Aubin; the final peace of 1381 was ratified at the altar of Guérande's
other remaining church, Notre-Dame-de-la-Blanche.

With that reminder of the past history of this ancient town, it is
time to see what it has to offer today. Stone-built houses, grey, and a
little grim. The collegiate church of Saint Aubin (though it lost its
position as a cathedral church, the Dean and Chapter continued in
being and secured for it the title of collegiate church), is a solid stone
structure, impressive but not beautiful and much spoiled by ill-
considered restorations to the exterior. The interior is much better,
mainly 12th century, dark and massive and perhaps a little frightening. The pillars have storied capitals of definitely Romanesque origin.
Then there is a jump of three or four centuries in the transepts and
the choir, which are rather heavily Flamboyant, then a further jump
in time with the furnishings none of which would seem to be later
than the 18th century. Finally there is a famous outside pulpit,
reached from inside, dating from the 15th century.

The tour of the ramparts comes next. Their total circumference
is a little less than a mile. If you start at the principal gate, the
Porte Saint-Michel (the eastern one) and carry on anti-clockwise, you
pass a succession of entirely delightful town gates and defensive
towers: *Tour Théologale, Tour Sainte-Anne,* the *Porte Vannetai se
Tour de Kerbénet, Tour de la Gaudinais* with gargoyle-decorated para-
pets, *Tour de l'Abreuvoir, Porte Bizienne, Porte de Saillé* and finally the
Tour Saint-Jean and the *Porte Saint-Michel* again. I cannot think
where one will find a comparable number of enchanting 14th and
15th century town gates and towers in so small a space. A few of
them have been all too obviously restored, but at least they are still
there to give the general impression of stepping into a past of five
centuries ago. A town which is only some 400 yards across can be
explored in depth (to use a somewhat horrid modern phrase) in
very little time. Where else can one find so many exquisite old
corners and streets and individual buildings in so limited an area?

Most of the moat has been filled in, but two sections on the northern side and one on the north-western are still there, to make an almost idyllic picture. The tall, arched gateway in its rectangular stone box, the plain stone walls with green plants growing between the stones to break the monotony of their grey surface, the banks of the moats and the bridge to the gate green with grass, and white and red with valerian blossom, and the water reflecting them all, and the sky as well – this is a picture which will live in the memory long after more dramatic scenes have been forgotten, a scene with a strange classical reminder when the sun shines strongly on the uniform, unexciting crenellations to give deep, regularly patterned shadows between them and make a frieze as exciting as any that ancient Greece has passed down to us.

Finally, a mile to the north is the *Moulin du Diable*, a beautifully preserved specimen of the old stone windmill of south Brittany. It is curious that a people with so little natural taste for architecture (nearly all the best in Brittany is borrowed from other parts) should have evolved the most beautifully proportioned and architecturally satisfying windmill. It is of the usual grey granite, with a short and powerful cylinder carrying a circular milling chamber of somewhat greater diameter, surmounted by a slated conical roof through which passes the shaft carrying the four sails.

The views from the ramparts may well have puzzled the observer, for though the landscape is not exactly beautiful, this section of the country was once the richest in the south of Brittany, and perhaps even of all Brittany. To south and south-west is the chequered pattern of the salterns; to east and north-east stretches La Grande Brière which is 10 to 11 miles long and about 6 miles broad at the widest point.

First, the salt marshes which run northwards behind the Croisic-Pouliguen peninsula. Coming south-westwards from Guérande towards Le Croisic on N 774 one comes to a most charming little village, Saillé on the edge of the marshes. The old stone houses, with heavily proportioned dormer windows and the least conventional of ground plans are pure Breton, and, like so many Breton buildings, are of no particular age. They are very picturesque and a good introduction to the traditional saltings on their doorstep.

The saltings are all below sea level at high water and protected by dykes. Water, as we have seen, reaches them by a sea-canal at Le Pouliguen and passes through roughly made but efficient sluice gates into shallow basins of odd shapes, called *fares, cobiers* or *adernes*. In these, a considerable portion of the water is evaporated and the brine is allowed to run into square reservoirs (*œillets*) with sides from 20 to 30 feet long. In these the sun finally evaporates the remaining water and leaves a layer of salt. The salt is scraped off in thin layers and carried to the mounds on which it will finally, weather permitting, dry right out.

These are assuredly Europe's most northerly salterns. Although the wind helps evaporate the water from the brine, it is above all the sun which is needed and in some years there is not enough to give any kind of worthwhile output. Nevertheless the average is still of the order of 30,000 tons a year: less than a century ago it was 80,000.

The view from Saillé therefore is of a vast plain covered with rectangular *œillets* which shine in the sun, alongside which are roughly conical mounds of dried salt which scintillate as if each had its own source of light. The flat plain gives the impression of being much greater in extent than it actually is, and if the not-so-distant horizon gives a touch of immensity to the view it is because it demonstrates with unusual clarity the curvature of the earth.

What gave the salt its immense importance in earlier days was not so much the product itself, as the tax successive governments placed upon it. The hated *gabelle*, the salt-tax, was instituted as early as 1286 by Philippe IV as a temporary measure. How rightly do the French say that *rien ne dure comme le provisoire*, nothing lasts as long as the temporary. Just on three centuries later, Charles V incorporated it in the permanent taxation of the country. Its collection was the source of almost unbroken disturbances and often loss of life. It took the Revolution of 1789 to put an end to it. The peasants needed salt as much for their cattle as for themselves, and the tax on salt took a large part of their income. It was a tax which bore most heavily on the poorest; to the rich it was never a burden.

From a plain inundated by salt water and providing in the past a fairly high standard of living for the workers and great wealth

for the dukes of Brittany and kings of France it is only a few miles
north-eastwards to the large water-logged peat marsh, La Grande-
Brière. Here, by contrast, life has always been exceedingly hard for
the inhabitants, who to this day must count amongst the French
under-privileged although many of the men work for good wages in
Saint-Nazaire. But they would not willingly exchange their strange
water-logged world for any other.

Access is limited to two roads able to take motor traffic. One
runs from Pontchâteau to, the other from Montoir-de-Bretagne
through, Saint-Joachim which is a substantial village near to two of
the 'islands' with a church whose high tower can be seen from afar
in this flat marshland. All around is a piece of Ireland – Galway, for
example – which 'has dropped from out the sky' on to the wrong
place. The inhabitants of La Grande Brière live off the sheep and
cattle which graze all the summer on the wide areas of bog. Peat
cutting, once the single industry of the marsh, is restricted to quantities sufficient to heat their own cottages. It used to be taken along
the rivulets, which make an intricate network, on to the bigger
canals. The peat was sold as far away as La Rochelle, as well as to the
nearer Saint-Nazaire and Nantes. Unlimited supplies of rushes
account for the high proportion of thatched roofs, but already
modern housing of a type to be seen in any French suburb is going
up alongside the old traditional cottages.

Swamps and over-green grassland, ditches full of wild flowers in
pastel shades, miniature hazel spinneys, isolated Breton cottages
and tiny hamlets joined by narrow roads, reeded meres and lazy
meandering waterways make up a scene no longer belonging to the
world in which we live, undramatic in form or colour yet full of
charm and enjoying the greatest rarity of all, a silence virtually
perpetual.

To those who would like to see a little more of this little-known land
north of the Loire and west of Nantes, I would recommend a continuation of the little road through Saint-Joachim as far as La
Chapelle-des-Marais and on to Missilac on the edge of the forest of
La Roche-Bernard. Here the vast château of La Bretesche was the
home successively of a remarkable number of the great families of

Brittany. A Laval, married to Isobel, daughter of the duke of Brittany, completed the original castle in 1430: then came the Rieux, Coligny, de la Trémoille, Haultemer, Lorraine-Chevreuse, Coislin, Lorraine-Elbeuf and Boisgelin families to bring the story up to the Revolution. It now belongs to the marquis de Montaigu. As for the castle itself, it was burned down in 1500, and rebuilt. Admiral Coligny lived in it in 1558. This Protestant connection caused it to be taken by the League forces under the duc de Mercoeur. They dismantled it completely. More rebuilding . . . and at the time of the Revolution it was described as being 'an enchanting place in which one could enjoy the best of company, all the advantages that wealth can buy and all the pleasures that it can bestow. The richness and elegance of the furniture, the magnificence of the hangings and the pictures, the wealth of mirrors and the gilding which decorated the rooms have become legendary'. Then, in 1793, a Republican column marched on La Bretesche, pillaged and destroyed the contents, hacking priceless art treasures to pieces with their swords, and finally setting fire to the fabric in many places. The solid walls resisted fire to a great extent and until late into the 19th century stood foursquare defying the elements as they had defied the hand of man. They made possible the present château, rather wonderfully restored at that time.

The tall main buildings, in the style of the last phase of domestic Gothic, face a 50-acre lake. At each end are strong hexagonal towers. Lesser buildings of varying heights link it to a stern watch tower which once protected a drawbridge. Around is a fine park, and inside the visitor may see many splendid pieces of furniture. It is still lived in, which makes it all the more agreeable to visit.*

From Missilac on D 2 to Saint-Gildas-des-Bois and across the Brest to Nantes Canal to the crossroads village of Lancé, down N 164 for 1¼ miles to where a narrow local road leads off to the right to the Château de Carheil. This is the exact opposite of La Bretesche, stern and imposing. Carheil is up to a point Gothic too, but a Gothic tempered by the first smiles of the Renaissance. Once it was a

* Since this was written it has been proposed and apparently accepted that the château should be sub-divided and sold or rented as flats. If this is correct, it will no longer be possible to visit it in detail.

Protestant stronghold, under Jean de Bolac, a man of iron will who dominated the surrounding district. The pastor of the local flock was one Cervin, as dynamic in the exercise of his religion as his master. 'Henceforward,' he would cry each Sunday in the course of his interminable sermon, 'henceforward the Ark of the Covenant of Jehovah is to be found at Carheil.' One hears no more of the Protestants after the revocation of the Edict of Nantes. In due course this very charming little castle (it had been, ironically enough, spared by Richelieu despite its Protestant background when he caused so many others owned by good Catholics to be pulled down) was bought by Madame Adélaïde, the dull, devoted sister of Louis-Philippe. It passed from her to Louis-Philippe's third son, the prince de Joinville and is still in the possession of the Orléans family.

Along the edge of the Gavre forest runs the road to Blain, where the well-preserved medieval castle cannot, at the time of writing, be visited. This is a pity, for it gives a wonderful idea of the size and strength of these great castles. It covers about 10 acres and, although some parts are older, the oldest complete portion is the immensely strong *Tour du Connétable* built by the great Breton warrior, Olivier de Clisson, towards the end of the 14th century. The Rohan family took over from the Clisson family and added much to the existing castle, including the drawbridge tower. The graceful Renaissance wing – the first purely residential part of the castle, was the birthplace of that Protestant duc de Rohan, son-in-law of the wise Sully who guided Henry of Navarre through the shoals and straits of his reign as Henri IV. In the next reign, this duc de Rohan was leader of the Calvinists, but it was not long before the family became Catholic. Most people will remember the part that Cardinal Louis-René-Edouard de Rohan played in the strange story of the necklace of the foolish Queen Marie-Antoinette.

From here, it is 25 miles to Nantes along a not very interesting road. Better by far, if one has the time, is to return to Saint-Nazaire by way of Savenay and Donges, and to take the ferry once again at Mindin – this time with the fresh water on the port side, and the salt water on the starboard side.

The River, South Side, to Nantes. Across the River, East of Nantes, and back to Nantes, North Side

L'Ermitage – Saint-Michel-Chef-Chef – Pornic – Pays de Retz – Salt marshes – Bourgneuf-en-Retz – Bouin – Machecoul – Saint-Philbert-de Grand-Lieu – The Lake of Grand-Lieu – La Chevrolière – Passay– Saint-Philbert-de-Bretagne, Vieillevigne, Montaigu – Tiffauges – Sèvre-Nantaise – Haute-Goulaine and Château de Goulaine – Basse-Goulaine across to Thouaré and Carquefou – Château de la Seilleraye – La Chapelle-sur-Erdre and Château de la Gascherie – Nantes

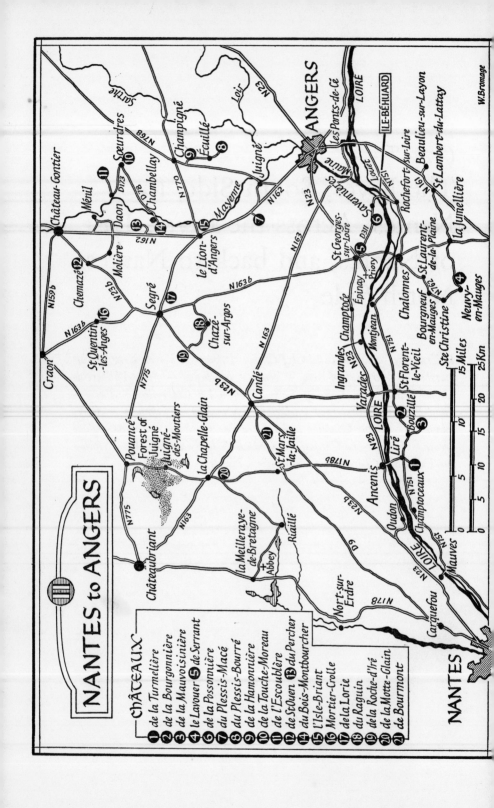

NANTES to ANGERS

CHÂTEAUX

1. de la Turmelière
2. de la Bourgonnière
3. de la Mauvoisinière
4. le Lavoir 5. de Serrant
6. de la Possonnière
7. du Plessis-Macé
8. du Plessis-Bourré
9. de la Hamonnière
10. de la Touche-Moreau
11. de l'Escoublère
12. de Serrant 13. du Percher
14. du Bois-Montbourcher
15. L'Isle-Briant
16. Mortier-Crolle
17. de la Lorie
18. du Raguin
19. de la Roche-d'Iré
20. de la Motte-Glain
21. de Bourmont

W. Bromage

Chapter Two

The River, South Side, to Nantes. Across the River, East of Nantes, and back to Nantes, North Side

At the beginning of Chapter One I wrote that Mindin, with one small exception, seemed almost the ideal place to begin the journey up the Loire. The one small exception is the difficulty of putting forward any acceptable reason why the English-speaking traveller should be anywhere near it at any time. It would not be unfair to describe it as being on the road from nowhere to nowhere.

The eastern road from it runs through Paimboeuf and then becomes particularly dull for the remainder of the 36 miles to Nantes. The other road, to the south, is a little more interesting. There are some impressive menhirs between L'Ermitage and Saint-Michel-Chef-Chef (a name nostalgically onomatopoeic, recalling the little trains of long ago which came puffing down from Paimboeuf to Sainte-Pazanne in the most leisurely way imaginable). What strange people by what strange means uplifted these colossal stones and left so little other record of their existence?

After a journey of only 12 miles, the road comes to an abrupt end in Pornic, a miniature seaside resort, with a miniature port accessible only at high tide, a miniature medieval castle which once belonged to the famous Gilles de Rais, or Retz, and miniature old houses rising up the hill. It is essentially *sympathique*.

On the way to the miniature golf course (miniature in the sense of covering a limited area and having only nine holes) is a magnificent dolmen – more properly perhaps *allée couverte* – fascinating even to those with little taste for the prehistoric, but remarkable in particular for being a double one.

The sinister figure of Gilles de Rais will be recalled at Machecoul and at Tiffauges, for there is little enough reason to believe that he had much to do with his castle at Pornic, beyond losing it in the sequestration of his property. The present building, much restored, began as a rebuilding after total destruction in the Breton Wars of Succession. The original probably looked from the port as if it grew out of the rock on which it stands. Now it stands as something planted upon it. Even the gentle and peaceful Pornic has its record of more recent wars. In the shadow of the Huguenot Cross, a work of the 17th century, in a little park to which there is no public access, 200 of the men of the Vendée slain by the Republicans at Pornic are buried. In the little resort's war cemetery there are almost equal numbers of graves of those who died for France and those who were killed at the sinking of the *Lancastria*, nearly 200 of each. It always seems to me that these shared graveyards are a bond of union which will last much longer than the day-to-day squabbles and disagreements which from time to time separate the nations.

From Pornic, D 13 carries one fairly swiftly through this *pays de Retz*, this country of the Rais family who were as important almost as princes, through Bourgneuf-en-Retz. The sea has receded from this one-time port, which now stands on the edge of marshes slashed across by tidal canals. If one has not already seen the salt marshes north of the river, it is worth the 5-mile run on N 758 towards the Ile de Noirmoutier, for Bouin is a quaint little place on the 'island' of the same name, but which of the *étiers* (tidal canals) amongst the dozens by which it is surrounded make it an 'island' is not at all clear. Both Bourgneuf and Bouin have a certain smell of decay, but in Bouin it is accompanied also by a certain picturesqueness which goes some way to compensate, whereas Bourgneuf seems much sadder. And Bouin has the marvellous light of these plains which stretch to the sea to an extent that the bigger place cannot rival.

One can carry through Bourgneuf-en-Retz and find Machecoul about 8 miles on; there is a direct road from Bouin to Machecoul also, and the distance is about 14 miles. Machecoul, Champtocé, Tiffauges, and the Hôtel de la Suze in Nantes . . . according to the evidence at the extraordinary trial of Gilles de Rais, these four were the scenes of appalling sex-inspired acts against young boys, and of their subsequent murders. In the records, the number is left uncertain, but Abbé Eugène Bossard, author of the first major work on Gilles de Rais, could write that 'many people estimate the number of victims at seven or eight hundred, which is possibly an exaggeration, yet one could say, if one pays attention to the confessions of Gilles and his accomplices, that there is nothing improbable about it'. To the careful investigator of the evidence, there can be very much doubt indeed whether there was even one victim! And this may explain why the ruins of his castle in this pleasant village, carry no aura of dark deeds and awaken no emotions. Many writers since Abbé Bossard have recounted how local inhabitants have been afraid to go near the remains of Gilles' castles, even in daylight, ever since. I have been unable to trace the existence of any authority of any kind for such statements.

It is 10 miles from Machecoul across the plain and a corner of the forest of Machecoul to Saint-Philbert-de-Grand-Lieu, a village of some 3,000 inhabitants. The village itself, raised a few feet above sea-level, is on the banks of a stream (the Boulogne) which flows northwards across the marshy flats into the lake of Grand-Lieu 2 miles away. Its chief interest is its very Breton church with stone spire, parts of which are as old as any other in France. Philibert was the founder of the historic monastery of Jumièges but, falling foul of the Mayor of the royal palace he was imprisoned in 674 and later banished. Freed, he founded a second monastery of his own on that island of Noirmoutier (the name means 'Black Monastery') so easily reached from Pornic and there he was first buried. The abbey church on Noirmoutier became a place of pilgrimage to the tomb of the saint, but with repeated Norse attacks on this coast it was felt that his remains must be sheltered elsewhere and were taken, in a leather sack, to Saint-Philbert-de-Grand-Lieu. This was in 836. In 858 they were considered to be in danger once again and were carried off to Cunault, on the Loire near to Saumur. In 862 the saint's poor, tired bones were carted off again, first to the abbey of Massay (near Vierzon), then to Saint-Pourçain (20 miles from Moulins) and finally to Tournus (between Beaune and Mâcon in Burgundy) and there, in the magnificent Romanesque church of Saint-Philibert they rest today in their shrine in the middle one of the three rayonnant chapels of the deambulatory. It is interesting to note that only at Tournus do we find the spelling of Philbert become Philibert, the usually accepted English form.

The ancient crypt in which his body rested is still there, and, in the nave and transepts above, remains of the Carolingian church equally of, or prior to, the time he was brought here may easily be traced. Most of the rest of the church was remodelled in the 17th century, but a visit is still worth while to see the stern nave, the alternating brick and stone courses, and the general air of great antiquity which leads many to believe that these portions are undoubtedly at least 1100 years old.

From Saint-Philbert-de-Grand-Lieu one looks out over a vast expanse of marshes, and on the distant edge of the marshes, the lake covers 17,000 acres. Much of it is reedy, but this does not prevent fishermen from propelling their boats through what looks at a distance to be a solid mass; elsewhere there are quite deep channels. If you have a taste for solitude and quiet, if you love fishing or contemplate a study of water birds, then make your way by a road going north-east from Saint-Philbert to a village called La Chevrolière and then north-west to the hamlet of Passay at which you can hire a boat to take you out on these quiet but melancholy waters. For both, the early winter is the best moment; though at that time of year you may well find that the lake has grown from 17,000 to as much as 22,000 acres.

From Saint-Philbert-de-Grand-Lieu one should head south-east for Saint-Philbert-de-Bretagne and Vieillevigne, then due east to Montaigu and Tiffauges. This last village stands on a little platform above the narrow valley of the Sèvre Nantaise and is well situated, but what visitors come to see are the quite considerable ruins of this important castle in which Gilles de Rais is supposed to have committed so many crimes.

Gilles de Rais was born in 1404, the heir to great fortunes which proved to be great misfortunes for him. His father, who died young, had named a guardian he thought suitable, but a wealthy grandfather (Jean de Craon) overruled the will and by his position and wealth secured confirmation of his guardianship of Gilles. Gilles had a fair education for the times, but was completely spoiled by the doting grandfather who, when the boy was only 13, arranged for him to be affianced to a Norman heiress whose wealth and lands would make the boy even more important in the world. The little heiress died before the marriage could be performed. Nothing daunted, Jean de Craon raised his sights, and Gilles, at 14, set his seal to a contract of marriage with Béatrix de Rohan at a ceremony at Vannes attended by all the nobility of Brittany. Once more a little bride-to-be died before the actual ceremony could be performed. So Jean de Craon tried again. This time he hooked Catherine de Thouars who would bring Gilles Tiffauges, Pouzauges, Savenay and Confolens and who knows how many great estates to round off Gilles' vast possessions. She was about 16 at the time, the same age as her fiancé.

Gilles was away at the wars, playing a courageous part in the final struggle between the Montforts and the Penthièvres for the right to rule Brittany. As soon as the war was over Gilles, was married to Catherine. The break in civil war was only temporary; it swelled into a national war between the king of France (or as much of it as acknowledged him) and the English. During the next six years Gilles distinguished himself in countless attacks upon English-held fortresses, but the general trend of fortune was against Charles VII who would shortly have decided to retire to the south of France had not Joan of Arc appeared. The period of Gilles' greatest glory had begun, for to him Charles gave the duty of watching over Joan at all times and of defending her in battle, which he did to such good purpose that when the king was crowned and anointed at Reims, Gilles was made marshal of France. He also had the honour of fetching the Holy Ampulla, which contained the oil with which all French kings were anointed, from the abbey of Saint-Rémi and returning it after the ceremony.

After Joan's capture, the only one of the French captains who had served with her, who had been her companions from the beginning, who seems to have made any attempt to approach her, was Gilles. He is known to have reconnoitred the surroundings of Rouen. Whatever he had in mind evidently could not be done: Joan had rubbed too many courtiers up the wrong way, and not all soldiers welcomed a country girl who won the battles they had not been able to fight successfully. It is at least possible that Gilles' devotion to Joan was resented . . . and remembered, not to his good.

With the death of Joan, Gilles became another man. There was one more courageous engagement, and then inaction. He became a man puffed up with pride, living always with all the trappings of luxury, living the part of the open-handed noble gentleman with such exaggeration as to make it difficult to believe in his folly. He began to run short of money – he who had been probably the richest man in Brittany, one with few rivals to his wealth in France as well. The property was there, but not the ready money. So the property was turned into ready money, at a tithe of its real value. Amongst those who bought great properties for very small amounts of money were the duke of Brittany and Jean de Malestroit, bishop of Nantes.

Eventually he sought the aid of necromancy. It was, of course, a sin in the eyes of the church, but one in which most noblemen had dabbled a little at one time or another. The philosophers' stone never appeared, nor any demons, but a number of necromantic experts did and in the end were the direct cause of Gilles' death. But he himself took the first fatal step. He agreed to sell a property of his, Saint-Etienne-de-Mer-Morte, to Guillaume le Ferron, who was protected by the duke of Brittany. Perhaps the money was not forthcoming, whereas Jean, the brother of Guillaume, was already in possession of the castle, and for this, or some other reason, Gilles determined to get it back. One Sunday, having posted troops to cover the castle, he burst into the church, drove Jean le Ferron out of it during Mass, forced him at sword's point to order his men in the castle to surrender, and then sent Jean away under guard to lie prisoner in the strong castle of Tiffauges.

This piled folly upon folly; under feudal laws, he now had the duke of Brittany as an open opponent; his action in interrupting the Mass with drawn sword and removing a man from the church was

One of the great
fortresses of the
Middle Ages, the
castle of Angers.
Deer still feed in
the deep moats.

The splendid keep
of Trèves stands
in a backwater
of the Loire,
separated from the
main stream by
one of the
innumerable sandy
islands.

Saumur, as seen from
the Loire. From the
right, the Gothic
Town Hall and next
to it a much older
and more warlike
part; then the 12th
and 13th century
church and, on the
hill, the powerful
white stone castle.

In this room of the
château de Langeais
the marriage contract
between Charles VIII
and Anne of Brittany
was signed in 1491:
their portraits on
wood stand on the
table.

an offence the bishop would not forgive. It was perhaps unfortunate that the king of France was thinking of cancelling the sales of Gilles' property to safeguard the interests of Catherine de Thouars, Gilles' wife. This would not please either duke or bishop, who might have to sell back at purchase price the great bargains they had obtained.

Jean de Malestroit set out on a pastoral visit, and used it to accumulate 'evidence' against Gilles, all of which was vague and much of it second-hand. Nevertheless, he produced enough to encourage him to send others on a secret inquiry. The bishop decided on arrest and trial of Gilles and his companions. In a letter addressed to the clergy, clerks and notaries public of the diocese he stated: 'It is now certain that Gilles de Raiz, nobleman, baron of the said place in the diocese of Nantes, has caused many innocent victims to perish and that upon them he has committed the sin of sodomy; that on many occasions he invoked demons, and made pacts with them and made sacrifices to them; that he has been guilty of heresy, of offending Divine Majesty, of confusing the Faith, and of causing scandal to many. . .'

The president of the tribunal of the Church which judged Gilles de Rais was this same Bishop Jean de Malestroit who had pre-judged him. The judge was Friar Jean Blouyn, Vice-Inquisitor of the diocese; the parish priest of Saint-Nicolas-de-Nantes appeared for the prosecution; three bishops were Assessors. There was no defending counsel. The one Assessor who was a layman was Pierre de l'Hôpital who was to preside over the ducal (civil) trial.

As regards offences on young boys, their abduction and disappearance, the evidence given was lamentable.

Nicole, wife of Vincent Bonnereau; Philipe, wife of Mathis Ernaut; Jehanne, wife of Guillaume Prieur of the parish of the Holy Cross at Nantes, recall on oath that they knew a son of Jehan Janvret and his wife, living at the house of Monsieur d'Estampes [brother of the duke of Brittany], the child then being about nine years old, of whose loss and disappearance they heard the father and mother bitterly complain, about Saint John's day two years back; thereafter they never saw the child again or heard where he was. They state that, for the last year and half or

thereby, they have heard it commonly said that the Sire de Rais
and his men abducted and killed little children. They also stated
that they had known a young boy, child of the late Eonnet de
Villeblanche and, over the last three months, to have heard the
mother of this child complain of his loss or disappearance, and
that since the mother's complaint they had not seen him. Further,
Raoulet de Launay, toolmaker, said that around the last feast of the
Conception, he made a quilted doublet for the child of the
said Villeblanche, who then lived in the house of Poitou, and
that it was Poitou and not the said Macée (*presumably the wife
of Villefranche, mentioned but not named in the preceding depo-
sition*) who bargained with him for the making of the doublet,
for which he was paid twenty sous; since then he has not seen
the child.

Such, then, was the kind of evidence collected on oath. In a
few cases, as in the last one above, a servant of Gilles is mentioned.
At no time is it claimed that he himself had any direct part in the
disappearance of a child.

Gilles denied everything. He treated the tribunal with such disdain
that eventually Jean de Malestroit excommunicated him. Then his
companions and servants were brought in. He had declared openly
to the tribunal that they would clear him. Instead, their evidence
was damning. They told of alchemy, and attempts to raise the devil,
which are often very funny. And they told well-rehearsed stories of
the abominations committed by Gilles upon little boys who all
found death at his hand. The witnesses, of course, were just innocent
bystanders. These accounts are so shocking that it is only recently
they have been translated out of medieval Latin into French from
the records of the trial. In Latin they appeared for the first time in
the 1880s.

If one believes them at all and accepts as low a figure as 200
victims, then the question arises as to what happened to the corpses.
The accounts given in the evidence are patently untrue and quite
impossible. You cannot burn 20 or 30 or 50 or 60 children's bodies
without any special furnace, or fuel, or place in which to do it
without anybody else in the castle being aware of what you are

doing. There is strong testimony that the 'powder' left over was scattered on the ground, but nowhere the slightest indication of how the bones and teeth became powder. If this part of the evidence is untrue, what is the rest worth?

Gilles de Rais, from defying the tribunal, overnight became a willing witness against himself. He confessed to everything, and more, to things possible and to things impossible. A good lawyer could drive coach and horses through his evidence. It was good enough, though, for the tribunal. Excommunication was lifted, Gilles granted the comforts of the church, and the right to be hanged before being burned. Nine years after Joan of Arc, he too went to the stake. It would be another sixteen years before Joan was rehabilitated. The family tried for a rehabilitation of Gilles, without success.

No person of reasonable intelligence and without preconceived ideas can possibly read the evidence of this trial without remembering some other extraordinary ones in our own time, complete with the brainwashing of which Gilles seems to have been the victim. Although it is obvious he had become a psychotic, I cannot believe in any of the evidence brought to establish murder of children. And as for his being a Bluebeard, that story belongs to the age-old folklore of many nations and there is not the slightest reason to believe that Perrault even thought of Gilles de Rais when he wrote his version of it. There is no contemporary evidence as to Gilles' appearance – no portrait, no description.

Such being the case, the remains of Gilles' castle of Tiffauges, which came to him in his wife's dowry, can carry no feeling of evil. The ruins are vast, covering something approaching eight acres within the outer walls. The best preserved part is the square keep of the 12th century, with a moat around, and another much later one, the *tour du Vidame*, a strong cylindrical tower of the 15th century with giant machicolations. There is a Guard Room and a Watch Room with good timber-work, and a 13th century chapel built on an 11th century crypt. All interesting and very typical of their times.

Two miles farther from Tiffauges on N 753 one meets N 148 bis;

a left turn on to this and in 10 miles one has reached Clisson, a most picturesque little town. In Clisson the Sèvre Nantaise and the Moine become one river and in the most charming way imaginable each is crossed by a 14th century, hump-backed bridge. From both bridges the scene is so photogenic with water and trees and old buildings (including the magnificent castle) that one could spend all day on either, finding new angles and delightful alternatives.

The original castle protected the marches of Poitou from intruding Bretons. Eventually the powerful Armoricans added Clisson to their own territories, and Clisson has been Breton ever since. The castle of which one sees the imposing ruins today was built by Olivier de Clisson the Elder when he returned from the Holy Land in 1223. Of Olivier II little is known but that he had three famous sons, Gauthier, Amauri and Olivier III, who all took an active and courageous part in the wars between the Penthièvre and Montfort factions, sometimes on one side, sometimes on the other. The important thing was not so much which side one took, but to enjoy a good fight. Olivier was the rival of Duguesclin, Constable of France and when the latter died he handed down the marshal's baton to his esteemed enemy. Charles VI confirmed Duguesclin's gift, and Olivier de Clisson led the French forces against the English. He died without leaving male heirs. The castle eventually passed into the hands of the dukes of Brittany, but its great days were over and century by century it frittered away. It was confiscated by the Republic in 1793. Then, two centuries and more since it had last seen a battle, the old castle became a front line again. First taken by the insurgents of the Vendée, then retaken by Kléber and the Republican soldiers, the castle suffered greatly, and Clisson was utterly destroyed.

The ruins of the castle may be visited and there is a *son-et-lumière* performance there in the summer, to which the complicated story attached to it provides an excellent script. But to most of us the best of Clisson is the confluence of the rivers in the shadow of the romantic ruins above.

Continuing along N 148 bis towards Nantes, one comes, again in almost exactly 10 miles, to a right-hand turning which leads to Haute-Goulaine, a little village on the edge of marshes. Here, the

Château de Goulaine presents one of the best remaining examples of the flowery Gothic of the second half of the 15th century which already foreshadowed the Renaissance. The façade, of the utmost elegance of design, ends in two fine towers with flattened angles. This building is entirely in the tufa of Saumur, which hardens with time and is in a splendid state of preservation. The two wings date from the beginning of the 17th century.

In almost every way, Goulaine is worthy of comparison with the finest of the better-known châteaux upstream, for what it may lack in exciting history it more than makes up by having been the home of the same family from the earliest times to the present day. In 1100, Alphonse de Goulaine was appointed arbiter between Philip I of France and Henry I of England. Whatever the difference between them was, he settled it so satisfactorily that they agreed his arms should thereafter carry three leopards *or* and *azure* for England, and one and a half lilies *or* (*fleur-de-lys*) for France. There are only a few stones which show the château of this early date.

Then there was young Yolande de Goulaine. Her father was away with most of his men fighting the English, but the English (with that perfidy which, as all Frenchmen know, is natural to them) came round the other way and besieged the castle. Yolande urged the handful of men left with her to fight to the end, and most reluctantly they did so. The siege lasted a month, and then shortage of food melted away the last inclination the men had to fight. Every day Yolande went to the tower to look for her father's troops, but every day was disappointed. The men became mutinous and were preparing to throw open the gates to the English. Yolande preferred death to dishonour and climbed to the top of the tower with the intention of throwing herself off it. As she prepared to make the fatal leap, she saw the sun dancing on the helmets and the swords and the lances of her father's men. And this, is much more likely to have influenced Perrault to re-tell the Bluebeard story than anything he ever knew of Gilles de Rais.

Christophe de Goulaine, Gentleman of the Chamber to Louis XII and François I, built the earlier part of the present château about 1480, and his son completed it in 1520. Later additions belong to the 17th century, when it became a marquisate. It was confiscated during the Revolution, then purchased by a Nantes ship owner, who sold it back in 1858 to the then marquis de Goulaine.

In it we find room after room, splendidly decorated, splendidly furnished. There is a *salon rouge* and a *salon bleu* with coffered ceilings and there is, as at Cheverny, a king's bedroom, only at Goulaine a king slept in it. When Louis XIV thought it advisable not to be too near Paris when Fouquet was to be arrested, he decided to attend the States General at Nantes and from 1 to 6 September 1661, he stayed at Goulaine, with the queen. And doubtless the Goulaine finances were very much the worse for the visit of the king and his Court.

Goulaine is open to the public all the year round, and the visit can be wholeheartedly recommended.

A country road runs from Haute-Goulaine to Basse-Goulaine, and on to join the river road (N 751) by the side of the Loire, which can be crossed by the first bridge above Nantes to Thouaré, where one takes the road to Carquefou. From this strangely named but otherwise unremarkable place one reaches two châteaux, La Seilleraye on the river side and La Gascherie (at La Chapelle-sur-Erdre) on the other. The Château de La Seilleraye was designed by François Mansart and is a good example of the neo-classicism of the 17th century of which he was both the prophet and the exponent. Madame de Sévigné, the eternal writer of letters, stayed in the château on a number of occasions and addressed letters from it. She had no great opinion of it: 'it has a big main building 30 *toises* long (a *toise* was six feet), two wings, and two corner pavilions'. The absence of any other comment fairly puts poor François Mansart in his place. It is true that the façade is extraordinarily plain – the only ornamentation is on the pediment which consists of vases out of which spring flames. Inside, however, it must have been very fine indeed, judging by what still remains of the *décor* of the time. The Louis XV wood-work, white on grey, is most decorative, and the staircase fit for a king's palace. It is now a hospital, but it is possible to see some of it, on application.

La Gascherie, at La Chapelle-sur-Erdre, can only be seen from the outside. It is a 15th century château on the backwater of the river, which makes an ornamental lake for it. The park is very pleasant, and from it one can gaze with wonder at the building. I am not sure when it was rebuilt, but it now appears in the guise of a mid-Victorian version of a late medieval building, quite remarkable in its own peculiar way.

The river Erdre is very difficult to reach by road, which perhaps accounts for its charm. When one does get to it, say at Nort-sur-Erdre, where one can get a boat, it is a haven of peace from the great city to which it is so near. One could spend many peaceful days exploring the network of big and little waterways. Our own road at the moment is not northwards to Nort-sur-Erdre, but 4 miles southwards to Nantes itself. For the moment, we can put the road maps away.

About Nantes I have a divided mind. It is a city, large by French standards, of a quarter of a million inhabitants. It is a thriving place, well built, with many attractive avenues and squares. It has a long and interesting history, and many ancient buildings worth the seeing. It is a port, and the coming and going of ships always adds interest. Yet somehow it just fails to strike the right chord. Perhaps because of the knowledge of the loss in recent years of so much that was old; the difficulties of parking anywhere near anything one wants to see and, in spite of all its activity, its air of being a dull provincial city.

Not only is it on the Loire, but three tributaries flowed through the town. Now only the Erdre is visible, and that for only part of its course towards its junction with the main river. The Loire, too, was divided into more branches than I can now remember. Little trains used to dart across the quays and shunt and pick up wagons and send car drivers nearly frantic with frustration. The last part of the Erdre is now invisible under a broad boulevard, and the other two streams have completely disappeared underground also. The trains run through tunnels and deep cuttings and are seen no more. The two city islands, Feydeau and Gloriette, are islands no more, but joined to the city on every side. Much that was picturesque – almost unique – has been sacrificed for a greater flow of traffic. One gets the impression that much of it has to keep circulating because it can't find anywhere to park.

Nantes is rich in history. In the struggles between the Montfort and the Penthièvre factions, Nantes first sided with the former, but in 1342 was besieged and taken by the opposing clan. Edward III of England unsuccessfully besieged it in his turn. In 1491, by the marriage of Anne of Brittany to Charles VIII, Nantes, with all the duchy, became French. It backed the Catholic League against Henry of Navarre, and when finally it had to give way to him as Henri IV of France, he made it the place of signature of the famous Edict, intended to ensure that Catholic and Protestant could live in harmony together. In 1789, Nantes declared for the Republic to come, and successfully resisted attacks by the Royalist and Catholic men of the Vendée. In 1793, under the Terror, the infamous Carrier for four long months carried out his campaign of persecution of all those under suspicion of being against (or only lukewarm for) the régime. I would suggest considerable caution in accepting all the stories of the *noyades*, the killing by drowning. Some are certainly true, but others, such as those about hinged doors in the ships' bottom, are clearly materially impossible – the ships would have sunk with their human victims and blocked the river, something which historically never happened. In this same year, the army of the Vendée was decisively defeated in an effort to take the town, but took it and held it for a short time in 1799. In 1830, Nantes was one of the first provincial towns to declare against the last legitimate French king, Charles X. In 1914, it was a principal supply base for the British, and later for the Americans. After 1940, it waged constant subterranean warfare against the German occupiers; it paid for it by the shooting of hostages (the boulevard which runs above what was once the course of the Erdre is named *Cours des cinquante otages*).

This is the shortest conceivable summary of a long and intricate history, which means that almost every old nook and corner of the city has its own story, and sometimes its own moment of glory. One sees the castle, for example, with a moat all round it, but originally on the south side it was the Loire itself which flowed peacefully by (whereas now the nearest point is all but half a mile away). And on the Loire, just below the castle, John Knox spent the long winter of 1548 as a galley slave of a rather unusual kind. His correspondence appears to have been considerable. To the con-

gregation of the castle at Saint Andrews he was able to send a force-
ful digest of a tract which had been sent to him, and to it added
quite long recommendations. Three of those captured with him,
were imprisoned on Mont-Saint-Michel, and wrote to him for
spiritual guidance as to whether they might, without hurt to their
souls, attempt to escape. He replied that they could, so long as there
was to be no taking of life in the attempt. They did escape, and they
did get back to Scotland. The mystery remains: how did he get his
incoming and outgoing correspondence carried to destination
whilst a prisoner? How, as a galley slave, did he get pen and paper
and the leisure to write at very considerable length? Somebody with
great power protected him and arranged for his release the following
spring. Who was it? There seems no answer.

He would have seen the castle from his galley very much as we
see it today; sturdy round towers and curtain walls, crowned by
battlements and machicolations, were part of the original fortress,
the one in which Gilles de Rais was imprisoned before and during his
trial. François II, last duke of Brittany, rebuilt and added to it. His
daughter Anne of Brittany, twice queen of France, was born in the
new château in 1476. She married Charles VIII in 1491 and, at his
death, his successor to the throne, Louis XII (1499), was married to
her in the château. It was in her time that the main dwelling, the
Grand-Logis was built. It is tall, towering over the battlements, and
very severe.

In the *Annales de Nantes*, under the year 1661, one finds that
'on September 5, the king arrested his *Surintendant des Finances*
(Financial Secretary), Fouquet'. The king was at the château de
Goulaine, as we have just seen, officially for the purpose of opening
the States General. One has to go back to 17 August to understand
the real reason for his presence. On that day he left Fontainebleau in
state, escorted by the French Guards, accompanied by the queen
mother, and went straight to Fouquet's château of Vaux-le-Vicomte.
The perfection of all he saw, the evidence everywhere of lavish
expenditure which exceeded all that he had so far ever spent on his
own palaces, convinced him that he should arrest Fouquet and bring
charges of peculation from national funds. Indeed, there was no
other way Fouquet could have got the money. In a whispered

conversation, the queen mother dissuaded him from acting on impulse. Better, she thought to arrest him well away from Paris and his powerful friends. So the king, through Colbert, pressed Fouquet to find ready money for the expensive journey, and squeezed him dry. Then, in Nantes, on September 4, the lieutenant of the king's Musketeers (d'Artagnan, of *The Three Musketeers* fame) stopped Fouquet's sedan chair as he was carried through the town and arrested him.

Fouquet was accompanied by a crowd of hangers-on. By the time d'Artagnan and his prisoner had arrived at the castle, not one was left to wish him well. From the castle, d'Artagnan accompanied him to Amboise, and from Amboise to Vincennes. On the way there was a little incident which throws a lot of light on the real-life d'Artagnan. Belle-Ile (mentioned in Chapter One as visible in good weather from Piriac) belonged to Fouquet, and was heavily armed. The king feared that the garrison, paid by Fouquet, would only accept a written order signed by Fouquet to deliver their fortress to the king's men. The king had instructed d'Artagnan to stop at Oudon, not far up-river on the way to Amboise, and there insist on obtaining from his prisoner just such an order. But hardly had they left Nantes when Fouquet remembered he had not made the castle over to the king, and that this might be held against him at his trial. He pleaded in vain to d'Artagnan to halt the coach at some place where he might write an order to the commander of the garrison. In vain he pleaded. 'His Majesty has instructed me to obtain this order from you at Oudon. You will give it to me there, and not before.'

Again, the king had wanted and expected a death sentence at the trial, but what could be proved against Fouquet was not nearly as serious as everybody had expected it to be. The judges therefore voted for a sentence of banishment. A very angry king had to announce that 'exercising the Royal Prerogative of Mercy, the penalty of banishment is mitigated to one of Perpetual Imprisonment.' As he took his prisoner from the Bastille to Pignerol in Piedmont, now Pinerolo in Italy (where he died), the cruel humour of this 'mitigation' escaped his humourless, disciplined mind: *je n'entends rien à toute cette affaire,* 'I understand nothing about the whole business,' he grumbled to all who would listen. He was not the debonair, quick-witted musketeer of the novel.

The man himself not wise nor witty –
His swordplay, though, exceeding pretty.

Nowadays the castle is almost entirely taken up by museums, the *Musée d'Art Populaire Régional*, the *Musée d'Art Décoratif* and the *Musée de la Marine*. Delightful as are the settings of these three, they cannot compare in interest with the *Musée Municipal des Beaux-Arts*, in a rather horrid, featureless building of the end of the 19th century. This museum is exceedingly rich in first rate examples of the work of artists ranging from Rembrandt to Raoul Dufy. There are three fascinating works by Georges de la Tour which alone would be sufficient reason to spend a while in the museum.

Near to the castle is the cathedral. Nothing remains of the 12th century Romanesque predecessor. The present one had its first stone laid by Duke Jean V in 1434. Building ended in 1938 with the completion of choir and chapels. As a building it shows the results one might expect from such protracted construction, in the century by century decadence of architectural inspiration. It suffered heavily from bombing in June 1944, but reconstruction has proceeded steadily and with great good taste.

The interior of the cathedral is very fine. Pillars have no capitals, rising in a single flight from ground to vaults. An unexpectedly light and elegant triforium runs above the arcades. The nave greatly outshines the choir, begun (in its present version which has had to be rebuilt after the bombing) in 1849.

The right transept holds a Renaissance jewel, one of the most satisfying and beautiful pieces of sculpture in France. It is the tomb of François II, duke of Brittany, and his wife, Marguerite de Foix, provided by their daughter, Anne of Brittany the work of Michel Colomb, the finest of Breton sculptors and the artistic father of Jean Goujon. It is in white, black and red marble. There is a life-size statue at each of the four corners: Justice, with sword and scales (said to be a portrait of Duchess Anne herself), Power, strangling a dragon of heresy, Prudence and Wisdom, double-faced, holding mirror and compass, and Temperance holding a lantern in one hand and a horse's bit in the other. All four are great works of art in their own right, most delicately executed. The twelve apostles are ranged in niches on each side of the tomb, attended by mourners. Upon it lie the recumbent figures of François and his wife: their feet rest on a lion and a greyhound, and three angels support their heads. It is all at once impressive and pathetic and majestic. Pathetic, because it is not their bones within the tomb. In the fury of the Revolution their remains were thrown out and scattered to the four winds. Instead, in 1815, the remains of Arthur de Richement, duke of Brittany and constable of France in the days of Charles VII were substituted.

There are many things to see in Nantes, and around it. One should go well down the north bank of the Loire, almost out of the city, and climb up towards the pilgrimage church of Sainte-Anne. From the Belvédère de Sainte-Anne, below it, there is a magnificent view over the port and shipyards. Nothing that one sees from the town itself has prepared one for this vast activity spread over a vast area. And although the boat trip up the Erdre from the Quai de Versailles up as far as Sucé is not really comparable with the outing in a smaller boat from much farther upstream at Nort-sur-Erdre, it is still worth taking.

Nantes took the Revolution very seriously, and two items of its revolutionary history make quaint reading. The first is dated 23 August 1790.

A society, The Friends of the Revolution, had been formed in England and had appeared to applaud the efforts of the French nation to renew its Government. The Friends of the Constitution in Nantes considered this as a call to reunite two peoples so long rivals and enemies, and decided to offer a banquet, at its own expense, to the English still living in and around Nantes.

At midday, August 23, 400 members of The Friends of the Constitution were already assembled at their meeting place. A deputation was sent to fetch their English guests who, on arrival, were greeted with loud applause. After many speeches, and replies to speeches, three artillery salvoes announced their departure for the open-air dinner. A procession was formed, which set out to the music of a military band. The President, accompanied by the English guests and the heads of the three Administrations in

Nantes, was in the centre. On arrival at the tree-surrounded open space where the dinner was to take place, the procession marched round the tables and took up position behind the President who laid a banner representing the entwined flags of France and England upon an altar. Inscribed upon the altar was a verse, which he proceeded to read aloud:

> O celestial Peace! O saintly Humanity!
> Kneeling before this thy altar, let France and England
> Swear to rally all the peoples of the Earth
> To the just Laws and true Happiness that only Liberty
>   provides!

Towards the end of the dinner salvoes of artillery, mingling with the sound of musical instruments, announced the most patriotic and philanthropic toasts.

Later, the President and one other member of the Society were delegated to proceed to London to present to Lord Stanhope and the members of the Society over which he presided the aforesaid banner and an account of the dinner, as evidence of our wishes for the reunion of France and England, for universal peace, and for the well-being of the world.

Did the president ever reach London? If so, how did Lord Stanhope receive him, if at all? Of this we know nothing. Nor do we know how much the dinner cost, though this was something which rankled when there was so little return for it. The annalist's second and last entry regarding this 'fraternal gesture' is dated February 1793. Very different indeed are its terms, eighteen months after the friendly dinner:

> However ill-placed our town may be for fitting-out privateers, resentment against the perfidy of the English, natural enough in a town which had so unrequitedly taken fraternal steps to induce that country to act in the interests of all humanity – which is the same as saying our interests – led to the arming of fifteen corsairs whose crews were voluntarily reinforced by the sailors of thirty-eight Netherlands ships and twenty-one English on which an embargo had just been placed.

One hears no more either of the dinner or of the privateers, for Nantes had other troubles to face. On 10 March following, the Republicans found all roads round Nantes cut by the rebels. The Catholic and royalist gentry of Brittany had risen against the godless Convention. The War of the Vendée had begun.

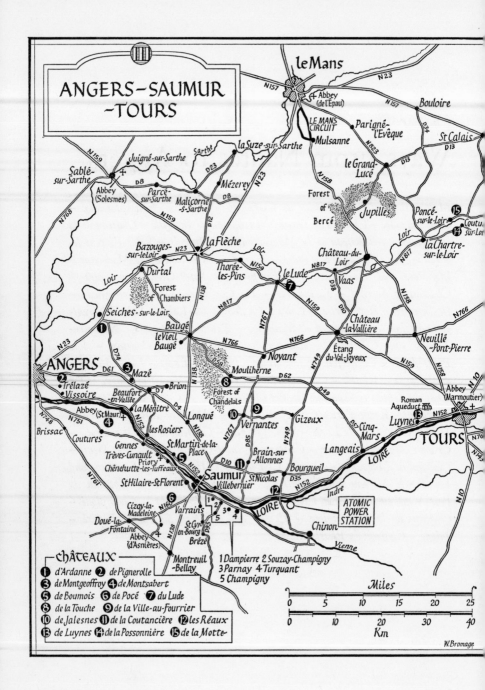

ANGERS–SAUMUR –TOURS

CHÂTEAUX

1. d'Ardanne
2. de Pignerolle
3. de Montgeoffroy
4. de Montsabert
5. de Boumois
6. de Pocé
7. du Lude
8. de la Touche
9. de la Ville-au-Fourrier
10. de Jalesnes
11. de la Coutancière
12. les Réaux
13. de Luynes
14. de la Possonnière
15. de la Motte

1 Dampierre 2 Souzay-Champigny
3 Parnay 4 Turquant
5 Champigny

Miles

Km

W. Bromage

Chapter Three

Ways from Nantes to Angers

From the estuary up as far as Nantes it is not easy to see the particular qualities which have made the Loire so admired a river. It is a consolation for leaving Nantes without having seen all one would have wished to see – and this is a universal experience – that for the first time one meets the river which one has been led to expect, broad, slow, usually shining silver or blue, meandering through a countryside so well wooded, so green and so rich in fine dwellings of past centuries that it belongs more to the fairy-tale world than to our own.

There is a country road following the right bank fairly closely: the going is not fast, but it is much more interesting than N 23 which hardly comes within sight of the river for the first 25 miles, whereas D 68 brings one close in after the first 7 miles.

At Mauves-sur-Loire suddenly there are rock cliffs the better part of 200 feet high, which give heavenly views over the Loire and the calm countryside. Little D 68 takes one past the Château de Clermont, a miniature palace in bricks built about 1630, surrounded by a park which rises to the cliff edge. Then at Oudon, standing at the confluence of the tiny river Hâvre with the Loire, a fine octagonal keep, surrounded by the ruins of a medieval fortress, seems to rear its proud head a hundred feet high against the sky. Inside, it is empty and one looks straight up its impressive height, looking for the marks of where each individual floor used to be. The fact that they have all disappeared long since does not prevent one from reaching the top, for there is a spiral staircase cut in the thickness of the wall. From the top one has the impression of looking to the very limits of the world, a green and pleasant world. The river itself is crowded with alluvial islands of such extreme fertility that nobody dares even contemplate cutting them away to give the river a better flow.

On a wooded height across the river is Champtoceaux, 240 feet up, long disputed between the dukes of Brittany and the counts of Anjou. This is almost the last connection with Brittany, and from now the styles and the history of Anjou take the place of those of Brittany. From the town's promenade there is a view over the curving river from Nantes right up to Saint-Georges-sur-Loire, which is only 11 miles from Angers. The remains of the powerfully fortified town of Châteauceaux, destroyed before Champtoceaux was built, are reached through a medieval gateway; to the right, a path edges the old fortress walls. Town and fortress were destroyed at the end of the succession of wars between the de Montfort and the Blois families.

Abandoning the river for a short distance, N 75 will lead from Champtoceaux to Liré, five miles away, on a little stream of the same name. At Liré there is a modern château, La Turmelière; in its grounds, between shady avenues of old chestnut trees, are the few remaining ruins of the château in which Joachim du Bellay was born and which he made for ever famous in one of the best loved of all French poems.

In my earlier book on the Loire, I risked an English version of this poem, for those who did not know it in French. I have polished the original, and it may be worth printing the new version in order to make sense of what follows.

> Happy the man, like Ulysses, who can attain
> A noble journey's end or, like he who won
> The Fleece, return in wisdom, travels done,
> And ever after with his kin remain.
> Alas! When shall I see the smoke again
> Rise from my hamlet in the morning sun
> Or when regain my house (my courses run)
> For which I would whole provinces disdain?
> Better the dwelling which my fathers made
> Than Roman palace pompously array'd;
> Better my slate than marble; better, too,

Than Tiber's flood this Gallic Loire of mine,
My Liré hills than mountain-Palatine,
Than rich sea air, the fragrance of Anjou.

of which the French is:

Heureux qui, comme Ulysse, a fait un beau voyage,
Ou comme celui-là qui conquit la Toison,
Et puis est retourné, plein d'usage et raison,
Vivre entre ses parents le reste de son âge!
Quand reverrai-je, hélas, de mon petit village
Fumer la cheminée, et en quelle saison
Reverrai-je le clos de ma pauvre maison,
Qui m'est une province, et beaucoup d'avantage?
Plus me plaît le séjour qu'ont bâti mes aieux,
Que de palais romains le front audacieux,
Plus que le marbre dur me plaît l'ardoise fine;
Plus mon Loire gaulois que le Tibre latin,
Plus mon petit Liré que le Mont Palatin,
Et plus que l'air marin la douceur angevine.

Caught up in diplomacy, backed by his powerful relatives, Joachim du Bellay was always too busy to return. Perhaps that is why his father's house fell into disrepair, and we are left only with his poems which have proved more durable.

A journey of a few miles only off the direct road, 2½ miles east-wards from Liré along N 75 brings one to Bouzillé; on leaving this village, the left fork leads to La Bourgonnière, the right fork to La Mauvoisinière.

The Château de la Bourgonnière is 19th century, with a sort of Victorian-Greek Ionic peristyle, because the original 15th century castle was burnt to the ground during the war of the Vendée. However, there are two happy remnants to be seen. A little to the left of the present building is a sturdy keep, over 100 feet high, an octagonal staircase turret, a fat cylindrical tower, heavily machico-lated. To the right of the château, an enchanting Renaissance chapel, younger by a hundred years than the warlike remains. In a centre retable is a statue locally widely venerated of Our Lady, between Saint Anthony and Saint Sebastian, admirably executed. The great curiosity here, however, is a statue of Christ, nearly 9 feet high, clad in a tunic, and contemporary with the chapel.

Very different is La Mauvoisinière, reached by the right-hand road. It belonged in the 15th and 16th centuries to a family closely related to that of Joachim du Bellay, by name La Bouteille, but the present château is later having been (by repute only) designed by Mansart. The gardens have recently often been attributed to Le Nôtre, though in fact they are the creation of the Marquis de Gibot in 1860. The statues which decorate these gardens are all that remain of the collection formed by the cardinal for his own château de Richelieu. There are 14 antique statues, 3 torsos, and a bust of Vitellius. Other busts exist, displayed on columns of red porphyry, in the courtyard of the Préfecture at Tours, but no other statues from the Richelieu acquisitions.

The marquis de Gibot had the excellent good taste not to change the architecture, but to leave its severe façade and projecting wings with no more ornament than turrets mounted on pendentives which belong to the original design. He also left the interior *décor* which perfectly reflects the taste of its time – the closing years of the 18th century.

Most of these country châteaux of Anjou are quite different from the more ambitious and palatial châteaux of Touraine, in that they were essentially places for permanent residence, whereas those of Touraine were all too often only places in which to stay for a season – often the hunting season. It was the land and not office at Court which paid for their upkeep. Even quite large ones, like La Mauvoisinière have a family air.

One can either return northwards along N 751 and N 763, cross the river on the very fine suspension bridge (1953) and see Ancenis, or else proceed westwards from Bouzillé to Saint-Florent-le-Vieil. Ancenis spreads over a wide semi-circle above the Loire, and the situation is delightful. It has some old houses, a few remains of the once powerful fortress, and an over-restored 15th-16th century church. If time is a consideration, it is better to push on to Saint-Florent-le-Vieil.

There is not much that is really old left in Saint-Florent, but there is a magnificent sculpture by David d'Angers in the church of the old abbey, a masterpiece whose style is a little out of fashion in this generation but which is bound to be fully appreciated again. And there is always the climb up the narrow streets and the vast view from the terrace to make the visit worthwhile.

A word about Saint Florent. The saint-to-be was a hermit in these parts until the end of his life – he lived to the fine age of 123. There are two schools of thought about this. The first maintains that he was so successful in converting the heathen around him that the good Lord kept on putting off his return home whilst there was still so much of this splendid work to do. The second puts everything the other way round. The Lord appeared to Florent in a vision and promised him he should live until he had converted 10,000 souls, after which the hermit did not see any particular reason to hurry in his task. In fact it came to an abrupt end when the chief of a wandering tribe was converted by Florent, and ordered his 3,000 followers to do the same, which substantially shortened the saint's life. His successor built an abbey where the hermitage had been, which prospered over many years until the greater abbey of Saint-Florent was built at Saumur.

On 4 March 1793, rebel bands of the Vendée tried to take Cholet, away to the south, and were repulsed by Republican troops. They were not definitely defeated, for they retired in good order on Saint-Florent, set fire to the district administrative office and seized its money: this was on that same day when the people of Nantes found that their road communications with the outside world had been cut. Rebel bands had overnight become the Army of the Vendée.

The following October Cholet was again the scene of violent fighting between the Republicans and the Army of La Vendée. A considerable number of Republican prisoners was taken. Finally, however, after heavy losses, the men of Vendée fell back on Saint-Florent. Bonchamp, perhaps their most distinguished leader, was mortally wounded. To gain a breathing space it was essential to cross the river, where the Republicans would not be expecting them. There were only a few old boats available, and they caused many casualties through being heavily overloaded.

So the men of Vendée built across the river the most extraordinary bridge that has ever carried an army. Doors, window-frames, planks, beams and all kinds of wooden oddments were fastened by cords (and withies, when cord ran out) to the most tenuous of stakes hastily driven into the sands. Sixty thousand soldiers, old men, women and children, under fire from a Republican post at Varades, worked day and night to build and keep in repair this fragile link. During the night of 17 to 18 October the bulk of the people crossed; the operation was completed on the morning of the 18th. On that day, Bonchamp died on the island in the river and, dying, cried, 'Mercy for the prisoners; that is Bonchamp's order.' Kléber, already distinguishing himself as a leader in the Republican Army, describes the result in his memoirs.

On the 18th, about 11 o'clock in the morning, our outposts along the road from Saint-Florent to Beaupréau reported a considerable number of men approaching: these were Republican prisoners, to the number of four or five thousand, all loud in their praises of their Liberator, Bonchamp, who was just about to draw his last breath. To get any idea of this event one needs to have seen this terrible yet touching scene, to have heard their accounts of their afflictions and of their hopes, and the expressions of their gratitude.

In a particularly cruel and bloody civil war this episode stands alone as an example of human kindness.

To the 14th century church of Saint-Pierre a 17th century octagonal bell-tower has been added. The severity of both makes the juxta-position less out of place than it sounds. In fact the view of the church is quite agreeable. At the end of the nave is Bonchamp's tomb. The dying man has raised himself on his left hand, and with his right is calling attention to his last order, which is inscribed below, 'mercy for the prisoners'. This was David-d'Angers' own act of gratitude. His father was amongst those soldiers saved by Bonchamp's generous act from eventual certain death. One must remember Bonchamps and his troops had passed through a country, their own country, smoking from the fires flickering in the ruins of what had been their own homes, for the Republicans (to use their own words) 'left behind ashes and piles of dead and nothing else'. And Bonchamp remembered his enemies as he felt his life ebbing away in the midst of 'a scene of pain, confusion and despair which compares with the awful spectacle which the world must behold at the Day of Judgement', as Madame de Larochejacquelein, who was present, wrote in her memoirs.

One crosses the river by bridge to Varades, crowned by the bulk of the Château de la Madeleine, a recent one for this part of the world, for the sake of the faster road to Saint-Georges-sur-Loire. If time is no object, the slower one on the south bank is much prettier, and the river crossing can then be made at Ingrandes, across a suspension bridge. This is where, officially, Brittany and Anjou meet. The church, post-1944, is very much in keeping with older buildings of the region, and a long salt depot with five arcades, a pediment and two end pavilions is good 18th century work. The great curiosity of Ingrandes is the *boire*, a dead-end branch of the river nearly three miles long which runs inland as far as Champtocé.

At Champtocé is the last of the Gilles de Rais castles, or rather the ruins of the last of his castles, which gives some idea of the vastness of his domains. He sold it to Jean V, duke of Brittany, in 1437, and there is no certain proof that he ever set foot in it himself after 1429. There are some pleasing 16th and 17th century houses in the little village. The road continues hilly and very pleasant as far as Saint-Georges-sur-Loire.

Saint-Georges-sur-Loire is not on the Loire but nearly 3 miles from it, and got its name from a 12th century abbey. All that is left to connect the present village with its abbey is a church in the classical style, with a Doric peristyle, and two other buildings of the 18th century. A little country road leads south-west to the old priory of L'Epinay: some of it is 15th century, though touched up in the 17th and 18th. Racine was once its Prior, and the French are fond of recalling, in this connection, his reference in his introduction to *Les Plaideurs*, to the law suit to which it led: 'neither my judges nor myself have ever properly understood it'.

By the main road it is only 11 miles from here to Angers, but there must be a halt at the Château de Serrant on the way. Almost at the

beginning of this book I mentioned Walsh who chartered the ship
on which the Young Pretender sailed in 1745. There is some confusion about his nationality, but the account the family accepted
was that he was an Irish nobleman, that he emigrated and settled in
Nantes where he made a considerable fortune which enabled him to
buy the château in 1749. This seems doubtful, although it is accepted
by many guide books. More probable in every respect is the more
detailed account to be found in the older histories of Anjou. When
James II fled from England to exile in France, the ship on which he
sailed had as Captain-owner one James Walsh. There is no suggestion of noble birth. In view of the notorious part he had played in
this exploit, he thought it wiser to settle in France. Recommended
by James II to Louis XIV and well received, he took nominal
French nationality and settled in Nantes where he developed a very
successful ship-owning business, which his son inherited. A grandson of the same name bought Serrant as early as 1730 from Madeleine-
Diane de Bautru, duchesse d'Estrées, sole surviving child of the
previous owner, the marquis de Vaubrun. When the son of the
second James, Antoine de Walsh (they had added an aristocratic
'de' with their increasing fortune), helped the Young Pretender
in his unfortunate venture, Louis XV, who had done so little to
help his cause, rewarded his helper by making Serrant into
a property giving right to the title of count, in 1755. It passed, by
marriage, into the hands of the duc de la Trémoïlle when the
direct male line of descent of the Walsh family came to an end
with Théobald de Walsh, comte de Serrant who, around 1820,
created the present gardens. It is still owned by the de la Trémoille
family.

All this, however, comes late in the history of Serrant. A very
early chapter, referring to the year 1111, shows that there were
already at that date Seigneurs de Serrant. The present château
belongs to three eras. The first, which includes the north tower,
the main building and the right wing, was begun in 1546. The plans
have been attributed to no less distinguished an architect than
Philibert Delorme, and this could well be right. In 1636, Guillaume
de Bautru raised the main building by another storey, and towards
the end of the century a second, matching, tower was built.

Just how Guillaume de Bautru found the money to purchase Serrant from the Rohan de Montbazon family is not known, but he even added Savennières, Bécon and Le Plessis-Macé to it and felt important enough to give himself the title of count, which nobody seemed inclined to dispute. He was the extreme example of the clever buffoon; he was liked because he encouraged people to laugh at him and flattered them by wearing the cap and bells of a court jester. He made Anne of Austria laugh, and that got him into diplomacy. He made Richelieu laugh, and that got him into the French Academy. Ambassador to England, to Spain, to Savoy, to the Netherlands, he died without issue.

Serrant passed to a nephew, who, as marquis de Vaubrun, became a distinguished general. The marquise de Vaubrun added the right wing and engaged Jules Hardouin-Mansard to design it and the chapel. Then, as we have seen, it was bought by James Walsh and some not entirely congruous alterations and additions were made. Further changes were made also by Théobald de Walsh when the gardens were laid out.

Today Serrant must rank as not only one of the very finest of the châteaux of Anjou, but as one rivalling the best of the châteaux of Touraine as well. Being a *Demeure Historique* it is furnished and lived in. The furniture is quite magnificent: it has few rivals the whole length of the Loire.

This superb Renaissance-style building (most of the later buildings were added to harmonize with the original ones) consists of three rectangular wings making three sides of the great inner courtyard, of which the fourth side is closed by a monumental gateway between two pavilions. The two exterior angles carry each a domed tower. The whole building is surrounded by water moats.

Immediately upon entering one is struck by its perfect proportions, beginning with a lovely staircase (supposedly from Philibert Delorme's plans) with coffered ceiling. Good tapestries line the walls of the dining-room, the Yellow Room is filled with beautiful furniture of the times of Louis XV and Louis XVI. In the library, which holds 20,000 books, above the fireplace, is a picture depicting the Young Pretender giving his instructions to Antoine de Walsh. In the duchess's room there is a fine Chinese-period Gobelins tapestry, and in the principal drawing-room (with a carved and coffered ceiling) is a very fine 16th century Flemish tapestry.

Apart from the almost breathtakingly lovely panelled staircase, the most striking thing of all at Serrant is in the chapel which J. Hardouin-Mansart designed. It is the tomb, by Coysevox, of Nicolas Bautru, marquis de Vaubrun, who was killed in 1675 at the crossing of the Rhine at Altenheim. On the sarcophagus are the marquis, reclining, and his wife kneeling – static, yet full of life. Above, apparently unsupported, Victory comes flying down towards them carrying in the one hand a trophy, in the other a shield. This must be considered one of the finest sculptures of its time and certainly directly comparable with the sculptor's best-known work, the tomb of Le Grand-Condé which is now in the Louvre Museum.

Having been duly impressed by Serrant and watched the sun sparkling on the wide lake, it is best to turn back along the main road (N 23) for the mile or so to Saint-Georges-sur-Loire and leave it on the minor road (D 311) going south-east towards Savennières and L'Ile-Béhuard. There is no château one can visit at Savennières, but instead a large and famous vineyard (*La Coulée de Serrant*) and a small church. The front elevation and the nave are almost unique remains of a church of the 9th, or at the very latest the 10th, century; their construction in courses of small stones alternating with brick in herring-bone design tells its own story. The Romanesque tower and choir are no later than the 12th century, and the quaintly carved beams of the aisle are quite modern in comparison – 15th century!

There is about this little church that indefinable but instantly recognizable atmosphere of a place of worship in which many, many successive generations have knelt and prayed, have sorrowed and have rejoiced. With it goes a feeling of separation from the outside world to which believer and unbeliever alike are susceptible.

A bridge below Savennières crosses three branches of the Loire. Just beyond the crossing of the first branch a narrow road turns off to the left: here is the Île Béhuard, one of the most agreeably quaint sites of Anjou. In a very short distance one arrives at the hamlet of the same name, and inevitably comes to a stop near a tiny church. The entrance is reached by worn steps, and it rises above a house, which must from all the visual evidence be of the 16th century. The strange little church appears to be of the 12th century (with much subsequent repairing); the use of pointed arches would not invalidate this supposed date. They occur, through a large part of France, in otherwise purely Romanesque buildings. This silt-covered island, of extreme fertility, was formed round a rock core, which here reached above surface level. The church, imitating on a smaller scale the ambitious abbey church of the Mont-Saint-Michel, was built as near the pinnacle of this rock as possible. Of the main nave, all the floor and part of the walls, in one place up to five feet in height, have been fashioned out of the rock. Another odd feature is the side nave, which runs at right-angles to the principal one.

Buhardus was a Breton nobleman attached to Geoffroi Martel (count of Anjou from 1040 to 1060) and on the death of his patron was so deeply grieved that he decided to turn away from this world. This island, and one of the other two grouped together here, belonged to him, and to it he retired with his wife and a monk of the abbey of Saint-Nicolas-d'Angers, his almoner. He bequeathed it to the monks of the abbey, who were given the third island by Garell, a knight in the service of Richard I of England, about 1170.

It was presumably about this time that the little church was built. It acquired a statue of the Virgin much revered and the object of many pilgrimages, and which Pope Pius XI incoronated in 1923. Both Louis XI and his son, Charles VIII, venerated this statue and made great gifts to the church which, as John Murray II wrote just a hundred years ago, 'by accident was forgotten at the Revolution and remains undespoiled'.

This is still the case. There is a most interesting 16th century panel painting of Louis XI hanging on the wall, there are naïve but charming ex-votos of many centuries to accompany it, some aged paintings (for which the light is quite insufficient), and the chains of Christian captives rescued from Algiers. In the Trésor are some old and beautiful silver pieces and ornaments, and in the church itself quaint statues, two baptismal fonts, choir stalls, a stained-glass window, all of the 16th century, and a poor-box of extreme antiquity which it is not possible to date accurately.

Though Notre-Dame-de-Béhuard has incomparably more to

offer the sightseer (and, indeed, the visit is of great interest) it has for me less of a religious atmosphere than the modest little church of Savennières. The visit also has its attendant danger. We did not pay enough attention to the fact that there was a coach parked not far away. We entered the church and almost literally stumbled upon forty or so pilgrims, just rising from their knees. Owing to the thickness of the walls, we had not heard them at prayer. We hesitated just too long. An enthusiastic gentleman in black had thrust hymn-sheets into our hands and propelled us towards vacant seats which were in the fullest view of the congregation. The priest gave us a smile of ineffable charm, which wrinkled his face up like a walnut.

There we were, trapped by our own inability to take an immediate departure in the face of them all. Led by the elderly priest, they had begun singing a hymn and one could see them individually. They were all dressed in respectable black. More than just respectable black: their black clothes positively exuded piety, men and women alike. There were about three women to every man, all elderly. I tried to make out who they were likely to be, and failed. Folk from a country town, that much was certain, but they all looked so alike that they might have been brothers and sisters. Some church con-fraternity, presumably, but why should they all look so alike? The mystery was never solved. For when their very long hymn, not very well sung, came to an end and the old priest turned round to offer up a prayer and they all knelt, we tip-toed away like thieves in the night, we hoped unseen. I doubt it though: I suspect many a pair of sharp eyes watched us through gaps between the fingers of the hands which covered their eyes and made rude comments afterwards on our flight. I was ashamed of our exit, justified only by my quick calcula-tion that if they were going to sing all the hymns on the hymn sheets, they would be there for a good two hours. The moral is, send out a recce party before entering a pilgrimage church.

Crossing the remaining two branches of the river, and taking a little road to the right, one comes to Rochefort-sur-Loire, a most pleasing old town whose atmosphere of peace is a little reminiscent of the pious air of the old lady whom nobody knows to have once been the Madame of a brothel. Rochefort is definitely not what it used to be. In fact where it is now was called Sainte-Croix, and Rochefort was a fort on one of the three rocky terraces which overlook it. It communicated by a bridge with a second terrace on which was a small walled town with a little fort of its own. This was Saint-Symphorien, and never was a saint's name taken in vain to quite the same extent as here. Saint-Symphorien was the town of 'the Pirates of the Loire', men who had served under the Guise family in the Holy League and finding the tide turning against them had seized Saint-Symphorien, ejected the inhabitants, and moved in with their women, their children and their booty. From it they raided the river and the countryside, bought themselves weapons and put Saint-Symphorien into such a perfect state of defence as it had never been before.

The pirates, under Hurtaud de Saint-Offange, made themselves feared even by as big a city as Angers, and as early as 1592 an effort was made under pressure from Angers to clear it. The siege was begun under the prince de Conti and continued under Marshal d'Aumont. By skilful use of their artillery, by constant sorties and above all by a perfectly organized system of repairing breaches as soon as they were made, the pirates prevented the troops from making any impression at all on the little town. Months passed, the autumn came, the troops were withdrawn; the cost had been high and for six years no further attempt was made to assault it.

It was not until June, 1598, that the matter was settled in the last way anyone would be likely to think of: Henri IV bought them out. For a large sum of money, they marched out of Saint-Symphorien, Henri's troops and demolition experts moved in, and town and fortress were razed to the ground.

The end of the story is no less improbable. The inhabitants drifted down to the tiny little village of Sainte-Croix and quietly settled there. They greatly outnumbered the original inhabitants, and gave their new home a name more familiar to them, Rochefort. But they made it Rochefort-sur-Loire to avoid confusion with the other Rochefort up on the rock. After this, they disappear from history.

One can climb up on to these rocky terraces, but the effort is hardly worth the reward, for the destruction was all too competently done, so that one can all too easily trip over the remains and hurt oneself, and it is a stiff ascent to reach the ruins. It is more rewarding to continue westwards on the road to Chalonnes-sur-Loire, with its always delightful views of the Loire and the islands. Chalonnes-sur-Loire has two fine ancient churches which have had, unhappily, to be largely rebuilt after war damage. The market days are Tuesdays and Fridays: this opportunity of attending a busy market in this part of France should be taken, for it is quite a spectacle. From Chalonnes, N 762 runs south-west to Saint-Laurent-de-la-Plaine, Bourgneuf-en-Mauges and Sainte-Christine. From there a little local road (D 149) leads on to Neuvy-en-Mauges and the Château du Lavouer.

One would not go to Le Lavouer for its architecture alone. It is a very simple building, which, with its splendid clusters of forest trees and grassland running down to two small lakes, is in many ways more akin to the English country house than to the more formal châteaux of France.

The region of Les Mauges lies parallel to the Loire to the south. Its sons became the most important leaders of the largely peasant army which waged the war of the Vendée. Some were men of the highest aristocracy, such as Count Henri du Verger de Laroche-Jaquelein; others, such as Jacques Cathelineau (born at Le Pin-en-Mauges, less than 5 miles to the west of Le Lavouer) were of no particular birth and rose by their own capacity for leadership. It was perhaps the most cruel and bitter civil war in a restricted area that France has ever known. On the one hand there was the fiery enthusiasm for the Republic of the young and conquering legions who had met and defeated the finest professional armies in Europe. On the other hand there were the deeply religious and royalist populations of parts of Brittany. It was all too often the musket against the scythe, the cannon against superior knowledge of the terrain. The counter revolution was put down by quite revolting means; but it is no less true that the excesses of the peasants gave the Republicans an excuse for their own cruelty.

No war has left such a profound and permanent mark on the people. The war with Prussia of 1870, although a century later almost, is not remembered in the same way, nor the devastating loss of life of the 1914–1918 war, nor the catastrophe of 1940 and the resurgence of 1944. The war of the Vendée is still more real to the Vendéens than any other.

This can be felt at Le Lavouer. The château became the headquarters of Jean Nicolas Stofflet, who though born at Lunéville in Lorraine, became a determined leader in the civil war. After two years of rebellion, he made a pretended submission in 1795, then took up arms again to be captured and shot at Angers in 1796. In this civil war there was always another leader to hand to take the place of one killed or captured. At Le Lavouer it was Autichamps, no less determined than Stofflet, though much less enterprising.

As was so often the case, the driving force at Le Lavouer was a woman. The property was originally in the ownership of a bastard branch of the great de Brissac family and at the time of the Revolution belonged to the Mabille de la Paumelière family. The lady of the house belonged to a most distinguished family, having been born a Mademoiselle Cambourg de Genouillac. As Madame de La Paumelière she took an active and distinguished part in this civil war. The château is still in the possession of the La Paumelière family.

Turning right on leaving Le Lavouer and its memories of 1793, and right again at the first fork, one eventually emerges on to the main road to Angers from the south, N 161, at Saint-Lambert-du-Lattay, a village whose principal claim to fame is that there is a *dégustation de vins*. The English word 'degustate' seems to have gone out with the 17th century, and if one attempted to use it in present days it would call to mind disgust rather than 'tasting for pleasure'. Do not be put off by it in this case at least, for what one 'degustates' here are the lovely little wines of the Coteaux du Layon, a river which runs south-westwards, parallel to and quite near the main road.

These rather heady little wines are very full-flavoured, perhaps too full flavoured to go well with very delicate dishes. On the other hand, they turn a snack into a feast, and, cooled, make a most refreshing and unusual apéritif by themselves. The Layon soon turns south-westwards after Saint-Lambert-du-Lattay, and there are some very pretty roads running between the vineyards which make a run round very enjoyable if one has an hour to spare before reaching Angers.

Otherwise N 161 continues towards the capital of Anjou which is here only 15 miles away. On it, the only further place of note is Les-Ponts-de-Cé, an historic and much rebuilt village which manages to have a single high street crossing four river bridges in less than 2 miles. The first crosses the Louet, which is not properly a river in its own right, but a branch of the Loire. The next two rivers are also branches of the Loire, but without separate names, and the fourth one is the Authion, a river in its own right. Three miles beyond the Authion, N 161 enters Angers which is on the Maine and not, as we have just seen, on the Loire.

And that is one way to reach Angers from Nantes.

There is another, longer and perhaps equally rewarding one to be taken north of the Loire, for which one takes N 178 through Carquefou, then along the edge of the marshes of Saint-Mars, to Nort-sur-Erdre which has been mentioned as a place for a boat excursion on the Erdre, 18 miles from Nantes. Continuing on N 178, there is a steady rise from sea-level for the next 11 miles to La Meilleraye-de-Bretagne which is nearly 300 feet up. Between a mile and a mile and a half from the village, on D 18, which runs south-east to Riaillé is a monastery of the order of La Trappe. It was founded between 1140 and 1145 as a Cistercian house, and the nave of the church is of this date. The remainder of the buildings are 18th century. In this remote countryside it is curious to find a strong connection with Dorset. The monastery was sold as National Property in 1793, but in 1816 was bought by a Society of Trappists who moved there lock, stock and barrel from Lulworth in Dorsetshire. It is best to return from here to N 178 for a quick run to Châteaubriant.

Châteaubriant is very ancient, pleasantly situated as a town, and bearing a name which is tremendously evocative. Yet I find it very disappointing.

To begin with, the site is not in keeping with the size and strength of the castle which is on a slight gradient rising from the town, instead of crowning some rocky tor. The quite charming little river Chère marks its northern boundary, but there is nothing dramatic about it. Little remains of the powerful 11th century circumvallation; some bastions survive, but so detached from each other as not to give much of a picture of a proud castle. The best remaining piece of the medieval building is certainly the strong square keep; there are

1 Saumur

2 The Vienne and the Loire (with the car ferry)

adjoining but usually incomplete buildings of the same age which, with the keep, make up the Grand Logis.

The second, and really quite distinct part of the castle, is the Château Neuf on the eastern side of the formal gardens which link the two parts. Built between 1533 and 1537 and well restored, these are very simple Renaissance buildings, free of the exuberance of Renaissance detail which, in the end, defeated its own object and turned taste towards neo-classicism. This simplicity in part is due to Breton reticence in architecture, for Châteaubriant is essentially Breton. Its favourite feature is the room in which the young, intelligent and all too pretty Françoise de Foix, countess of Laval, is supposed to have been shut up for ten years (with a child who soon died) in a black-hung prison for having too well pleased François I, whose mistress she became.

François's love did not long endure, the duchesse d'Etampes came, saw and conquered. Françoise hung about the Court, broken-hearted, until a disapproving husband took her away to Châteaubriant. As for the rest of the story, I have not been able to trace it back to its source: it seems suddenly to have sprung into general knowledge, self-generated. It seems just as likely that Françoise de Foix shut herself up in her black-hung chamber. What were the alternatives for a still-young woman who had been for a time the most powerful in all France, and now was no more than another discarded mistress? A convent, suicide, or living death? One day, perhaps I shall find the key to the origin of the usually accepted fable.

From Châteaubriant to Pouancé is only a distance of 10 miles along a very fast road (N 775), which ought to give time in hand for some of the diversions needed to see interesting places which cannot easily be placed in any kind of logical order.

The old fortress of Pouancé is most picturesque. Largely 13th century, when all the most imposing fortresses of the Middle Ages were built, altered and added to in the 15th. In addition to the castle, the town was protected by its river (La Verzée) which expands north and east into the Etang de Saint-Aubin, to the south into the Etang de Tressé and to the south-west into the Etang du Fourneau. The castle is on the north-east of the town, the direction from which its garrison, men of Anjou, could expect the arrival of the men of Brittany, their usual enemies.

There are still eleven of the original towers left, some round, some square and some hexagonal, as century by century military fashions changed, and the general view is imposing. The little town is full of charm, with a 16th century church on the Place des Halles which has come straight from an illustration to a fairy story. The little street which faces this house passes under the old town clock gate (Porte de l'Horloge) of the 14th century, and if the 19th century Romanesque church is not by any means true to style, it has all the naïve charm of a country girl dressed in all the wrong things to go to the city.

N 178 bis runs southwards from Pouancé, through a part of the forest of Juigné, and on through La Chapelle-Glain. A little to the south of this village, close to a considerable mere, stands the imposing Château de la Motte-Glain, whose name points to a much earlier castle on the site. The *motte* was the mound, often artificially made, on which the earliest fortresses were built if there were no convenient rocky heights on which to build it. These very early fortresses were mainly of timber, and the *motte* disappeared with the increasing weight of stone fortresses. Certainly the present one is not on a *motte*, being a rebuilding of the very end of the 15th century.

Returning to La Chapelle-Glain, a right turn on to N 163 puts one on the road to Candé, a well-situated but not very memorable little town. N 23 bis, south-west, is crossed by D 185. Taking it to the right brings one to the Château de Bourmont, which has a quite fantastic history. Here is, in good part medieval, a château which was set on fire fourteen times in the war of the Vendée! The moats are set about by little towers, the gate is protected by a heavy tower, the original chapel is still there, as are the rather delightful service buildings which line the courtyard: all those genuinely belong to earlier times. In the reconstructed main building also is the old Guard Room, spared by the flames. On one wall is an inscription, *Vive la République Française*, left by some Republican soldier on one of the occasions when the château passed into their hands. Here the Marshal de Bourmont was born, who is considered to have betrayed Napoleon in 1815, to have been the enemy of Ney when he was brought to trial, and ended by triumphantly taking Algiers for the Bourbons in 1830. This did not bring him the favour of his fellow men, who remembered all too well his desertion on the eve of Waterloo, so he spent the rest of his life – sixteen years – sitting at home in his castle planning and overseeing the repairs and the restorations. One must agree that he did it well.

Back to Candé and out north-east by N 23 bis to the little village of Roche-d'Iré (château in Louis XIII style, with a very fine wood retable of the end of the 15th century in the chapel), where a local road, D 203, leads to Chazé-sur-Argos where the delicious Manoir de Raguin hides its unexpected treasures. An older manor house was almost totally rebuilt by Guy du Bellay at the beginning of the 17th century.

The result is a piece of architecture which runs counter to all that one expects in France. It is, in detail, totally disordered with no symmetry at all. By some curious architectural alchemy, it is also completely charming. Hard by a narrow square tower is a round turret with a tall, round, slated roof which is unexpectedly carried on upwards by three slender columns bearing what can most graphically be described as an umbrella, surmounted in its turn by a tall cross. Then, on the other side of the square tower is a three-storey elevation below a very tall slated roof – perhaps a variant on a Norman model – whose two lower storeys carry Romanesque windows but whose upper ones are tall rectangles below a triangular pediment. The whole thing is completely absurd, and positively lovable. The mixture is due to various generations of two noble families of Anjou, who have added and altered through the centuries, the Beavau family and the Contades family whom we associate more readily with Montgeoffroy.

Guy du Bellay's most famous effort, however, was not exterior but interior, *les chambres dorées*, the gilded rooms. Happily they are still there to be seen, for otherwise they would be impossible to believe in. They are reached by a fine stone staircase; they are completely panelled, and covered with grisaille decorations on a background of gold leaf! Guy is supposed to have paid 15,000 *livres* for them, an enormous sum in his day. It was the very height of eccentricity to spend a considerable fortune on just two rooms of a quite modest gentleman's country house.

From Chazé, on D 184 north-east to Marans and then northwards up N 161 bis to Segré, an unexciting modern town, well situated where Argos and Verzée meet to form the Oudon, a substantial tributary of the Mayenne which flows through Angers. A right turn just before the southern edge of Segré takes one to the Château de la Lorie. It is another curious mixture of the centuries, without the unpretentious charm of the Château de Raguin, but with some very lovely features which have to be seen separately to be admired. To begin with, the surrounding park with its fine trees is a delight; it is all set about with little lakes which reflect the façades of different parts of the very grandiose whole.

Towards the end of the 18th century one Charles-François Constantin was Provost-General of Anjou. He married money – and this must be almost the first recorded case of the European with position marrying the American heiress to a fortune. She was American-born of French parents who had made a substantial fortune in America. With her money he was able to build a very luxurious mansion for himself. The Revolution left not much of the château undamaged, but the ballroom in the grand Italian style can still be seen with its wealth of different marbles and its endless mirrors. The Minerva courtyard also remains; its noble proportions give the visitor an idea of what La Lorie must have been in its heyday.

After the Revolution La Lorie came to vivid life during the ownership of the duke and duchess of Fitz-James (the name came from a natural son of James II of England, Marshal Berwick, made duke of Fitz-James by Louis XIV in recompense of the services he rendered France as a general in the French service). Life in the château was one continuous fête and it was ever filled with guests. Later it passed to the marquis de Saint-Genys who enlarged, restored and redecorated it. He bought, and brought to La Lorie the marvellous wood panelling from the château de Vitry, home of Cardinal Dubois, minister of Louis XV. The gardens were laid out by a master landscape-gardener, Edouard André. The formal gardens, rich in good statues, some noble elevations and much fine detail reward the visitor to this great château.

Northwards up N 23 bis then left on to N 163 bis, until just before

Saint-Quentin a few miles up, then along a narrow road to what remains of Mortier-Crolle, home in the past of the very top provincial families. It began with Clisson family, passed into the hands of Bertrand Duguesclin (cousin of the constable of France), whose daughter had it as part of her marriage settlement when she married into the Rohan family. Marshal de Gié (born Pierre de Rohan) lived part of the time here, part at La Motte-Glain, and the tapestries with which he used to ornament both (they travelled with him) have ended up in the castle of Angers.

The last owner of Mortier-Crolle was Anne de Rohan, whose love affairs with outstanding men of the first half of the 17th century were uniformly disastrous to them. Henri II, duc de Montmorency, thought himself too great a nobleman to be toppled from his supreme position. He was led by the most sickening of royal conspirators, Gaston d'Orléans, into a plot against Richelieu. Louis XIII did not hesitate to take his life for it. The comte de Soissons, son of Condé, was assassinated; de Thou and Boutteville died on the scaffold like Montmorency. Anne lived to see her own son die the same way. She lingered on, haunted by what ghosts and what memories it is idle to conjecture. Perhaps there were none: 'she did naught in her life but follow her own desires'.

Mortier-Crolle was allowed to fall into unworthy hands, who let it fall also into almost total disrepair. Ruins remain of walls and towers and, miraculously complete, the main building survives though bereft of its corner pavilions or towers. A quaintly covered porch strikes an original note, but for the rest it is a plain building as one would expect from the end of the 15th century, awaiting the impact of the Renaissance. The entrance, a little fortress in itself, is flanked by two fine round towers. Despite its historic interest, I would hate to live in it: I feel I would dream of Anne de Rohan and not pleasantly.

At Craon, some 6 miles to the north, up N 178 bis, is a very lovely château with a really beautiful French-style garden, very little known and of no real historical interest. Built entirely of the white tufa of Saumur – the stone which, with the passage of centuries, becomes whiter than white – in a typically French unity of design it fits perfectly into its setting of gentle slopes front and rear, grass covered for the latter, rigorously ordered garden for the former.

Once a fortress stood on this site, but it was demolished by the order of Henri IV, in 1604. Not until a century and a half later was the present château begun, for the Marquis d'Armaillé. It consists of a central rectangular block, flanked by two square corner pavilions a little in retreat of the main building, with a large terrace fronting the whole. It bears a substantial resemblance to Montgeoffroy, which was just a little later in date, but is on two floors to Montgeoffroy's three.

This very lovely and symmetrical building was the work of Pomeyrol, an architect not widely known. The rather stolid exterior sculpture is by Lemeunier, and it is claimed that David d'Angers worked on the interior woodwork. This is almost certainly a confusion of generations, for Jean-Pierre David was not born until 1788, whereas the château dates from just before 1760, and nothing inside bears the hallmark of a very great sculptor, but only of a very competent wood carver. This exactly describes Jean-Pierre's father, known as an ornamentalist rather than as a sculptor.

Twelve miles to the east by N 159 bis is Château-Gontier; from here a fast main road (N 162) could take one in 27 miles to Angers. With only slight deviations, no fewer than nine interesting châteaux may be visited if one is content not to speed down this main road.

First, then, south-west on N 23 bis for just over four miles to where one turns right into the grounds of the Château de Saint-Ouen, a little before the road enters Chemazé. It is a magnificent mixture of styles, built in 1505 by an aristocratic monk, one Guy Le Clerc de Goulaine, Abbot of La Roë, confessor and counsellor of Anne of Brittany. So, in the simple style of the reign of Louis XIII, a little chapel was built, and beyond it a very charming house for the abbot, with tall and narrow windows and a hexagonal tower within which curls the staircase, and a basket arch above the main door.

Then, suddenly – and apparently only ten years later, Abbot Guy decided to build again and filled in the space between chapel and manor house with an uninhibited dwelling displaying all the decorations that the Renaissance had brought. To the left and to the right, lived and prayed the man of the Church; in the centre lived the statesman.

The effect is amazing and amusing. The 'new' château has a square central tower four stories high and two narrow wings two stories high with mansard windows in the sloping, slated roof. The square tower ends in an open and very Italianate arcade, with admirable corner domed turrets; everywhere are fluted pilasters, carved foliage and delicious rosettes and highly ornamented pediments above the windows. The château, too, is in white stone, which the grey schist of the older buildings sets in high relief.

Inside, there are some very fine rooms, and a noble staircase circles up the square tower. In the ground floor dining room is as fine a fireplace as still remains from the early days of the French Renaissance.

From the village of Chemazé, take D 588 to the south-east for a couple of miles, to a hamlet called Molière, where six roads meet. Continue over the crossroads on D 588 for about the same distance again until it meets N 162, the main road from Château-Gontier to Angers. Turn left northwards up it for about a mile, when, on the right, D 611 will take you westwards to La Magnanne and the village of Ménil.

The Château de Magnanne is pure Louis XIV style, balanced to a hair's thickness, virtually unornamented and with a general air of the strictest regimentation. Never has a man's name been given to an architectural style with better reason. *Le style, c'est l'homme*: in this case the style is indeed the man himself: rigid and orderly in thought, hard and unbending, totally unsentimental, and in the long run a big bore . . . *and* I would include the architecture of Versailles in that category.

Some years ago, to my joy, I picked up off a book box along the Seine a transcript of the king's own personal instructions as to how to see his new gardens at Versailles. The *Manière de voir les jardins de Versailles* is a military manual. 'Mount the seventeen steps to the terrace. Look to the right at the Grand Trianon. Look to the left at the Apollo Basin. Look straight forward at the Grand Canal. Turn round, descend the steps and take the path, left, to the Jardin du Roi.' No time here for stopping to smell a flower, observe a bird, or look at the sky. The background to it all, the grandiose, dull palace, reflects the man for whom it was built.

All these little Versailles are too small to be big bores in the same way as Versailles itself, but they can be little ones. This one is, outside, and not made any better by unhappy restorations. But, as at Versailles, the interior detail is magnificent. The marvellous wood-work is Regency – French Regency of course, the period when Philippe d'Orléans ruled for the under-age Louis XV, say between 1715 and 1723. Four splendid panels from paintings by Nicolas Lancret – Water, Earth, Air and Fire – are of the same period. Furniture upholstered in tapestry-work and other furniture signed by the great names of the 18th century make this, to my mind, one of the most rewarding of the visits to the châteaux of Anjou.

If, from Magnanne, you go up into the village of Ménil and turn right in the centre of it you will come to a little ferry which takes you and your car across the Mayenne, a substantial river. One of the pleasures in rural France is taking a ferry, for usually they cross a river at points where once there were fords and which, therefore, are not necessarily linked to any busy thoroughfare. Rather the con-trary, it is more likely to be a little country road which was built to meet the ferry terminal each side. Of course, there is no point in being in a hurry. You will get across the river eventually, but there are salutations to be exchanged, a passenger or two visibly hurrying along the approach road to be waited for, perhaps an unwilling cow or horse to be coaxed on.

Once across the Mayenne, you take the road which will turn right (southwards) to lead you to Daon. The village is beautifully situated on the river and is surrounded by châteaux of past centuries. In particular, the Château de l'Escoublère, 1½ miles north-east, is interesting for its early date and appearance.

It is obviously 15th century, very simple and a little stark. It is unkind but not unfair to describe it as a fortified farmhouse on a big scale, and moated. The main building, in rough stone, has rectangu-lar windows; an external octagonal tower holds the staircase. It is flanked by four round towers, two with pepperpot roofs and two with little domes and lanterns. One enters through a fortified gate-way leading to an outer courtyard with a graceful well, surmounted by a cupola carried on four little columns. It is inscribed with the date: 1475. This seems early for such a delicate piece of work which could more easily be ascribed to the later Renaissance period. On the other hand, an inscription on the main building gives the date as 1570, which must be a re-building or an extension in the same style as older parts for, as we have seen with other châteaux, Anjou was very sophisticated in its architecture of noble houses – and this one was built for the Duguesclin family. If you have to look the name up anywhere, it is also often spelt Ecoublère, the 's' in Escoublère being silent.

A little road eastwards from Daon goes to Soeurdres, where there is a 16th century country-gentleman's house now no more than a farmhouse. La Touche-Moreau, tall and severe, is a little dilapidated but none the less still a very fine example of an early Renaissance country house. Brick and stone alternate and contrast pleasantly with the marble window ledges. There is a delightful turret on one corner which springs up at the height of the top of the first floor windows and overtops the roof to which it is linked by a most unusual and ingenious piece of rafterwork, slated over.

From Soeurdres, a south-westerly minor road (D 78) crosses the Mayenne again at Chambellay, runs through the village, and picks up the main Angers road about 2 miles from the river. Up N 162 for a little more than another mile and a turning to the right will be seen which leads to the Château du Percher. This is a most interesting building, for though the feeling is in general that of Flamboyant Gothic, part at least of the disparate buildings belong to the early Renaissance.

The proportions of the various parts bear little relation to each other and one's first feeling on seeing it may well be one of mild bewilderment. Here is a little Flamboyant chapel, with an octagonal turret suddenly appearing over the west door on a corbel. There are two main buildings at right angles to each other. In the centre of one is a tower which begins life as an octagon, then decides to simplify things for itself by becoming square. The main staircase starts in it at ground floor level, then – as if deprecating the tower's change of plan – abandons it for a round turret which starts half way up the building on a squinch. The gable windows are surmounted by richly carved pediments and there is everywhere a wealth of happy detail.

Southwards down the same N 162, passing the D 78 crossing, a turning to the left after the one to Chambellay takes one to Le Bois-Montbourcher, an altogether more spectacular château than those which have just been described. It is marvellously situated on virtually an island site on a vast lake, edged by an approach avenue of fine trees. It is very difficult to put an exact age to it, but the 15th, 17th and 19th centuries have all played their part, and there has certainly been some over-enthusiastic restoration. The towers by the water's edge would seem to recall an original fortress. There is one wing which has no physical connection at all with the main buildings of the château and it is not clear how this came about. It is composed of a low central building and two end pavilions, one much higher than the other. This (which has been much less restored than the other), is probably the original residential building, erected within the ring of protective walls and towers of the fortress. In the interior, there are some good pictures and much interesting furniture.

On leaving here, one runs southwards again to Le Lion-d'Angers, where the church, once the abbey church of Saint-Martin, has a Romanesque nave, a modern choir in the manner of the 13th century, architrave mouldings in geometrical patterns of the 11th century on the western portal, and remains of 16th century frescoes on the walls of the nave. N 770, going north-east, crosses and gives access to an island, L'Isle-Briant, where far more people go to see the races on an excellent track than to see a rather fine 18th century château. Taking this road to Champigné (7 miles), then N 768 southwards and a turning left about a mile from Champigné one reaches the Château de La Hamonnière, a most pleasing pre- and post-Renaissance building.

The first of the two main buildings was built for Antoine Hamon, who gave his name to the property. He was an obscure gentleman of Anjou, but the 15th century house is a model of good taste and a quite beautiful illustration of the last phase of domestic Gothic. The pointed gables of the mullioned windows and the usual flat-sided tower to contain the staircase are here in perfect proportion to the building as a whole.

The Renaissance building, built for Antoine Legay is much more complicated. The windows all have semicircular arches, the roofs have a double slope, the lower being carried on a corbelled balustrade, and the staircase is carried in a strong square tower, with highly decorated mansard windows.

Southwards down N 768 and another left hand to Ecuillé, just south of which is the interesting and decorative Château du Plessis-Bourré (*Plessis* = a walled property; *Ménil* or *Mesnil* = an isolated farmstead or homestead). It is square, with a round tower complete with pepper-pot roof at each corner, a tall main dwelling occupying all of one side, a chapel a fortified gateway to what used to be a drawbridge and dependencies facing the main dwelling, byres and stables on one of the other sides, and more dependencies on the fourth – the whole protected by a water moat.

This is a very large château and properly comparable with many of those better known which are in Touraine: if this one reminds you, for example, of Langeais it would not be surprising.

It was built by Jean Bourré between 1466 and 1472. He was the favourite minister of Louis XI, and Intendant of the Royal Finances to Louis XI, Charles VIII and Louis XII. He must have been a very honest man, or an exceedingly clever one, to have been Minister of Finance under three separate sovereigns without ever being disgraced. First he had a château near Segré, then he built Langeais for Louis XI, and finally Le Plessis-Bourré for himself with the memories of Langeais still strongly in mind.

When he bought the property it was called Plessis-aux-Vents, as doubtless the winds blew hard and cold across the plateau. First the broad moats had to be dug, then the very pleasing grey stone brought from afar, then the bridge built to end at the drawbridge and then local springs had to be found whose water could be made to flow into the moats. In 1487 it was all finished and he was able to receive Charles VIII and all his suite in the style to which they were accustomed.

This is a remarkable château, almost unique in that it is all of one period with the exception of some of the dependencies altered at the time of Louis XIII, and that the old wooden bridge has been replaced by a stone-built one. What is also exceptional is to find a château of this size virtually all of one design and fabric of the period when the first thoughts of comfort were affecting the medieval fortress.

In some ways the last of the castles west of Angers to which we come is the most evocative of all. Here we have the firmest reminder how deep the roots of history run in this green, well-watered and well-wooded land. It is another *plessis*, and this one almost certainly did begin with the *palissade* from which the earliest *plessis* got the name, the fence of stakes all round a property. In all cases, doubtless, a more substantial defensive wall soon replaced the wooden pales. It is Le Plessis-Macé.

To reach it from Le Plessis-Bourré it is best to go back to Ecuillé and then N 768 again, which is taken southwards to Juigné where the river is crossed. At Juigné, one must take the road by the church northwards, towards Pruillé and, at the road junction before arriving there bear left and cross over the main road (N 162) to Le Plessis-Macé on the other (western) side.

Towards the end of the 11th century some kind of building was put up here by one Macé, which seems to have been a contemporary form of the name Mathieu, and it is this property which presumably had its palisade. He ended his days as a Benedictine monk at Angers, but not before he had acquired a family to inherit his estate, which they continued to do until the end of the 14th century. It passed by marriage to the Beaumont family in the 15th century, but by this time the Hundred Years War had played havoc with it.

Louis de Beaumont began a fifty-year task of renovation, for when he died his son carried on. This first rebuilding began in 1453, at the end of the Hundred Years War, with the repair of the 12th century walls and towers. Then came the turn of the main residence – two blocks of buildings at right angles – the chapel, and the dependencies. The result of their work is, roughly what we see today. We know that before 1483 it was fit to receive Louis XI and his Court. Later, both Francis I and Henri IV came and hunted from this château, which, by the latter's time, had passed into the hands of the du Bellay family. It is believed that Joachim du Bellay wrote the *Olive* sonnets at Le Plessis-Macé.

Then it became a farm and was not kept up at all. It might well by this time have collapsed entirely if the Countess (Theobald) Walsh, wife of the head of the great Walsh clan of Nantes, had not seen it, admired the still magnificent remains, and again rebuilt it. The work began in 1876.

What may now be visited are the whole of the exterior, the chapel, the keep and some of the living rooms. Inside, there is little enough to see except the flamboyant Gothic woodwork of the chapel, for all the contents were sold by auction in the last years of the last century, but the buildings themselves are admirable, illustrating as they do the very end of a period of architecture which the brilliance of the Renaissance outshone.

It is unlikely that many readers will wish to visit all these châteaux of Anjou. Yet they represent only a selection from the full number, and take no account of those still to come east of Angers. I have tried to make the selection eclectic, so that all readers will find one or two châteaux which will be certain to interest them.

This part of the Loire is relatively seldom visited and I have tried to show that it has its own treasures, not those one finds in Touraine proper but their equal in everything but royal associations.

It is a lovely part of France, but all in subdued tones. There is nothing very dramatic here, but pleasing countryside, low hills, an infinity of streams. I remember it – and see it vividly in my memory – more easily than I do many far more picturesque parts. It has two great and increasingly rare blessings: it has been unspoiled by too great a prosperity, and for those of us who live in or near cities or under flight paths to airports, almost miraculously silent.

Angers: Ways from Angers to Saumur

Angers – Trélazé and the slate quarries – La Ménitré – Abbey of Saint-Maur – Les Rosiers – Gennes – Saint-Martin-de-la-Place – Château de Boumois – Angers – Beaufort-en-Vallée – Longué – Saint-Barthélemy-d'Anjou – Pignerolle – Mazé – Montgeoffroy – Brion – Seiches-sur-le-Loir – Château d'Ardanne – Château du Verger – Chambiers forest – Durtal – Bazouges-sur-le-Loir – La Flèche – Sablé-sur-Sarthe – Solesmes abbey – Le Mans – Epau abbey – The Le Mans circuit – Moncé-en-Bélin – Château du Lude – Noyant – Linières-Bouton – Pontménard forest – Mouliherne – Vernantes – Baugé – Le Vieil-Baugé – Jalesne – Château de la Ville-au-Fourrier – Les Ponts-de-Cé – Brissac – Doué-la-Fontaine – Montreuil-Bellay – Asnières abbey – Le Puy-Notre-Dame – Vaudelnay – Château de Pocé – Coutures – Château de Montsabert – Bourdion – Saint-Rémy-la Varenne – Saint-Maur abbey – Le Thoureil – Gennes – Cunault – Trèves – Saint-Macé priory – Chênehutte-les-Truffeaux – Saint-Hilaire-Saint-Florent – Saint-Florent abbey

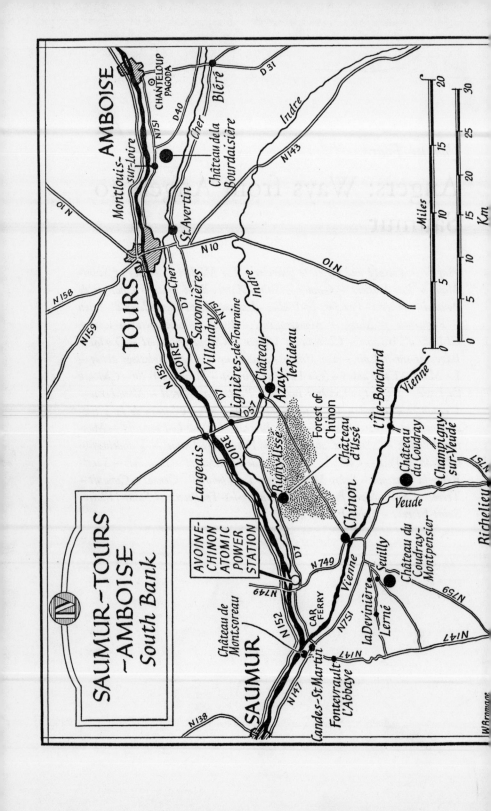

SAUMUR–TOURS –AMBOISE *South Bank*

IV

AMBOISE

CHANTELOUP PAGODA

Bléré

Indre

D 31

N 751

D 40

Cher

Château de la Bourdaisière

N 143

Montlouis-sur-Loire

N 10

St. Avertin

N 10

OIN

TOURS

N 158

N 159

LOIRE

Cher

D 7

Savonnières

N 15

Villandry

D 7

Lignières-de-Touraine

Indre

Château Azay-le-Rideau

D 57

LOIRE

Langeais

D 7

Rigny-Ussé

Forest of Chinon

Château d'Ussé

Vienne

L'Île-Bouchard

Château du Coudray

Champigny-sur-Veude

N 751

AVOINE-CHINON ATOMIC POWER STATION

Chinon

Veude

Château du Coudray-Montpensier

Richelieu

N 151

N 749

Vienne

Seuilly

N 152

Château de Montsoreau

N 751

Lerné

la Devinière

N 759

CAR FERRY

SAUMUR

N 147

Candes-St-Martin

N 147

N 138

Fontevrault L'Abbaye

N 147

Miles

Km

0 5 10 15 20

0 5 10 15 20 25 30

W. Bromage

Chapter Four

Angers: Ways from Angers to Saumur

Angers bestrides the Maine about half way down its length – though 'its shortness' would better describe the full course of this river which, from its beginning at the junction of the Mayenne and the Sarthe to its end as it runs into the Loire below the city, measures barely 7 miles. Here again, we meet the French uncertainty about the length of their rivers: Larousse indicates 8 kilometres, 5 miles, and Quillet-Flammarion gives 10 kilometres, 6·2 miles. Neither figure is compatible with a mid-stream measurement on a big-scale map!

Angers is a most agreeable, historic city with a number of fascinating features. Do not be put off by old descriptions of 'black-visaged Angers'. These date from the days when beam-and-plaster houses were aproned with the black slate quarried at Trélazé, only a few miles away. There is hardly one left now to be seen and stone houses replaced most of them even before the Revolution.

Even that is comparatively late in the long history of the capital of Anjou. Of its days as a Gaulish city we know little, but in Roman times it was a civilized place with public baths, circus and arena (the Rue des Arènes keeps the name it took from the latter). Under Roman rule, it was for three centuries called Juliomagus. In 471, under Childeric I, city and province passed into the hands of the Merovingian kings from the count who still ruled them in the name of Rome. In the 10th century the rule of hereditary counts began; they included Foulques Nerra to whom are attributed a great number of ancient towers throughout Anjou and Touraine, some of them justly. When Henri Plantagenet came to the throne of England

H

as Henry II, through Matilda's marriage to Geoffroi Plantagenet, the long and fruitful connection between Angers and England began, one of whose most permanent and interesting results was the creation of the Angevin style of architecture. Angers was lost to England by the unhappy King John. Although Henry III was confirmed in his title of count of Anjou as late as 1259, effective control remained essentially French. In 1481, after the death of 'good King René', the last duke, who had abandoned Anjou for the Kingdom of the Two Sicilies, and his kingdom for the county of Provence, Anjou passed officially and without contest to the Crown of France.

The limits of the old city are clearly marked by the line of broad boulevards which link the old centre with the new districts on both sides of the river. The fantastic old château which overlooks the quays on the east bank must rank, for itself and for its contents, not only as the first place to see in Angers, but also as one of the essential places to be visited on any journey to the river Loire.

One cannot say, as Coleridge wrote of Xanadu, 'so twice five miles of fertile ground with walls and towers were girdled round,' but with a long, roughly pentagonal, perimeter of tall, thick walls and taller towers (even though now truncated) enclosing pretty gardens, many a visitor brought up on the English poets must have remembered those lines. The perimeter, in fact, is about 1025 yards. The towers number 17, and they run to 70 or 80 feet high. They splay outwards at the base, which gives them the shape of the leg of a sailor's bell-bottomed trouser. They have a strange ringed appearance, for though mainly built of the strong but ugly slatey-coloured schist the dull monotony which this would provoke is relieved by bands of white stone.

The moat is very broad and immensely deep. As one approaches over the bridge to the portcullis entrance to the castle one looks down unexpectedly far. A second look, if one has not been prepared for it, is inevitable. Has the first glance deceived, or are those live and active deer deep down in the now dry moat? They are; there has been no ocular deception. This gives the measure of the width and height of the moat. They mark the site of a famous menagerie kept by good King René.

Something else becomes apparent, too. The tree-tops visible above the lofty walls are not those of giant specimens planted in the enclosed gardens. They are the tops of trees which grow in gardens arranged in shallow recesses between the outer and the inner skin of the perimeter wall.

The chapel dates from the early years of the 15th century and is one of the best preserved in Anjou, at least as far as the vaulting and its carved keystones are concerned. The buildings as a whole are in good repair, of real interest and well worth the time spent on them. But they are all eclipsed completely by the greatest treasure Angers has to show, one of the greatest in the world. Duke Louis I of Anjou commissioned from Nicolas Bataille, the greatest weaver of tapestry of his age, the full story of the Book of the Revelation of Saint John the Divine. The cartoons from which Nicolas Bataille worked were commissioned from the painter in ordinary of Charles V of France, Hennequin of Bruges. They were woven between 1373 and 1380.

The story is not complete, and at times the cartoons did not follow the chronology of the book with absolute faithfulness, but by and large it is a complete work of art, extraordinarily sophisticated for its time. The horror may be less felt than when the cartoons were painted, but at least it is properly grotesque and always a little frightening. The balance of the designs, the mastery of movement, the great art shown in never letting the detail swamp the subject proclaim Hennequin of Bruges to have been a great interpreter of the subject he was given.

I would like one day to have the time and the money to be able to spend the winter in Angers, or sufficient to spend 83 different days studying the 83 subjects of the tapestries, after a careful re-reading of the book at the rate of one a day. I have never yet had the time and opportunity to consider them individually as interpreters of the mystical thoughts of Saint John (if, indeed, they were his), nor to work out in my mind how else these interpretations could have been made . . . say by a William Blake. In fact Blake comes to my mind all the time in connection with these works of art: across the centuries there is much in common with the mystics of Byzantium, of the middle ages, of the 17th and 18th centuries. The link between the Primitives and the Moderns are these works of the closing years of the 14th century.

The Grande Galerie was specially built for them in 1952, of materials identical with those of which the castle itself is built, the lighting most carefully studied and the choice of the dark red of the woollen velvet background most successfully arrived at after many trials. The windows are also tinted, but very slightly, and the result is that all can study the tapestries in virtually ideal conditions. You can hire a receiver, with tapestry by tapestry commentary in French or English: it is very well done, and adds immeasurably to one's appreciation. In the Logis du Gouverneur, there are a number of other tapestries, including a delightfully surrealistic *Lady at the organ*. There she sits, on a vast carpet of flowers, this aristocratic young lady, in her magnificently embroidered robe, playing a portable organ, with a boy working the bellows. At the other side of the organ, a most elegant young gentleman, holding the words and music in his hand, is singing to her playing. There are two other boys: one is swinging a cat by its tail (which must have added a quaint counterpoint to the efforts of the lady and the singer), and the other romping with a dog. The whole thing is done with an enchanting lightness of touch; it is absurd, deliciously absurd, so that one is apt to remember afterwards rather than remark at the time with what mastery of the art the tapestry has been woven.

The cathedral, 12th and 13th century, is a fine Gothic structure with much good carving, but remarkable in particular for what must be the finest Romanesque stained glass windows still to be seen in France, relics of a previous cathedral, painstakingly put together again for this later one, at some time and by some person unknown. They are finer, and certainly easier to see, than those of Le Mans cathedral, earlier in date and perhaps even richer in texture.

There is much else, too, that merits a longer stay in Angers than one is usually prepared to make. There is the Préfecture, with its unexpected background. The administration of the *Département* has, since 1790, been lodged in the remains of the oldest Benedictine abbey in Anjou! If early charters are to be believed (which is not quite always the case), it was founded by a Merovingian king, Childebert, in 535. It was then rebuilt in high Romanesque style in

the second quarter of the 12th century. Finally, it was rebuilt once
again in the last quarter of the 17th century.

If, in the main, it is the rather delightful buildings of this last
reconstruction which constitute the Préfecture, some of the ambitious Romanesque work still remains, and by far the most impressive
part is the isolated tower, known still as the *tour de Saint-Aubin*.
It is a square tower of enormous strength thanks to the thickness of
its walls, and it had a double purpose. It was, in the first place, a
campanile separate from the abbey church. In second place it was a
place, strong as the keep of any castle, to which the monks could
retreat for safety in case of attack. It communicated with the abbey
church by a passage. It is not surprising, in view of its almost military
purpose, that there are few openings in the thick wall below the
height of a three-storey house. At this height the thick corner
buttresses thin out and take the shape of the four slender turrets with
slated *flèches*, which mask the change from the square of the tower to
the octagon of the top storey. The slated octagonal roof is waiting
for its spire, and has been ever since it was built, which in one way
detracts by its unfinished air, and in another way increases its appearance of almost menacing strength.

Still to be seen are a little gem of a 15th century house, the
Maison d'Adam, the beautiful town house (*Logis Barrault*) built in
1487 for Olivier Barrault, Treasurer of Brittany, which now houses
museum, art gallery and library, two other churches (Saint-Serge
and La Trinité) which are both ancient and interesting, and a third
which must be unique. It was the chapel of the priory of Saint-
Eloi, partly Romanesque, now used by the French Reform Church:
an example of broad-mindedness by all concerned. There is, too, the
once abbey church of Saint-Serge, with an early 13th century choir
in perfect Angevin style.

Wandering through the streets of Angers will show you many
more ancient houses, many more ancient churches and chapels and
remains of monasteries. So much more than Nantes does this city
retain its past that it is difficult to believe that once the larger city
was even richer in old buildings.

From Angers to Saumur there are so many variations of road

possible that it is very difficult to choose between them. To make a complicated matter as simple as possible, the main ones will be taken separately, beginning with those on the north (right) bank of the Loire. The first is, in fact, one that hugs the river quite closely for the 18½ mile journey.

If you leave Angers by N 152, a small detour at the Carrefour de la Pyramide (the pyramid dates from 1743 and commemorates the completion of a levee to hold back flood waters of the Loire) to Vissoire and Tréblazé will provide a sight more remarkable than beautiful and, if you have taken the precaution beforehand of obtaining a pass from the *Ardoisières de Trélazé* Head Office, at 52 Boulevard du Roi René, at Angers, a quite unique experience – a visit to some of the oldest (700 years) and most extensive slate quarries in the world. The quarries stretch for 3 miles and some of them are now being worked at a depth of over 1,000 feet. Some 4,000 workers are employed.

These are the slates which gave 'black Angers' its unkind name. They are the slates characteristic of all the lower reaches of the Loire. They are considered to be of the highest quality to be found anywhere; something approaching two million roof slates are sold from here every year. The quarries have been completely modernized and in equipment compare favourably with the most advanced coal mines.

Back, via the pyramid, to N 152 which, three miles farther on, meets the river and then follows it. The broad river is dotted with islands and islets; villages, woods and farms on the farther bank look most attractive. Why does whichever bank of a river one is not on always seem so much to be preferred to the one being followed? At La Ménitré is a manor house, or quite small château, dating from about 1450, ascribed to good King René and lived in by his second wife, Jeanne de Laval. Across the river is a fine view, which includes the ruined abbey of Saint-Maur, the first of the Benedictine rule to be established in France. The road follows thereafter a long, slow river bend before arriving at the bridge which links Les Rosiers on the right bank with Gennes on the left bank. Wise people (if it happens to be on one of the days when they feel they can afford a good lunch) will have arranged to take their midday meal at the former.

Les Rosiers is very picturesque. There is, for example, something quite uniquely pleasing, even romantic, about a suspension bridge. No doubt the delightful curve of the supporting chains seen against sky or water has much to do with it. First, then, Les Rosiers has its suspension bridge. It also has the most charming 13th century church with a decorative Renaissance spire (dated 1538). It has pretty old houses in its Grande-Rue, which isn't really as grand as all that. Above all, it has two restaurants. I regret to say that it is known to far more people for these two restaurants than for bridge or buildings.

To take them in alphabetical order, the first is the Hostellerie des Ducs d'Anjou, where one eats royally in a 16th century manor house, in which one is well but not stylishly served. The other is the Hôtel Jeanne de Laval, a much less impressive building, but where one also eats royally and is served a little more ostentatiously. Both are medium-priced – above rather than below – and both have three of the crossed spoon and fork symbols which in the Michelin guide signify 'very comfortable restaurant'. Why does the Jeanne de Laval have one Michelin star for good food and the other not? I find this impossible to understand, for with two such close rivals for the same class of trade, there is absolutely nothing to choose between their very high standards of food. It was at the Hostellerie des Ducs d'Anjou that I first tasted Champigny, not a great wine but an exceedingly pleasant one.

Whenever you can find a small village with two good restaurants in rivalry with each other, there you are likely to eat extremely well at a price reasonable for the kind of restaurant and the kind of food. It is something worth looking for, as those who have been to Les Eyzies, in Dordogne, will remember.

About 3 miles along the river from Les Rosiers, and just beyond the riverside village of Saint-Martin-de la-Place, one comes to the Château de Boumois. In part this is a fairy tale castle in bright white stone below deep grey slated roofs, with round towers, fat and jovial below their conical dunce's hats. But turn round to see the side that faces the open country and the jovial air has disappeared entirely; the Gothic elevations make one think of tall, gaunt women with tight-lipped mouths.

Boumois belongs to many different eras. The corbelled sentry-walk of the gateway towers was built for use in a war-torn closing of the Gothic age: the corbels continue along the Renaissance buildings as a decoration. On the inner courtyard, the Gothic has already taken on an Italianate look that the Renaissance will continue and alter into something French. The staircase turret, well lit by mullioned windows, is all angular, and almost touching it is a round turret corbelled at first floor level. During the 17th and 18th centuries windows more in the taste of the times were introduced. The pretty little chapel, with its own campanile, is 16th century, and the dove-cote 17th. The Guard Room has a ceiling like the inverted hull of a ship. The elaborate carving of the wood and the metalwork of the staircase door make it a little art gallery of its own.

There are, inside, many articles having belonged to or been associated with the hero of Boumois, Aristide-Aubert Dupetit-Thouars. He was born in this castle in 1760 and joined the French navy before he was 18. He saw much service in the Mediterranean and off the coast of Africa. When the Count of Lapérouse, the French explorer, met his death in the Pacific in 1788, it was the Chevalier Dupetit-Thouars who organized the search for such survivors as there might be of the two ships which made up Lapérouse's expedition. Meanwhile he was given command of *Le Tonnant* and took part in the disastrous (from the French point of view) attack by Admiral Nelson on the French fleet at Aboukir. A cannon-ball took off one leg. With immense presence of mind he ordered his men to place him upright in a barrel of sawdust so that he should not bleed to death. Die he did, and soon, but still calling to his men, 'Don't lower the flag! Don't lower the flag!'

Despite France's total loss of Canada in 1763, many Frenchmen continued to visit it, and amongst them was the Chevalier. This was in 1795, three years before his death. He became enthusiastic about this new country, and Niagara before all else in it. He was disappointed, as one learns from the book on his travels, which he wrote immediately on his return, that he was not allowed to visit Quebec and Montreal, and had to content himself with long conversations with French-Canadians whose courage and fidelity impressed him. He ends his book in an atmosphere of melancholy.

I do not know why I begin to feel so little at my ease in a country which unites vast size, noble-minded inhabitants and the most attentive hospitality. Does the English atmosphere bear heavily on the breathing of a Frenchman? Is it due to my regrets at the sight of these fine lakes on which the French first launched ships worthy of their size now having to carry that same flag which has so recently been hoisted over Pondichery and our finest strongholds in the West Indies? Is it the vexation, which I must keep within myself and never show, of seeing Canadians in a condition of subjection to their fierce conquerors?

Indeed, it cannot have been easy for men of action, men of the intense patriotism of the Chevalier, to see France's overseas possessions being taken over by the British one after the other. A man seldom gives himself away so much as in his writings, and the Chevalier emerges as forthright, honest and most likeable. And he was only one of three remarkable men of the same family. His elder brother by two years, Louis-Marie Aubert Dupetit-Thouars was an outstanding French botanist and a member of the Académie des Sciences. He did not enter the navy, but travelled much, and wrote several books on his discoveries in his own field in Madagascar, Réunion and Mauritius (which was then still French). Then there was their nephew, Admiral Abel-Aubert Dupetit-Thouars. He entered French history by taking over Tahiti in 1842 and making it a French protectorate.

The historic château of Boumois, standing so proudly by France's greatest river, had in fact little enough history to be proud of until the two generations of this family shed lustre upon it.

It is only 5 miles from here to Saumur, and it is a good fast road, carrying less traffic than one would expect. From it I took a colour photograph the one to which, of all the hundreds I have taken taken in France, I come back to the most often. The white clouds are dancing across the blue sky – the luminescent light blue of the Loire. In the foreground is a corner of a little vineyard, with the vines in exuberant leaf of a delicate green. There are a few pear trees faintly dotted with the white points of unopened buds. In the middle ground, more fruit trees and some larger ones make a green screen. On the horizon the white castle of Saumur silhouetted against the sky, more woods, and the tall, thin spire of a village church. This, to me, is France eternal, and the very quintessence of the long Loire valley. There is nothing here that an artist could not have painted a hundred years ago, two hundred, three hundred: nothing but the pale sky and the bright white clouds, the vineyard and the orchard and the light brown earth, and the castle on its hill.

The second alternative road from Angers on the right bank is not very much longer, being in all no more than 32 miles, and it includes one of the most interesting of all the châteaux. It starts off as the Longué road (D 61), becomes D 4 at Beaufort-en-Vallée and N 138 at Longué. These 'D' roads are avoided by some motorists as they are usually shown thinner on the map than the 'N' roads. My own experience has been that they are good roads throughout the land of the Loire (as far as Nevers at least), not always so broad as but usually so much freer of traffic than the 'N' roads that I have often arranged a whole day's run on them. 'N' of course signifies the *Route Nationale*, the major highway, 'D' means *Route Départementale*, a road of secondary importance; the third category, 'V.O.', *Chemin Vicinal Ordinaire*, is sometimes very *ordinaire* indeed, being intended only for inter-village traffic.

Just past the first little village beyond Angers, Saint-Barthélemy-d'Anjou, the Château de Pignerolle (or Pignerolles, or even Pignerol; there is no uniformity in the spelling) is situated up a little side turning to the left. If you have not known about it beforehand you will be in for a great surprise, for there, before you, is the *Petit Trianon*, somehow strayed from Versailles. And no modern imitation, either, but glorying in all the elegant workmanship of the 18th century.

It is not an exact replica, but a design suggested by the *Petit Trianon* of Jacques-Ange Gabriel to his brilliant pupil, Bardoul de la Bigottière. It is not quite square, but deeper than it is wide. There is a peristyle of four fluted Corinthian columns which support a projecting balcony. There are, for the ground floor, tall rectangular windows surmounted by triangular pediments. The ornamental balustrade of the balcony is continued round the building.

This amusing home was built for the Avril family almost at the end of the 18th century. This highly remarkable family managed, for almost a full century, from generation to generation to generation, the world-famous *Académie d'Equitation de France*, French Riding Academy, at Angers. Members of the most distinguished families attended the courses at the Academy, and they came from every civilized country. Riding in those days was the mark of a gentleman: you could tell a man's breeding by the way he rode.

Around the new Trianon was a vast park, with the entrance guarded by two very elegant octagonal pavilions. In it was a fine orangery, and a great number of good statues, for the Avril family were people of good taste. It is a good thing there were none left to see the sad end of their delightful property.

In 1939, the Polish Government-in-Exile were temporarily installed in Pignerolle, but driven from it by the German Army in 1940. It was then commandeered as an Army H.Q. by the Germans. When they left, of the multitude of statues in the park, two remained. The house was a shambles. It is not even certain that only the Germans were to blame, for French families made homeless by bombing took over the huts and shelters left by the Germans.

Despite this, Pignerolle is worth seeing, even though it be only from the outside, for it is quite intact and quite lovely, and it promotes thought. Did, for example, England ever have a similar dynasty of king's equerries? And if so, would they have run a riding school for profit?

Fourteen miles on, 1 mile north of the village of Mazé, is the noble Château of Montgeoffroy, high up in the list of the very great châteaux of France. It is not only a beautiful building, but for its décor and furniture I think it is probably the most interesting of all. Cheverny must be a close rival, but there is an atmosphere of a family home about Montgeoffroy which the more ornate Cheverny does not quite succeed in imparting. Indeed, I know of nothing comparable with Montgeoffroy for a complete, accurate, intimate view of the domestic life of a great family at the end of the 18th century.

The château stands at the top of a long, gentle slope covered with green fields; it is a tall, simple and elegant building, with centre bay and end pavilions in projection. The end pavilions are visually connected with the two wings of dependencies at right angles to the main building by single-storey squares. These dependencies themselves end in two squat round towers with conical roofs, on the very edge of the stone balustrades which follow the curve of the two crescent-shaped moats. Only the front, as one approaches this virtual *cour d'honneur*, is open; the drive goes straight on through the gap in the balustrades, which end in pedestals carrying stone urns. Farther down the hill, away from the house, are the fine wrought iron gates.

Château de Montgeoffroy

Louis-Georges-Erasme, marquis de Contades, was born in 1704 in the 16th century château which the present one has replaced. He entered the army and eventually became maréchal de France 'for', as his enemies said, 'successfully losing the battle of Minden'. On the triangular pediment of the centre bay the trophies of his wars are carved, but are of no help in determining in what battles he *was* successful. However the old château was pulled down in 1772 and the building of the new begun in March, 1773. Minden had been fought in 1759, and forgotten.

Material was brought from the derelict châteaux of La Roche-Thibault and La Singerie. Ashlar was brought from Durtal and Chênehutte-les-Tuffeaux, freestone from Baugé. Seven years later, in August, 1779, it was ready for the flock of cabinet-makers, decorators, and upholsterers who arrived from Paris . . . and who left it exactly as we see it today.

The rooms are handsome and well-proportioned, but there are no long galleries, no *salons* the size of a concert hall, nothing designed deliberately to impress by its size, or elaborate gildings, or wealth of rich hangings. The old marquis wanted a house to live in: this he got, and this it remains. The furniture is by the great Parisian furniture-makers of the time; it still represents perfect good taste. And so do the curtains, and so do the colours of woodwork, wall-coverings and everything else about it. How much of this the old man was responsible for is difficult to tell, but many of the orders were issued by his niece, and she may well have been the good genius of the house.

It was furnished in 1779. Ten years later came the Revolution. The old marquis still lived on. How then did all this escape the destructive wrath of the revolutionaries, the senseless breaking up of works of art which accompanies most revolutions? A portrait in one of these miraculously preserved rooms gives the answer, at least in part. It was a room occupied by Madame Hérault de Séchelles; the portrait is of a very handsome man, her son, whom Carlyle called 'one of the handsomest men in France'. Hérault de Séchelles was a member of the old Paris Parlement, and took his place in the National Assembly. Then Marie-Jean Hérault de Séchelles was on one of the committee chosen to formulate a new constitution. He was twice President of the Convention.

Whilst he lived and was protected by Danton, his mother's friends were safe. Danton, flattering himself that he was still too powerful to have any cause for fear of his own life, sat by as Hérault de Séchelles was arrested. Then Danton was taken away to prison. He and Hérault de Séchelles met at the foot of the guillotine. 'Our heads will meet in there', said Danton, nodding at the basket placed below the neck-rest of Dr Guillotin's famous machine. And a few minutes later they did.

This was in April, 1794. The Contades family's powerful protector was no more. True, the marquis still lived, and his age was perhaps some protection. These must have been days of great anxiety none the less, for they could hardly foresee how quickly the great upheaval of the nation was to settle. The following year the old man died, and the following year also the Directory came into being and the Revolution was over.

This is at least some good part of the answer to the question as to

how it all survived, but I see from some notes taken at the château
itself that there seems to have been some kind of official sale to the
local notary – an honest man devoted to the family – of the château
and all its furniture, and that he sold it back to them when they
returned to live in it. In other areas and with other noblemen, this
might not have been much of a deterrent, but obviously the family
were well liked, and too far from big towns for urban mobs to come
and incite the peasants to orgies of destruction.

The Cenotaph of the old marshal is in the chapel, part of the old
château (it dates from 1543), in which there is also a fine stained glass
window of about the same period, with a particularly pleasing version
of the adoration of magi and shepherds. In the dependencies on the
opposite side of the courtyard are some interesting old carriages used
by the family in times past; the 18th century litter is probably the
only one left to be seen in France.

At Cheverny, where the king had his *droit de gîte*, the right to a
room ever kept ready for his arrival, no king ever came. At Montgeoffroy, where there was no *droit de gîte*, the king came and was
treated as one of the family (which must have been a great joy to him)
and had a mild gamble on cards or backgammon: the table, left as it
was when last the king played there, is carefully dusted each day,
and put back just as it was – or as near as anybody remembers it to
have been.

When the new lady of the house takes over, the Majordomo comes
to her and proffers her the inventory of the furniture and hangings.
It is a book which he shows to visitors with great pride, for it goes
back to the 18th century and hardly needs to be amended at all.
Nothing that matters has changed since then, and this makes
Montgeoffroy a living thing without parallel. Indeed, looking for a
modern note, all I could find was a single photograph of a very
handsome and still young couple whom I took to be the present
owners. I have no idea when it was taken, nor does it matter, for in
that house time is immaterial.

I think everybody leaves with regret such a superb dwelling-place,
where even the kitchen, adorned with great numbers of shining
copper pans, is a lovely room in its own right. The regret is softened
if one returns to D 4 and continues for a few miles south-eastwards to

Beaufort-en-Vallée. This little town is on one of the richest plains in Anjou and is built round the ruins of a powerful fortress built (or, more properly, rebuilt) by Count Guillaume-Robert de Beaufort, the father of Pope Gregory XI, in 1346 . . . and good King René re-rebuilt one of the towers just a century later. Although the church dates from the 15th century, with 16th century additions, it was heavily rebuilt at a bad time in the late 19th century. However, the 1542 bell tower, nearly 150 feet high, is a splendid piece of work, and 16th, 17th and 18th century architecture figures in others of the buildings of this pleasant and prosperous townlet.

A particularly fine church, illustrating the first development in Anjou of the Gothic style, is at Brion, just a little over two miles due east, by D 7. Brion is on a rise, and looks out southwards over the plain, down to the Loire. This mixed Romanesque and Gothic church, with transept and choir in the then new-fangled Gothic, was fortified during The Hundred Years War, and the crenellations on the apse still remain. To avoid a return to the main road at Beaufort, D 211 can be taken almost as far as Longué, from where 10 miles of the fast N 138 bring one to Saumur.

Journey number three goes a little farther to the north, and if it does not include another Montgeoffroy (and there is no other), it does lead to other interesting places. First it takes N 23, leaving Angers towards the north-east, for nearly 12 miles. Just before arriving at Seiches-sur-le-Loir, the Château d'Ardanne is to be found on the right-hand side of the road. This is a very early specimen of the once-fortified residence, few of which have been allowed to endure in their original state. To see it one has to ignore the unhappy late 19th century would-be Louis XIII house, and then admire the keep of the old house, built above a broad porch. Alongside is the octagonal stair turret. There is also a two-storey round tower with pointed slated roof on either side of it. All these are a genuine 14th century production, quite beautiful in their own Gothic way.

Seiches-sur-le-Loir itself has nothing very remarkable to offer except the usual air of self-satisfaction which one expects from a French market town deep in the country, and the advantage of being planted on the banks of a pretty river. Just to the north of it are the fine remains of what must once have been a very splendid castle of the Rohan family, where kings and queens were received by the proud Rohans as if the monarchs were the ones on whom the favour was being conferred. *Roi ne puis, Duc ne daigne, Rohan suis:* king I cannot be; duke I will not demean myself to be; a Rohan I remain. The dependencies and their towers and stair turrets are left of the marvellous 15th century residential fortress built by Pierre de Rohan, better known as the Maréchal de Gié. It was deliberately pulled down by Cardinal Louis René Edouard, Prince de Rohan-Guémenée, towards the end of the 18th century, for what reason cannot now be known. Why a castle where his ancestors had received in state Charles VIII and Charles IX, Henri IV and Louis XIII, a castle which rivalled in its size, its beauty and its furnishings anything that the kings of France had built themselves in the Val de Loire, remains a mystery. Cardinal de Rohan ('Diamond Necklace' Rohan), protected by the armour of his own arrogance and stupidity, was unassailable. Nothing penetrated that did not flatter his vanity.

Even now, these servants' quarters have a noble air and do a little to recall the modestly named Verger (Orchard), whose outer wall was 2½ miles round, which had two sets of moats, and luxurious buildings surrounding a huge square courtyard where there was ample room for all the war games.

One can return direct from Le Verger to N 23 without going back to Seiches and have a quick run (partly along the edge of the forest of Chambiers) to Durtal. This little town on the Loir was once entirely fortified. If you leave from the Place du Marché you will see what is left of the original ramparts built by Geoffrey Martel, count of Anjou, in the 11th century. You then go under the magnificent Porte Véron to reach the castle; this deep archway, protected by two round towers belongs to the era of the first rebuilding of the castle, during the reigns of Henri IV and Louis XIII. It completely dominates the north bank of the Loir. It is now a hospice, but may be visited.

The road cuts across a loop of the Loir to reach the little town of Bazouges-sur-le-Loir. The partly 12th century church, for example, whose wooden vault is decorated with late 15th century paintings, and the delicious little castle right down on the bank of the Loir

The forbidding castle of Luynes, on the far side of the river looks out across it over a vast area of green meadows, typical of this part of the Loire valley.

Ussé has a delicate grace attained only by a few of the other châteaux of the Loire.

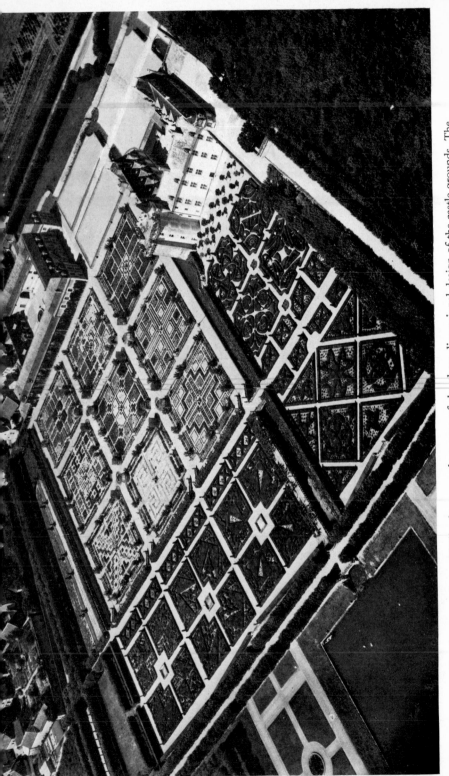

The flower gardens of Villandry are only a part of the three-dimensional design of the castle grounds. The original château was rebuilt in 1532, much altered in the 19th century and restored in the present one.

which demonstrates the way a king's chamberlain lived at the beginning of the 16th century. The two main blocks of buildings were much altered in the 17th century, and one Louis XII pavilion has been rebuilt in our own times, but the general impression must be much the same as when it was built, and the 16th century chapel and the sturdy machicolated towers at the entrance are just as they were.

As you come into La Flèche from the west, the main road leads you up to a crossing in the very centre of the town. If you turn down to your right, you will find a bridge over the Loir and some pleasing glimpses of the winding river; if you turn up to your left, your way will soon be blocked by a very substantial building and you will be obliged to turn either right or left.

This town began life as a medieval fortress in the middle of the Loir. Then a priory came, and a town began to form. In due course it came under the overlordship of Charles de Bourbon, duc de Vendôme. He died in 1536, and next year his widow came to live at La Flèche and built herself a comfortable residence, of the kind the Renaissance had just brought to France. Fifteen years later, Antoine de Bourbon with his wife Jeanne d'Albret took it over. They left in mid-May of 1553 for Pau, where their son was born on the 13th of the following December. So if France's favourite king was born in the old château at Pau, at least he was conceived at La Flèche, for the son was to become Henri IV. And it was he who first gave his château at La Flèche for use as a place of education. He presented it to the Jesuits, in 1604. They made it the set of buildings that one sees today. At its peak, it counted some 1500 pupils; many of them became men of learning and importance, and none more so perhaps than Descartes. In the long run it may be that his most remarkable gift to the progress of the world was his work on Analytical Geometry, perhaps the most powerful instrument of research any single person has put into the hands of men of inquiring minds. He himself probably thought it a mere trifle compared with his philosophical writings. Certainly his *Discours de la Méthode* has influenced profoundly the French way of thought, and probably given Frenchmen the reputation for logic which facts do not always bear out. Logical development from a single undeniable premise: to this day this is

I

the way the students at the great French Ecole Polytechnique (which turns out the most influential civil and military engineers and artillery officers) are taught to think. Its dangers are epitomized by the case of an old friend of mine, very much my senior, who, from the theory of vortices, argued himself back into a belief in the Trinity. Unfortunately the pre-Einstein theory of vortices was blown sky-high by later knowledge but whether this very eminent electrical engineer lost his belief in the Trinity as a consequence I never dared to ask.

Descartes came into this Jesuit school at eight, and at first the keenness of his intellect and his swift progress in all the subjects he was taught – languages, mathematics, astronomy even – endeared him to his teachers, but they came to be bitterly disappointed in him before he left. He became openly dissatisfied first with their, and then with all, doctrines and scholastic methods. He himself has described how as soon as he left college he forsook all books and tried to discard from his mind all that he had been taught, so as to make it more readily able to receive impressions of truth, no matter from whence they came.

The great 17th century buildings which you may visit now (on application to the concierge) are virtually the same as those which Descartes knew, but they no longer house a Jesuit college. The Jesuits were expelled from France in 1762, and the college was taken over and run as preparatory school for the distinguished Ecole Militaire in Paris. It is not clear just what made Louis XVI decide to use the premises to house a civilian college, which he did in 1776.

The college was shut down at the Revolution. Under Napoleon, it opened up again, until in 1808 he made it a *Prytanée militaire*, which it remains to this day. And what does this mean? It doesn't mean what it says, for a Prytaneum was the public hall of a Greek state (or city) in which the sacred fire was kept burning. In Athens, it was the hall in which distinguished citizens, foreign ambassadors and the successive presidents of the Senate were entertained at the public charge. In practice, the *Prytanée* was an invention of the Revolution as an institution to which the sons of officers could be sent free to be educated to the standards of the entrance examinations to the *grandes écoles*, such as the Ecole Polytechnique or the Ecole Militaire. The much restored, Jesuit-style chapel is light and pleasant.

In a niche above the gallery of the north transept are the ashes of the hearts of Henri IV and Marie de Médicis, or all of them that could be collected when the original organs were burnt by the Revolutionaries. The rest of the buildings, always in excellent taste, seem in some way dulled and diminished by the use to which they are put. This may be solely because there are too many of them, all in the same style. This is possibly a purely personal reaction, which others may well not experience.

From La Flèche, there is a long way round to Saumur which can be most attractive. If I hesitated long before including it because it strays rather far from the Loire, the visit to Le Mans, however short, finally seemed to me so important that it deserved a space in this book.

It begins with a swift 16 mile run north-west up N 159 to Sablé-sur-Sarthe. The little town is built on both sides of the river, where two tributaries flow into the Sarthe. It is one of the prettiest situations anywhere to be found in this country of rivers. It is worth looking at some pleasing old houses on the way up to the château which may be visited, but only by prior arrangement with the owner. Jean-Baptiste Colbert, the efficient but unlikeable Minister of Louis XIV, bought himself the title of marquis, which was attached to a 13th century fortress (or what remained of it) originally belonging to the Craon family. It was a nephew of the great man who built the present imposing château, making use of the supporting walls of the old one. It is very faithfully in the Louis XIV style, a big rectangular building with a centre pavilion given additional prominence by a very tall roof. The very agreeable gatehouse, well fortified, was built in the 14th century.

What one comes to Sablé-sur-Sarthe to visit is not in the town itself, but 2 miles away to the north-east. It is the famous abbey of Solesmes. It was established as early as 1010, as a modest little priory. Its activity continued through the centuries, but gently rather than demonstratively. With the Revolution, all the congregations of Benedictines were dispersed, and it was not until 1833 that the monks returned, under the famous Dom Guéranger, to make it once again a place of study, contemplation and prayer. In the great flurry of anti-clericalism which divided France down the middle in the late 19th century, the monks were driven out again in 1880. They went on living in and around the town for 15 years.

They returned in 1895, and began their rebuilding and extensions in 1896. They had been, and continued to be, the driving force behind the restoration of some of the finest old abbeys in France, such as Saint-Wandrille in Normandy, Sainte-Madeleine-de-Marseille, to be transferred in 1922 to the splendid Abbaye de Hautecombe, in Savoy, and to the building of others abroad, including Spain (Silos) and England (Farnborough). In 1901 they were once more driven out for an exile that was to last more than 20 years, during which they created the abbeys of Oosterhout in the Netherlands and Quarr, in England on the Isle of Wight.

In 1922 they returned, one hopes, without fears of any further expulsion. Since then the congregation has quietly found world-wide fame for their work in bringing again to vivid life the delights of Gregorian chant, of which their choir is now beyond doubt the finest exponent. They have also greatly encouraged the other arts and have themselves shown that modern art and sacred art, far from being incompatible, can be two aspects of the same thing.

The monastic buildings cannot be visited, but enough can be seen of their external appearance to realize that a return to the style of the 13th century can marry happily with a degree of modernization. The abbey church may be visited, and should be if only to see the carvings known as *The Saints of Solesmes*, the earliest of which dates from 1496, the latest from 1550. There are four groups, each surrounded in a framework of architecture and sculpture which is half-way between the old Gothic and the new Renaissance world. The groups are: The Entombment of Jesus, Christ disputing with the Doctors, The Communion of the Virgin and the death of the Virgin. Their artistic excellence has caused them to be attributed by many to Italian artists, but if this was so, no record of it exists. Without a record to the contrary, one must give the credit to the monks themselves.

Sung Mass must always be a memorable experience at Solesmes, and for the Christmas Eve midnight Mass and the Easter Masses, all seats in the church are booked, certainly for weeks, probably for several months, beforehand. I have not heard one myself, but the late Gordon Cooper described the Christmas Mass which he had attended as a service 'of great majesty' and perhaps the most satisfying spiritual experience he could remember. As a highly experienced travel writer, who had been nearly everywhere and seen nearly everything, he was not often carried away by new experiences. In all the years I knew him, he never spoke to me of anything comparable.

And now, 20 miles of straight road (N 23) to Le Mans, much of it through forest land. And at journey's end, a thrusting, thriving provincial capital of great antiquity, shopping centre for the rich agricultural district around, with enough of its own industry to make it a balanced city, and a place whose name is known to millions who have longed to pass through the turnstiles of the world's greatest annual road race, the Le Mans Twenty-four Hours.

The cathedral stands on the summit of a hill (as ideally all cathedrals should) and is surrounded still by a number of the old houses which have clustered round it for centuries. It actually breaks through the Gallo-Roman walls, and one can only guess for how many centuries before Rome came this hilltop carried walls or ditches for its defence. The cathedral is completely absurd, and I have a very great affection for it. Its individual components have been allowed to retain their individuality; each is good of its kind and even externally each stands alone, happening to be neighbours of other parts of good design, but nowhere welded with them into a congruous whole. The result is a cathedral which attracts the same kind of sympathetic affection as does a mongrel dog, who all too clearly shows his mixed descent.

For example, the choir towers above the nave, and no effort has been made to smooth out, or hide, or conceal by adding some extraneous architectural device, the fact that they do not belong to each other. The nave, which originally had a painted wooden vault, is Romanesque despite its pointed arches. One is accustomed to think of Romanesque style as automatically having round-topped arches and of Gothic having necessarily pointed arches. In fact the Gothic style depends on many things; essentially it is the style of the filled-in skeleton. The thin bones take all the stress; between them the infilling need bear no weight and can be no more substantial than the glass of the large windows. Romanesque depends upon the solid wall, with which remarkably lofty results could be obtained, as the extremely tall pilgrimage church at Saint James of Compostela so admirably shows. The nave, then, is no later than the 12th century; the arcade under the aisle windows are of the 10th or 11th, and some Roman-type parts of the outer wall undoubtedly belong to the original church of the 8th or 9th century.

By 1063, something approaching the present cathedral had already been completed in the Romanesque tradition. It was complete even to its transept towers. These did not last long; history interfered with architecture. Le Mans had long been the capital and principal residence of the counts of Maine, when William I of England, William the Conqueror, in the course of his quarrels with his neighbours grouped around his Norman possessions, seized the city. It was whilst he was busy with the conquest of England that the men of Le Mans, who had been deprived of their very special and important privileges, rose against him. Twice more they rose against him, twice more he repossessed himself of it. It was while he was in residence in Le Mans that he found the transept towers interfered with his views from the upper windows of his palace across the place, and had them removed. When Henry II, who was born in Le Mans, came to the throne, the privileges were restored to the towns-folk. Then Philip-Augustus took it, and later John of England re-took it. Then he lost it, and eventually it was ceded to the widow of Richard I (Richard Coeur-de-Lion), Queen Berengaria of Sicily, who did a great deal for it. Her tomb, brought from the abbey of Epau, is in the south transept.

Twice the Romanesque church suffered heavily from fire and in 1217, Louis-Philippe then being in possession, permission was asked and granted for a much larger choir to be built, which would necessitate extending the cathedral beyond the Roman walls.

The choir is splendid, with its soaring apse, its girdle of chapels and its double ambulatory. Of its period, there is nothing finer in France, for it is even more magnificent than Bourges. Coming out of the older, more solid-looking nave, into the lighter, loftier choir, is stepping into another world, the world of soaring Gothic. The stained glass is not as fine as that of Chartres, but it is a worthy rival of it.

There is another church in Le Mans which richly rewards the visitor, that of Notre-Dame-de-la-Couture. It gets its odd name from the name of the abbey which it served, the *abbaye de Saint-Pierre et Saint-Paul de la Couture de Dieu*, and *couture* means neither 'sewing' nor 'sowing' but is used in the sense of culture: 'the abbey of Saint Peter and Saint Paul for cultivating the knowledge of God.' Not only is this church architecturally rich in examples of several centuries of the middle ages, but it also has good pictures of the 16th, 17th and 18th century and some good 16th and 17th century tapestries, and a 10th century crypt whose pillars carry extraordinarily archaic capitals. In the crypt one gets a rare feeling of a place of worship used regularly for 1500 years nearly, for the first chapel was built here at the end of the 6th century.

It is a far cry from this antiquity to the Le Mans racing circuit, on which the first 24-hour road race was run in 1923, but on the way there one more visit of antiquarian interest is worth the making (all the more that it also takes one to a good, modestly priced meal).

The Abbaye de l'Epau is on the western outskirts of Le Mans, on the left bank of the river Huisne, amongst green fields. The approach is along a narrow road, and opposite the entrance to the abbey is a pleasant little restaurant where, one Sunday, we ate a delicious, well-prepared and nicely-served lunch in very pleasant surroundings at a price which would have been the double in Paris. It was a First Communion Sunday, and two parties were celebrating the full acceptance into the rites of the Church of a young girl. The girls in their very formal, long white dresses were enchanting and not entirely displeased to be the centre of family attention. With that inborn sense of the right manners for different social occasions which characterizes the French, both parties were at the same time gay yet constrained. Lunch had come to an end and the oval sugared almonds, white, or tinted in pastel colours, without which no baptism or First Communion can be held in France, were handed round. Where else, would the little girls have been quietly told by their mothers to offer them at the table of foreigners they had never seen before and would never see again? The day was hot, the lunch was plentiful. The little girls disappeared, and reappeared in their petticoats, and seated themselves again without the slightest trace of self-consciousness nobody taking the slightest notice. And that also struck me as a social grace.

Across the road and into the abbey grounds, where once again the centuries roll back. Here, in 1230, work began on a Cistercian abbey, paid for by the benefactor of Le Mans, Queen Berengaria, a widow for already over 30 years. Here are the few arcades still surviving from the cloisters, here the sacristy, with 14th century paintings still on the walls, but difficult to comprehend, and here the capitulary hall, divided into nine bays by columns whose capitals are carved with foliage. Here are the vaulted refectory, kitchen and cellar, and here the plain but beautifully proportioned abbey church in the Cistercian pattern – six chapels opening on to the transept and, at the east end, a rose window of the 14th century.

This was the resting place Berengaria chose for herself. Poor Berengaria, she had no luck. Daughter of Sancho VI, king of Navarre, she was brought up in one of the most civilized Courts in Europe. Richard Coeur-de-Lion had already paid court in Pamplona to one whom the chroniclers describe as 'a prudent maid, a gentle lady, virtuous and fair, neither false nor double-tongued'. Queen Eleanor, Eleanor of Aquitaine, escorted her to Sicily. In Sicily, Joanna, the widowed Queen of Sicily, arranged to escort her as she followed her husband on the crusade. They were married at Limasol, in Cyprus, in 1191. It would not be true to say that she never saw her husband after the honeymoon, but certainly she saw very little of him for the eight remaining years of his life, and lived under the complete domination of Eleanor (who usurped her title as 'queen of England'), the most formidable woman in the history of the middle ages.

She built Epau for the Cistercians, and there she was buried. Why then is her tomb in the cathedral at Le Mans and no more than a plaster cast left where the original should be? The sad answer is that the people of Le Mans, 'fearing lest the English should fortify the monastery', destroyed it in 1365. Although it was to some extent rebuilt in the closing years of that century, it never prospered as the other monasteries of the Cistercian Order did, and fell into such neglect after the Revolution that it was thought wiser, soon after the Restoration of 1818, to move an object of such historical interest to the cathedral of the town over which she had ruled with kindness.

The Le Mans road racing circuit is just outside the southern edge of the town. The present circuit is 8·364 miles and has twice been shortened. When it opened in 1923 it went right into Le Mans, giving a hairpin bend in a street setting more like the Monte Carlo Grand Prix than the road circuit used today. My first attendance was with the original circuit still in use: my second was also the first year (1929) of the circuit from which that bend had been eliminated, but this still left houses lining some small part of it. In 1932 the present much shorter circuit came into being.

In all the intervening years, the atmosphere remains identical, with fresh waves of new enthusiasts eager every year to enjoy their first Le Mans (the first is seldom the last, and attendances go up and up). Not all go for twenty-four hours of undiluted motor racing, though some do. In the centre of the circuit are restaurants, bars and buffets, many fairground amusements and the *Village*, usually empty, which comes to life for the two days of racing with shops, displays, a police station, a post office, and a motor museum. Access to all this is through tunnels or over footbridges. One 'side' of the roughly oval circuit is N 158 (main road from Le Mans to Tours) from which the rest can be visited – except of course in the middle of June, on practice days, and the two race days.

Those who admire old cars must consider me very lucky to have seen the race in the days when there were giants in the land – the green Bentleys of the late 1920s. And luckier still to have been in the pits time-keeping as these massive things roared through the night with headlights we would hardly today put on anything faster than a well-pushed pram. Charles Faroux, for more years than I can say the race organizer, asked to be allowed to drive one during practice and came back with the apposite but unkind remark that 'Britain always did build good battleships'. In fact it needs a study of results to realise that Bentley did not always win easily. My own interest was in the Chrysler team, and in 1928, though a Bentley won, it was with a leaking radiator that in another few laps might have put it out of the race, and the American Stutz Bear Cat which came second had lost two out of its three gears and could not have continued much longer whilst 'my' two Chryslers were closing in from third and fourth positions. Finally both the Bentley and the Stutz did just manage to last the course, but the excitement of a young man helping with the timekeeping in the pits can be imagined as the rumours of the bad condition of the two bigger and faster cars were brought in by breathless well-wishers of ours can easily be imagined. At one moment, victory seemed within our grasp, but Christian Lie (who had entered them) would not have the 'all out' signal given. There was over 100 miles to make up on the Bentley and almost as much on the Stutz. To make that up, our cars, with their much lower top speed, would have had to be pushed beyond the danger point. Christian Lie wanted them to finish, to show their reliability at high speed. At the time, I was desperately disappointed, but I now know he was right. The drivers were even more indignant; it was not only for their prestige; there were money considerations as well.

Such are the excitements of Le Mans; they remain much the same. It is only the speeds which differ. In the first race (1923), the winning Chenard-Walcker averaged 57·2 miles per hour. In 1928, the winning Bentley averaged 69·1; in 1933, an Alfa-Romeo pushed the figure to 81·1, and a Bugatti to 86·85 in 1939. Top speed fell in the immediate post-war races, but in 1953 Jaguar put it over the 100 m.p.h. mark for the first time (105·8). In 1963, a Ferrari averaged 118·1.

Coming out from the Le Mans circuit at Mulsanne, a road to the right leads to Moncé-en-Bélin; coming out of this village, one can turn left on to N 767, the road to Le Lude. This little town is 22 miles almost due south. It is on the Loir which, as we have seen, joins the Sarthe just above Angers; the united stream then joins the Mayenne, which from there to the Loire is called the Maine. There has been a village here since prehistoric times, for it commanded the road from Laval to Tours, as well as controlling traffic on the river. Whoever held Le Lude and Vaas, 8 miles up, was master of the approaches to Tours and as far up the Loire as Blois.

At this point, Foulques Nerra comes into our story. This turbulent duke of Anjou was the greatest builder of castles of all time. He was also one of the very greatest of strategists. Over fifty years he continuously and almost always successfully held in check his bitter and more powerful rival, the duke of Blois. He did it with a force usually much smaller than his enemy's by his strategy, which included the building of a great number of fortified towers (mostly of wood, on *mottes*) in commanding positions. He lived from 971 to 1040, and the Quillet-Flammarion dictionary describes him bluntly as 'powerful, warlike and tyrannical', but he was a far more complicated man than that. Three times for certain, and almost certainly a fourth, he went on pilgrimage to Jerusalem – no small undertaking in those days, which throws light on a different facet of his character.

When his father died, Foulques Nerra came into possession not only of Anjou itself, but of certain other properties which were highly embarrassing to his unfriends. Anjou was a rough circle round Angers, marching with Brittany on the west, Poitou on the south, Touraine on the east and Maine on the north. The actual delimitations were the source of endless quarrels, wars, seizures, acquisitions by marriage, and general uncertainty. In various ways the Foulques had acquired properties in Touraine, of which Amboise was the most important and the most troublesome. Less than 16 miles from Tours, on the Loire and on the road from Tours to Blois, only 23 miles away, it was a strategic toothache to the ambitious Count of Blois, who could only by roundabout ways get to his other possessions without the goodwill of the Counts of Anjou. To Foulques also it was a headache because his great enemy, the count of Blois, could stop relieving his garrison there at any time.

At incredible speed he built his towers. All, or nearly all, started as woodwork on a *motte*. Three (Chéramen, Cormillé and Mont-boyau) have completely disappeared because they were never converted to stone keeps. But that still leaves no less than 18 others, and probably more. He built them to command rivers and roads; he built them north of the Loire and he built them south of the Loire. By marching from castle to castle he could move his small army at great speed from one end of his domain to the other, whilst his opponents were spied upon and fought at every turn. Had he lived beyond that illness which cost him his life at Metz on his return from his last journey to Jerusalem, he would have taken Tours and split the county of Blois into two separate parts. This, however, the culmination of his plans and wars, was left to be done by his son, Geoffroy Martel.

The kingpins were of all his system of fortifications Le Lude, north of the Loire and Montrichard, south of the Loire. The latter he created for himself, the former he inherited. There is no certain date to be put to Le Lude. It is reported as having helped to repel the early Normans, but this first fort had disappeared in Foulques' day. He built another one, supposed to have its foundations where the terraces of the present château have since been made. After this came another medieval fortress, said to be of the 13th century, whose deep and cavernous cellars remain beneath the present château, which is itself of four different eras.

As soon as one approaches this becomes all too evident. This square castle, with a round tower at each corner is almost unbelievable. To the south is a rather beautiful genuinely 16th century façade. To the north, is a Gothic façade; to the east is a Louis XVI façade; to the west is the main entrance and bridge over the dry moat. We will draw a kindly veil over some of the restoration work, well intended, but with all the architectural sentimentality which marked the mid- to late-19th century.

The exterior of the building shocks many who see it for the first time. The gardens, on the contrary, delight everybody from first view to last. The lawns and parkland, cut by a scintillating stretch of the river, lead up to thick bands of woodland trees. Down on the river bank is given the most original *son-et-lumière* performance in France, usually from just before mid-June to the end of September, at week ends, on Thursdays as well in July, on Tuesday and Thursday as well in August. The five centuries of history of the present castle are presented by a company of 300, in costumes of the period, with ten red-coated huntsmen playing a fanfare on their horns, with cavaliers on land and a state barge on the water, with ballet, and with luminous fountains. Small wonder that Le Lude has won an *Oscar du Tourisme Français* and is a laureate of Prestige de la France.

The best of the château itself is inside. Here are some very precious and lovely things, as well as some horrid over-restoration. Le Lude is still lived in, and has the warmth and the illogic of a real home, such as that modern importation, pampas grass flowers in a noble

19th century Chinese vase on an 18th century veneered table, with 17th century silk-upholstered chairs around. This no château-museum would ever dare to present, but these delightful touches give Le Lude a most human appearance. There are some interesting costumes and splendid items of decoration of many centuries. Altogether, despite its disparate façades, Le Lude is a most rewarding place to visit.

Continuing down N 767 through Noyant to Linières-Bouton, on the edge of the forest of Pontménard, a 7 mile there-and-back run to Mouliherne, justified by a little church of great interest to those who make any study of architectural development. The walls of the nave show the narrow courses of the 10th or 11th century, whilst the vaults of nave and transept show the new light touch which had developed in Anjou in the 12th and 13th century. The crossing carries a bell tower of the 13th century, lit by wide bays. The pillars of the apse have historiated capitals. This delightful old church has so far mercifully escaped the attention of thoroughgoing restorers. On the south-west side of the village, there is a pretty 16th century château, high on the slope, the Château de la Touche.

One can either return to Linières-Bouton and from there go on down N 767 to Vernantes or prolong the excursion into the deep past of Anjou by going another 9 miles up to Baugé. The little town is deeply enshrined in the past. It has grown up around one of those early fortresses built by Foulques Nerra, this time to command the valley of the Couesnon, which flows into the Authion (one of the rivers the bridges of Ponts-de-Cé cross). On the foundations of this or a subsequent fortress, Yolande of Aragón, the mother of King René, built the existing château which is now the *Mairie*. The 68-step staircase, in a multilateral turret with flattened angles, is a fine piece of engineering as well as a beautiful architectural feature. The ribbed vault is in a palm-leaf design, bearing the combined arms of Anjou and Sicily.

The Rue Anne-de-Melun, on to which the château faces, is continued by the Rue du Docteur Zamenhof, and there one finds the Hospice Saint-Joseph, founded in 1643. The collection of decorated faience pots in the dispensary (which may be visited) of the 16th and 17th centuries is remarkable and it is difficult to think

of another as good. In the Rue de la Girouardière, south of the
16th century church, is the *Chapelle des Incurables*. Here is a remarkable
relic, dating for certain from the 13th century, and supposedly made
entirely from wood from the true Cross. It was brought from
Constantinople by one Jean d'Alluye to the now vanished abbey of
La Boissière and transferred for safety to its present resting-place.
Pieces of the true Cross are very numerous – enough, one feels, to
build another Noah's ark. This particular one is of more than usual
interest, in that its size is so much greater than any other which
has come to my knowledge, and is double-armed. This form became
the heraldic emblem of the counts of Anjou, and from them passed
to the House of Lorraine. Then it became less known as the Cross of
Anjou, and eventually known only as the Cross of Lorraine, from
which it became the emblem of the Free French Forces in 1940, and
is now to all effects and purposes a national emblem.

But how and why did it get its double arm? In heraldry, this
design is known as the patriarchal cross, but all my attempts to find
the chronology of the 'Cross of Anjou' have been unsuccessful. This
particular one is no longer the plain wooden piece that it once was;
during the 14th century it was ornamented with two golden cruci-
fixes and medallions adorned with pearls and precious stones.

Baugé is a small place, and one can enjoy sauntering through the
old streets in which there are quaint old houses. Le Vieil-Baugé
is 1½ miles to the south-west, and though the church is old, with 16th
century 'improvements' and a twisted and leaning spire of some
interest, it does not live up to its antique name.

The run through the forest back to Mouliherne and down N 767
to Vernantes is much more beautiful than the main road run through
Longué and enables one to see the lovely old stone spire (15th
century) and bell tower (12th century) of the one-time church
which is now the Mairie. A peep inside at the cenotaph of the Lords
of Jalesne (or Jalesnes), a 17th century work of slightly florid
sculpture helps to make the visit even better worth while. What is of
very real interest is the château de Jalesne, not much more than half
a mile to the west, but one would have to inquire about the possibility of visiting the beautiful exterior, to which tree-lined avenues
lead, and which is cut off from the outer world by particularly deep

moats. The tall and slender chimneys, the high and steeply sloping roofs, the corner pavilions, the turrets rising from pendentives, the round gable windows, give a truly 17th century air to this handsome château. Little is lost if one does not approach it, for 19th century alterations are all too visible close to it. These come from the days when Monsieur Ackerman owned Jalesne. He was an Alsatian by birth who had settled in Saumur. There he taught the local wine-makers how to use the *méthode champenoise* to make their good still wines into a not very good imitation of Champagne. As sparkling wines go, sparkling Saumur is not bad and sells very widely, but I prefer the sparkling Vouvray from just up the river and would much sooner drink Saumur as a still wine.

If Jalesnes is not to be seen, then you can console yourself with the Château de la Ville-au-Fourier, something more than a mile to the north-east of Vernantes. It all belongs to the earliest Renaissance and consists of two buildings at right angles to each other, flanked by cylindrical towers. It is not very striking, but genuine and rather sweet. It was built by the grandson of Jean de Broc, who was cup-bearer to Louis XI, a post of great confidence because of the sinister possibilities it offered if the king should happen to have offended the bearer. All that one knows of its history is that Marie de Médicis and Charles IX slept there; we do not even know if they slept well or badly.

After Vernantes, straight down N 767 through much woodland, on to N 138, and Saumur.

There remains only one other way of reaching Saumur from Angers, and that is the southern route over the bridges of Les Ponts-de-Cé, and for the moment straight down N 748, though only for 5 miles, to Brissac, a very charming castle, quite different from anything yet described.

Charles Cossé was born in 1505. He became a professional soldier, captured Le Havre from the English in 1563, and died a marshal of France. Artus Cossé, born in 1512, became a professional soldier, took a prominent part in the victory of the Catholics over the Protestants at Moncontour and died in 1582 a marshal of France. Charles de Cossé-Brissac, born about 1550, became a professional soldier, surrendered Paris to Henri IV and died in 1621 a marshal of France.

It was the last marshal of this remarkable military family who spent his declining years rebuilding Brissac. In the middle ages Brissac was a barony belonging to the influential Chemillé family and then to the powerful de Brézé family (Diana of Poitiers was the wife of a de Brézé). Towards the end of the 15th century, it was acquired by the father of the first Charles. What the cash value of opening the gates of Paris to Henri IV was to Charles de Cossé-Brissac cannot be known, but it added immensely to his standing and by the time he retired from active service in 1606 there was ample money to rebuild Brissac.

The duke (for Brissac had been raised by a grateful king to the status of a property which conferred a dukedom, this being the French system) intended to make a clean sweep of everything and to start again from the foundations. Unfortunately for his plans, the two strong cylindrical towers defeated all attempts to pull them down by hand. Gunpowder would have been the answer, but was not considered safe to use, which in view of the totally unscientific methods of manufacture was certainly a wise decision.

So to our joy, we see today the new building squeezed into the space between these formidable primitive towers, with which great liberties have been taken since the new château was begun as a residence. There is doubt about the architect, and for once we have too many names to choose from instead of the usual anonymity, but the most probable man is Jacques d'Angluze, son of the king's architect at Fontainebleau. To carry out his designs, he surrounded himself by many others: Charles Corbineau was the principal collaborator and many consider him to have been the real architect.

Between its two round towers, a vast mansion was begun, strangely modern in its proportions, being seven storeys high on a comparatively narrow front. The original intention was to make the whole vast château in the same style, with a return wing to form the second side of a huge square courtyard.

Alas, the de Cossé-Brissac money ran out, for exterior magnificence was being matched by interior magnificence, and the rear wing was built in the much less exuberant and expensive manner of the

Year after year Honoré
Balzac came to stay in
the château de Saché and
the surrounding country-
side figures in many of
his novels.

Once belonging to
Henry I of England and
later to Henry III,
Montrésor was rebuilt in
1395 and again at the
beginning of the 16th
century. It is one of the
most gentle looking of
the pre-Renaissance
châteaux.

The lower floor of the gallery across the Cher, the famous feature of Chenonceaux. The wall medallions are superb examples of Renaissance art.

Architects and masons of four different centuries worked on the château de Chissay and this elevation is now unbalanced, but the decorative corner towers are very handsome.

style of Louis XIII. It is probably an advantage. The Renaissance effect of the early part tends to remind one of a wedding cake, much aided by the whiteness of the tufa and the facility with which it could be ornamented with foliated scrolls. All the château completed in the same way might have been too much of a good thing. As it is, the contrasting styles give it great charm.

Château de Brissac

The interior is quite magnificent. The large and beautifully proportioned Guard Room, with its wooden beams carved in a rich profusion of designs, bedrooms with tapestry-hung walls and discreetly carved doors, the family portrait gallery – there have now been twelve ducs de Cossé-Brissac – and early four-poster beds, one of which at least has tall human figures by way of posts and crouched ones by way of feet, as well as other old and interesting furniture.

Brissac has one moment of royal history. Henri IV divorced his first wife, Marguerite de Valois. He had married her only to strengthen his hold on the Crown, as she was the daughter of Henri II and Catherine de Médicis. He took as his second wife Marie de Médicis, 20 years younger. After the death of her husband, she was Regent during the minority of their child, Louis XII. The day came when there was war between mother and son.

K

There was a battle at Les Ponts-de-Cé, held for the queen, between the soldiers of the two sides. The queen's men were driven so easily from it that nobody could take the battle seriously, and it has gone down in history, not as the Battle of Ponts-de-Cé, but as *Les drôleries des Ponts-de-Cé*, the frolics at Ponts-de-Cé.

And that night Marie de Médicis and Louis XIII were reconciled, and slept under the same roof, the gorgeous roof of the château de Brissac. The reconciliation lasted not very much longer than the battle.

If the Château de Brissac were upstream from Saumur instead of downstream, I am sure it would be high up in the list of those it is a 'must' to have seen. Brissac makes me think that perhaps it would be a good thing if travel writers today were allowed to give the terse and useful warnings which their mid-Victorian predecessors allowed themselves. Of the Hôtel de la Poste at Brissac, John Murray II had only three words to say: 'dirty and dear'. There is still an Hôtel de la Poste at Brissac, but I can assure readers that it is neither dirty nor dear.

Should it be your intention to make an excursion from Saumur itself along the river bank, then it is worth continuing along the fast main road (N 761) across the rich plain, between fields and bits of vineyard and woods, for the 14 miles to Doué-la-Fontaine, one of the most extraordinary villages it is possible to visit. 'La Fontaine' is not a fountain, but one of the innumerable natural springs which mark the beginning of the little river Douet. They fill two vast reservoirs, each only just short of measuring 150 by 100 feet, cut out by hand in the rock, it is said, in 1768. There must, I feel sure, have been excavations already in existence for it to have been the hand work only of a single year. Doué is in part built over old quarries, which were worked by the Romans. The southern extension of Doué, inseparable now from it, is Douce; at Douce is a famous arena, with its stone seats cut out from the solid rock. It is now generally believed that these were in fact old quarry workings following a stepped pattern, a process used by the Romans. These were certainly used for theatrical purposes in the 15th, 16th and 17th centuries.

There is a pleasing 15th century church (Saint-Pierre) and some rather dramatic ruins of the old collegiate church (Saint-Denis) of very pure Angevin style of the middle of the 12th century. There are also the remains of the castle walls, high above the town, which are in their turn dominated by a huge *motte*. One can guess at once, and guess right, who was the constructor of the *motte* and builder of the wooden tower which stood upon it: Foulques Nerra.

One can well go straight from here to Saumur, only 10 miles on a good road, but there are some minor places of interest. They are not of great importance, but the surroundings are so delightful that if there is time, it is well worth visiting them.

Straight down the same road, N 761, for seven and a half miles, and there is one of the most enchanting villages in all Anjou. The river Thouet, which edges Saumur and flows into the Loire just downstream from it, here broadens out and makes a picturesque pool in which castle and church are reflected. Then Montreuil-Bellay rises upon the hill behind, largely within 13th century walls. From the river, fortifications, castle, church and town buildings make a picture straight out of earlier centuries, with nothing to mar the illusion.

It is probably needless to say that the original castle here – a stone and not a wooden one this time – was built by Foulques Nerra. He gave it, as was so often the case with him, to a reliable friend and follower (with feudal reservations, naturally), Giraud Berlay which later became distorted into Bellay. In the 15th century, the counts of Melun who then owned it began building the present castle, and walling the town. Its long list of noble owners includes some with which the history of France is repeatedly studded: d'Harcourt, Orléans-Longueville, Cossé (before being Cossé-Brissac) and de la Trémoille. In more modern times, it was bought by the infamously miserly Niveleau, whom Balzac (with some exaggeration) immortalized as Le Père Grandet.

Few places have more royal names linked with them, though none of the occasions of their visits are of any particular historical interest; six kings, from Louis VIII to Louis XIII, lodged within these walls. But Montreuil-Bellay comes into history when the duchesse de Longueville and the duc de Richelieu were exiled to it in the days of the Fronde.

As you cross the bridge to come into the town, you will see a little upstream, an old mill. Access to it from the town is through a fortified gate, through which is an old Benedictine priory and the ruins of a 12th century church. Curtain walls fell down to the stream itself from the priory; both were pierced by fortified gates through which the streamside path had to pass. However, we are concerned with the road that continues the bridge and runs right through the town. It enters through one old town gate, and leaves through another. On the right-hand side is the little Rue du Château, which leads to the deep moat of the castle. To one side is the castle's lovely little 15th century church, with a single nave. To the other side is the gateway to the castle. The gate is between two tall thin towers. Through the gate one comes first to the old castle, rebuilt in the 12th century on the site of Foulques Nerra's tower, and modernized in the 15th century. Then, towards the river, is the new castle, with towers and with turrets, straight out of an illuminated Book of Hours.

You may wonder why I have not included Montreuil-Bellay and its towers and turrets and old churches and town walls as a place that it is important to see. In itself it is, but the castles can only be visited when the owner is not in residence. It would be disappointing to arrive at the gate and be turned back.

There is one other piece of sightseeing on the way to Saumur. Up N 761 towards Doué-la-Fontaine for 3½ miles, then a right turn on a local road to the remains of the Abbaye d'Asnières. The abbot's chapel, with its very ancient carved flagstones, and tomb statues, of the 14th century, and other later ones in stone and wood, make the visit worthwhile. It is really as good a way as any other to get to Saumur, as a continuation of the local road brings you out on to the Doué-la-Fontaine to Saumur main road (N 160). There is an earlier detour which I recommend to those who have a taste for the early Angevin style in churches. This entails a few miles down D 88 to the south-west on leaving Montreuil-Bellay, then a turn right on a local road to Le Puy-Notre-Dame. The village is at the top of a hill, and for long was known as Le Puy-en-Anjou, but in view of the enormous number of pilgrims to Le Puy-en-Velay, it took a closer link with it.

The church is the most perfect example of the purest Angevin style of the 13th century, with side aisles as lofty as the nave, and the square choir, and the ribbing which distinguishes the style. The church possesses one of the many Girdles of Our Lady, brought back from Jerusalem. One of its qualities is to ease the pangs of child-birth. For this, it was carried in great state to Anne of Austria when she was about to be delivered of Louis XIV. Nearly five feet long and two inches wide, it is undoubtedly oriental in origin and made of linen and silk. Clasps and covers, jewelled, are of much later date, mainly 16th century. A pilgrimage is still made to it each year, on the Sunday next after September 8. From here there is a direct road through Vaudelnay on to N 761, emerging exactly opposite the little road to Asnières.

Just aside from N 160, a mile or two from Saumur, on the left, is what remains of the severe castle of Pocé. The most interesting feature is the formidable gateway, an individual fortress in itself. Only one other of the 15th century buildings remains, a square dwelling which does not live up to the rather fantastic entrance. Then, high on its hill above the town, the Château de Saumur shines in the sunlight against the blue sky and the white clouds.

The short way from Angers to Saumur, via Brissac, is to go north-east from Brissac to N 751, on D 55, then take N 751 to the right for 2½ miles, as far as Coutures, and turn left up the local road to Montsabert. The castle belonged to Jeanne de Laval. The widowed Bertrand Duguesclin, Constable of France, needed a new wife. Jeanne de Laval was very young indeed, and very rich indeed. Overcoming any reluctance to marry a girl straight from the school room (she was fifteen) and setting aside any high-falutin' ideas about marrying a wife for herself and not her money, Bertrand at nearly sixty years of age married the little girl with the big name and the big fortune. The Montsabert one sees today is not the one he lived in for a time with Jeanne, but one built by his successors in the two following centuries, yet it is exactly as though he had lived on to supervise the rebuilding. It is singularly heavy for its time. It remains a fortress, with heavy square towers, and round towers, and crenellations and machicolations; no feminine hand has been at work to soften the warlike elements into the decorative ones of so many other contemporary castles. This makes Montsabert highly interesting, for really only Montsoreau compares directly with it. The inside cannot, mercifully, be visited. It is used as a *Colonie de Vacances*, a summer home for the children of needy parents – a quite admirable French institution. Only it is better not to know what the little darlings do to the inside of the place.

From Montsabert we can go straight up to Bourdion and Saint-Rémy-la-Varenne, nearly on the river. Alongside is the abbey of Saint-Maur, an historic place with a long history, but suppressed at the Revolution and badly in need of the rebuilding undertaken by the Benedictines in 1890. Hardly was it finished than they were exiled in 1903, and in recent years it has been occupied only by a small seminary. Saint Maurus was a follower of Saint Benedict in the 6th century, but there is much doubt if the Maurus who settled on the banks of the Loire was the same person. Saint-Maur itself was famous above all for the learning of its Benedictine monks from the 17th to the 19th century. There are many remains of past centuries still to be seen here, and not least perhaps the ultimate ruins of a circular Roman temple that Saint Maurus (whichever one it was) transformed into a Christian chapel.

Some of the furnishings of Saint-Maur are to be found in the old waterfront church of Le Thoureil. At Gennes, a bridge leads across to Les Rosiers. High up on an escarpment are the remains of a fine old church – really old, for the walls at the transept are 7th century, or 8th century at the latest. It is not used now, and a little sad to see, but the view over the Loire in both directions is so soft, so green, so gentle that one tends to sit and gaze for far longer than one intended.

The road now follows close to the river, and approaches Cunault. What is left of a 9th century priory is the large and evocative 12th century church, wonderfully preserved for its age and not anywhere being spoiled by too obvious or ill-judged renovation.

At very first sight, though, one finds a flaw. The central square tower is not a fit. It is a very pleasant piece of work in its own right but it has, as it were, come from the wrong box of bricks. The reason is that the tower is a century older. Presumably, when the older church was demolished, there was not enough money to build a new tower, so the old one was left and the rest of the bigger church was built round it. But it is a very handsome tower, with three arcaded storeys, and a spire four centuries later than the 11th century tower itself, but remarkably apposite to it.

The beautiful pillars and historiated capitals are rightly the glory of Cunault: foliage, human beings, mythical monsters follow each other on the capitals with imagination and masterly carving. No less remarkable, and enjoyable, to my mind, is the general impression of height, and spaciousness. Altogether this must rank amongst the greatest of Romanesque churches still extant, and one that all should see.

Next to Cunault is Trèves, once a separate place but now joined to it. Like Cunault, Trèves has a fine Romanesque church of the 11th century, but in detail it does not bear comparison with its neighbour. If the church at Trèves were a long way away, the comparison would be easier on it. Trèves also has a fascinating priory, the *Prieuré de Saint-Macé* which may not, unfortunately usually be visited as it is private property. This is a pity, for the quaint chapel has two porches, and one would like to examine it more closely.

The very name of Trèves was an invention of Foulques Nerra, one of his few jokes to come down in history. According to the Chronicle of Saint-Florent, Foulques was on one occasion marching on Saumur, still held by Gelduin of Blois, when the latter sent a herald to suggest a truce. *Ut trevas faceret*, says the chronicler. Foulques' small army was at a place called Clémentiné because its church was dedicated to Saint Clement. There he halted, and sent word that he would like to make a truce (*faire une trève*). So he built himself a new fortress there, and called it Trève, *quod trevas nuncupavit*, as the Chronicler of the abbey of Saint-Florent wrote.

You may be told that the splendid tall keep, almost exactly 100 feet high, is the very one that Foulques Nerra built. This is simply not true and could not be, historically or architecturally. Instead we must accept it as the work of a chancellor of France, Robert Le Maçon, and part of a great castle he completed in 1435 on the site of Foulques Nerra's original, which may well have been of wood. Apply at the house at the foot of the tower and find the energy somehow to climb to its top. The view is worth all the energy expended, many times over.

Chênehutte-les-Tuffeaux gets its name from the vast quarries (in which mushrooms are now grown) of tufa, excavated underground, whose stone gives the whole Loire valley its very special appearance. The old priory here, which occupies a commanding position above the river, is now a three-star hotel, and a good one, which seems far better than just leaving it to fall into ruins.

At the twin villages of Saint-Hilaire-Saint-Florent we are closing in on Saumur. The Cavalry School cannot be more than 1½ miles away. The little villages are shut in by slopes which are completely honeycombed by caves. It is in these caves that the still wines of Saumur are made sparkling by that Champagne method which, as we have seen, Monsieur Ackerman brought to this part of the world.

The old abbey, in which the Chronicle of Saint-Florent was written – a most useful one for the long forgotten history of Anjou, but maddeningly deficient in dates – is now the *Couvent du Bon Pasteur* where, on request, you may visit the 11th century crypt, for the sake of the delicate designs of the capitals. By this time you are likely to be too impatient to arrive at Saumur itself to stop yet once again.

A little over a mile, and we pass through the gateway to what most people think of as The Valley of the Loire, and the royal châteaux and the familiar names and the sights which photography has made familiar to millions who have not yet seen them.

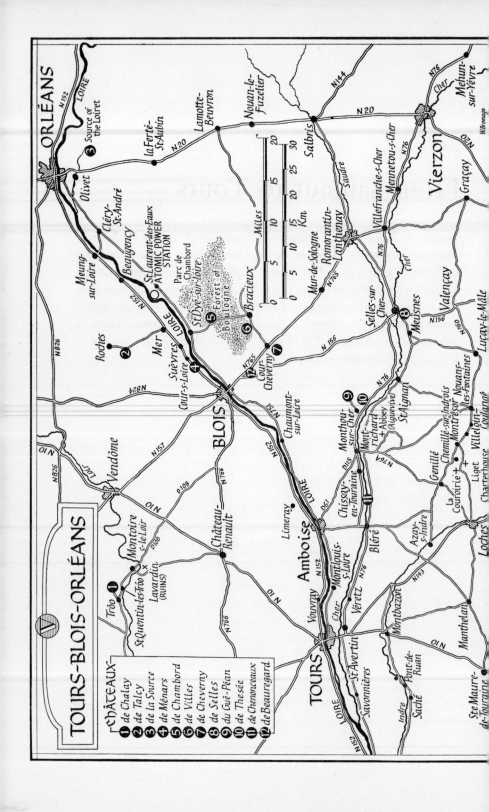

Chapter Five

From Saumur to Tours

Saumur from the river is very imposing. Its white tufa stone houses look so clean and welcoming, the really forbidding castle is so unreal in its whiteness that it is impossible to associate it at first glance with war and cruelty, the turreted Hôtel-de-Ville, almost exaggeratedly Gothic, the short, solid, four-sided tower of the church of Saint-Pierre, surmounted by a thin, sharp spire, a slated lance-head ready to transfix any air-borne enemy, and tall grey roofs, and little towers peeping up here and there, make a picture of urban splendour in miniature.

It is a town dealing very largely in wines and, as we all know, wine towns are always agreeable and friendly places. Despite the apparently endless and rather ugly main road which sweeps across and runs dead straight through the town on a north-east to south-west axis, it is really very small – it is only that N 138 runs through it at the angle which gives it the greatest depth, and falsifies the idea of size. It is built mainly on the left bank of the Loire, a little on the island in the middle of the river (it used to be two islands, the Ile Millocheau and the Ile Offard, but they got joined together), and a little around the railway station on the right bank.

On the left bank, the town is contained between the Loire and the Thouet, which (as we have seen) meet only farther downstream at Saint-Hilaire-Saint-Florent, but all the old part of the town runs down the slope to the Loire, away from the Thouet. If we start from the bridge towards the castle, we first pass the relatively modern theatre to reach the Hôtel de Ville. When you come close to it, you can see that it is not quite pure Gothic of the early 16th century, but carries a good admixture of 19th century Gothic-style additions, including a very un-Gothic clock. The older part, with bartizans on its corners, machicolations and amiable little turrets looks like a tiny fortress from outside, but the courtyard elevations are decorative and domestic. Farther along the river, Saint-Pierre is a basically late-twelfth and early thirteenth century building, with a west front rebuilt after a disastrous fire in 1674, when no attempt was made to match the old. The new front is conspicuously of its own period. If you walk up the hill behind the church, there are old streets with ancient houses which give purpose to a quiet saunter.

The first hereditary count of Blois was the Norman Thibaud or Thibault, brother to Rolf of Normandy according to some historians. He fought more with his wits which were often no less lethal than warriors' weapons. He has gone down in history as Thibault the Trickster. What was there before his time we do not know for certain, but we do know that Saumur belonged to him at the time of his death in 977.

This normally unconquerable fortress of Saumur which Thibault left to his descendants was a thorn in the side of Foulques, being situated right inside the nominal borders of Anjou, astride a good road and dominating the river where an island cut the width of the stream into lengths easily bridged.

Foulques was on the other side of the Loire when he learned that the count of Blois had just left Saumur to besiege the Angevin fortress of Montboyau. Instantly collecting all available troops, doing forced marches to Angers where he crossed the river, and back up the left bank, he fell upon the town and took it, and then made the fortress his target. Every able-bodied man from the town, every available soldier left behind by Gelduin of Blois, was shut up in it, but Gelduin had taken too many away. The walls and gates could not be fully manned. There were two gates, the western one on the town side, the eastern one on the side of the slope where Foulques had arranged his troops. The monks, however, had their own secret weapon. It had long, they said, been traditional to confide the guardianship of the eastern gate to the highly venerated relics of Saint Doucelin and Saint Florent. This proposal was accepted by acclamation, and the defenders rushed off to the western side.

This showed both a touching faith in the venerable relics and a not very intelligent military appraisal of the situation. The eastern approach was much the easier of the two for the attacker, and unlike the western side would not call for scaling ladders and all the paraphernalia of siege warfare. Not unnaturally, Foulques and his men broke down the eastern gate and entered the fortress.

They were stopped dead in their tracks by the sight of the shrine enclosing such holy relics, surrounded by guttering candles, and of the black monks prostrated in fervent prayer. The superstitious men would not advance beyond them. Foulques, never a man to be deterred by details, ordered them to pick up the shrine, with the utmost reverence, and convey it to a sheltered spot near by. And then he marched into the fortress and took the men of Blois by surprise, and treated them very badly, if the monks' chronicle is to be believed. They had reason to be anti-Foulques, for their monastery within the fortress took fire, and Foulques would do nothing to fight it. The monks took the remains of the holy Saint Florent to safety. Foulques promised them a bigger and better home for the saint's relics in his own city of Angers. They and the relics were put on a boat to sail down with the current to Angers, but at Trèves the boat stopped and nothing could get it to move. Foulques went so far as to call Saint Florent 'an impious lout', but it was useless. The relics had to be unladen on the left bank of the Loire, within sight of Saumur, and there Foulques built the promised monastery.

And Foulques the builder rebuilt the castle after the fire, and it lasted until the end of the 14th century, and then again after rebuilding until the 16th – that is, what we see today.

The château, which has four splendid corner towers, is an irregular four-sided construction, of which one side has been destroyed and left open. The Decorative Arts Museum occupies the whole first floor of both the completely restored wings (the château was badly damaged in 1940, but the restoration has been very well done), and the second floor by The Horse Museum, *Le Musée du Cheval*. The former is a very good one for a town of this size, with some particularly excellent porcelain. As for the latter, if you consider the Horse only as a useful but not highly intelligent quadruped, you will not enjoy it very much. If, on the other hand, you consider the Horse as an intelligent and treasured friend and the highest form of animal life, outside man, then you will find the Museum highly interesting.

Also to see are the Romanesque Notre-Dame-de-Nantilly, and the quite delightful *Jardin des Plantes* which falls down the slope from the château in a series of terraces garlanded with vines. To walk down through these beflowered terraces towards the Thouet is one of the quiet joys of a visit to Saumur.

Saumur has, in the Hôtel Budan, another of those comfortable, hospitable middle-grade hotels which one always remembers with a smile. It is quiet, and the food is good, but above all one remembers it as a place where the client is always a human being. By and large, the more expensive the hotel, the less one feels this.

Crossing over to the right bank of the river, and taking N 152 upstream, one comes after 2 miles to a road to the left, just before arriving at the village of Villebernier. This leads to the admirably picturesque Manoir de Launay. There is a fat little stone tower with a tall pepperpot slated roof and a chimney apparently added as an afterthought, a stone built oblong house (quite small) continued by what were possibly the stables. These boast a wide door with a pointed arch and ancient beam work above and on the gable end.

This was where good King René used to escape from the cares of office (if, indeed, he ever allowed himself to be worried by them) and with his best loved friends would lead the life of a well-to-do gentleman. The pastureland around was used for friendly tournaments, and for sitting around in the sunshine listening to each other's poetry, or playing and singing. It is so unpretentious, so unspoiled still, that I find it most moving. But then I hold the unpopular view that an amount of escapism is a most valuable thing in life and that to use the word as a reproach shows a total lack of understanding of human needs, though like everything else in life, it needs to be enjoyed in moderation.

Back to N 152, and the next 4 miles to cover. It is another turning to the left to be found, signposted for Varennes-sur-Loire. One must go through the village and straight out the other side for 5 miles where, just before coming in to Brain-sur-Allonnes, the Château de la Coutancière is situated on the left of the road.

Neither Brain-sur-Allonnes nor La Coutancière is mentioned in any guide book I have been able to consult, and the tragic event which took place within its walls is wrongly attributed to another château altogether – Montsoreau, on the opposite side of the Loire.

In 1579, La Coutancière belonged to the Sieur de Chambes, count of Montsoreau, governor of Saumur. The countess of Montsoreau, a proverbially gracious and intelligent woman, attracted to this château the nobility and the intelligentsia of this part of France. She could not refuse a welcome to the governor of Anjou, even though he was Louis de Bussy-d'Amboise, a man of conflict, a formidable swordsman and greatly feared duellist, a main instigator of the massacre of Saint Bartholomew, and a reckless bully. He was then aged thirty.

The unfortunate countess not only received him, but fell in love with him as well – the attraction of opposites. Bussy-d'Amboise was amazed, delighted, and unbearably proud of his conquest. With full details, he wrote the triumphant news to his friend the duke of Anjou. And François of Anjou recklessly passed on the account to his brother, Henri III. In front of all his courtiers, His Majesty thought fit to make a mocking reference to the deceived husband. 'The governor of Saumur', he said, 'our Master of the Royal Hunt, must be a very bad huntsman. He has let his own quarry fall into de Bussy's snares.'

As the cynical monarch must have known would happen, the word was carried to Saumur with the speed of a racehorse. The count could also be a man of action. He made his wife write a letter to de Bussy, making an assignation. In the presence of his wife, he and (or so the story goes) eleven of his men, attacked de Bussy on arrival and though the culprit killed some of his opponents, a dagger-blow in his back from the count finished him off. At the same time, others of the count's men murdered de Bussy's companion, a lieutenant of the Sénéchaussée of Saumur, and therefore directly in the king's service. Nevertheless, no action was ever taken against the count. The king, it was whispered, was glad enough to be rid of Bussy-d'Amboise.

The pretty and witty but foolish countess did not spend the rest of her days shut up in the castle, mourning for her dead lover, hating and hated by her husband. On the contrary, they lived much more happily thereafter, and she gave him several children and continued to be a much esteemed hostess.

Since those days the moat of this château, which is really more a manor house, has been filled in, the old chapel has gone, and with it the covered way from house to divine service. But there it still is, the Château de la Coutancière, and though the bloodstains have long since gone, metaphorically they remain.

On the return journey, the left turn a little below the château, on to D 10, brings one straight into Saint-Nicolas-de-Bourgueil and then to Bourgueil itself. If the time of day is suitable (and the suitability can be elasticated in such a case as this) a stop should be made for a *dégustation de vin*. Bourgueil makes an excellent red wine, one of the best of the Loire. I cannot say *the* best, because Chinon across the river makes a very similar one. They can be very difficult to tell apart. When I am there, and taking both at different meals, I can easily distinguish the softer finish and flavour of the Chinon from the slightly more robust and fruity Bourgueil, but once I have left the standards of comparison behind, I should not be very certain of turning back a bottle of Bourgueil because it bore a Chinon label.

Both of these wines are suitable for the traveller and sightseer; they are strong enough to be satisfying, but light enough in body not to induce after-lunch sleepiness.

It would be best to turn back from Bourgueil a little way along the road to Saint-Nicolas-de-Bourgueil and go straight down the first road on the left to Les Réaux but unfortunately one has to take the less pretty road (N 749) and turn off the right at Le Port-Boulet, for the railway line cuts the other one and there is no way across it. One is, at that point, in sight of one's destination. Life can be very trying. However, it is not much of a deviation, and the outcome is well worth it.

Les Réaux is a black and white checked château, one of the few of its kind in this part of France. It is all in brick and stone. Red and black bricks are used to contrast with white stone courses, the whole highly patterned effect being strongly reminiscent of some of the Norman châteaux and manor houses. Guillaume Briçonnet built it at the end of the 15th century. He was the son of a famous mayor of

Tours, Jean Briçonnet who was also an Intendant of Finances. To this same powerful family of financiers belonged the Catherine Bohier, née Briçonnet, whom we have to thank for Chenonceaux. Having built his beautiful Plessis-Rideau as it was then called, Guillaume was made archbishop of Rheims, and was never able to live in it. A later owner, Gédéon Tallemant des Réaux, gave it his name in mid-17th century. It has been very much altered, and has lost its moats, but is still so original, so pleasant to look upon, that it is worth going to a little trouble to look at it.

From there, on to N 152, and away up by the river bank, facing almost at once the vast Avoine-Chinon atomic plant (better seen from the other side and at a more flattering distance), and in 12 miles reaching Langeais.

Langeais is a most agreeable little town in its own right, with a handful of antique houses of real charm, busy streets, and its own royal castle, and in the grounds of the castle we do genuinely find the remains of a very early tower – a stone tower, naturally – of the redoubtable Foulques Nerra.

In 992, Foulques took the town from Eudes of Blois, and built a tower to defend it. Then its history is uncertain until we find that in 1044 it was in the possession of Thibault II of Blois.

The first major rebuilding of Langeais, about the middle of the 13th century, got off to a bad start. It was begun by one Pierre de Brosse. This remarkably able man began life at court by becoming barber to Louis IX. He was, therefore, a man in whom Louis had absolute confidence. The king's taster was his protection against poisoning of food or drink: against the barber's razor, laid against the royal throat, there was no protection at all if the man were not to be unconditionally trusted.

Louis' son, Philip the Bold, was brought up to trust the father's barber and unofficial councillor. He admired Pierre's wisdom in public affairs. As soon as Louis died, Philip made Pierre de Brosse his minister. Then came disaster.

Philip's young son died. As there seemed no particular reason why he should have done according to the medical knowledge of a backward age, it was inevitably assumed that he died of poison. Pierre de Brosse accused the child's mother of the crime. For a man

L

of his experience and good sense, this seems a most extraordinary thing for him to do. Even if he had full knowledge of how and why she did it (if she did), he must have known that the chances of convincing the king were very small, and the danger to himself very great.

As he must have expected, the queen retaliated by accusing Pierre of the crime, and she won the day. The trusted minister of two kings was tried, found guilty and hung upon the gallows at Montfaucon.

Except for the basic facts of the counter accusations and the trial and its result, the records of this strange business are depressingly incomplete. One would so much like to know the background. What were the relations between minister and queen which led to the double accusation? Was there jealousy, or love turned to hatred, was there a struggle for power? All kinds of surmise are warranted, but the records do not show at all why either party should have wanted to murder the child, which seems to be so motiveless that one is forced to disbelieve in anything but a sudden virus disease, or peritonitis. Perhaps, simply, a grieved father made it known that he believed the boy had been murdered, and minister and queen accused each other in self-protection.

In the reign of Louis XI, between the years 1465 and 1469, another minister, Jean Bourré, took over the ruins of the Pierre de Brosse château and built one of his own, which is one to be seen today.

In The Hundred Years War, Langeais fell to the English on several occasions. Finally, in 1427, the troops of Henry VI agreed to sell it for 2,500 golden écus, on condition that it was totally dismantled 'except for the old tower'. And this is how the remains of the Foulques Nerra tower are still to be seen alongside the 'new' castle built in 1465.

The entrance to Langeais is stern indeed. On a narrow front, in a narrow street setting, and two great round towers, joined by a narrow building in which a cavernous entrance below a pointed arch is protected by a drawbridge, present an unwelcoming face to the outside world. The furrowed brow of this unwelcoming face is a well protected sentry-walk around the towers and along the front of the linking building. This is the most forbidding entrance we have yet seen, perhaps more forbidding than any other we shall see.

Yet when you come out on the other side, the mask of war has become a mask of peace. The front is the full Gothic fortress. The inner façades are bare and simple, but they are not war-like. As yet the decorative elements of the Renaissance which is just beginning have not reached them, but the bountiful fenestration, the charming gable windows, the tall chimneys, tell of more peaceful days and the desire to turn the fortress into the comfortable residence.

The château belongs to the Institut de France, the last of a long, long list of owners, and it has done well by it. Here Anne of Brittany became queen of France for the first time when she married Charles VIII, and in the very room are their portraits painted on wood. Everywhere are great fireplaces of the era, and furniture that might well have belonged to it, and tapestries that, though faded now, were bright with colour when the 'new' château began its life. The sentry-walk gives an exact idea of what it was like to be on guard duty high up, and look for signs of movement in the green countryside around – the flashing of lances, the glistening of metal helmets; the sound of many horses could be heard from afar up here. Have a look at the royal bedroom, and remember that curtains round the bed were as much a necessity as a luxury, for cold draughts rampaged all night long, and all day long too, through corridors, under doors, round pillars, and particularly up and down stairways.

As you come out from the visit of the castle, there is a pleasant little formal garden at the foot of a mound. And this mound, which still carries the remains of a keep, must be the original *motte* on which Foulques Nerra built *his* castle nearly 1000 years ago. And if the ruins we see are not those of his keep, I would prefer not to know it, but to be able to go on thinking this is a direct link with him.

For the 2 or 3 miles which separate Langeais from Cinq-Mars-la-Pile the road cuts across a bend of the Loire and joins it again exactly opposite the point at which the Cher runs into it. Just beyond the village are the remains of a once splendid château and beyond that, on the top of a slope, the mysterious *Pile* dominates the scene. It is a square tower, with sides measuring 13 feet across; it is nearly 100 feet high, and surmounted by four pinnacles. There were five, but one was blown off in a great windstorm in 1751. It is usually described as being of Roman origin, and dating from the 3rd or 4th century, both of which assertions are exceedingly dubious. As to what purpose it can have served, there are endless guesses but no facts to support them.

The mystery surrounding this structure is not lessened by equal uncertainty regarding the name of the place where it was erected. Some think that the *Cinq* of *Cinq-Mars* referred in some way to the five pinnacles; that there might have been a fierce battle here in which five generals were killed and whose deaths are thus commemorated. There is no evidence of any kind of such a battle. Others believe the name to have been derived from *Campus Martius*, as the Romans are known to have had camps along this stretch of the Loire, probably at Langeais. Still others maintain that it was named in honour of the consul, *Quintus Martius*, though he had no known connection with Gaul. Gregory of Tours refers to a church here, founded by *Saint Médard*. In the earliest written record, it is referred to as being *in parochia Sancti Medari de Pila*: that was in 1218. Rather later records show other versions: *Saint-Mars, Cinq-Maars* and *Cinq-Mars*.

There is some evidence to be obtained from the tower itself. It is solid, the core being of undressed stones deeply embedded in cement. The surface is of brick, arranged in coarse patterns. That the quality of the materials was good is evident from the continued existence of the tower, and this would point to a Roman origin. Against this, I think it impossible for the brick ornamentation to have been Roman. It is too crude altogether even for the days of the decadence of Roman art. Also, there is no Gallo-Roman relic even remotely resembling it.

It seems not unreasonable to think that this may be the work of later invaders using Roman constructional techniques yet being totally lacking in Roman artistic feeling. Many, many years ago the authors of the *Tableaux chronologiques sur l'Histoire de Touraine* searched for historical data which might go some way to confirming such a theory. Their suggestion was that this monument marked the limit of the territory the Roman General Aetius had to cede to the invading Alans in 439, and that the enslaved labour with which the Alans built it knew how to mix Roman cement but had all the Gaulish lack of artistic sense when it came to decoration.

For the next 5 miles upstream, to Luynes, the road runs nearly all the way close to the river. The village is very ancient, with a number of rock dwellings and three or four 16th century houses. The market retains its 15th century woodwork, doubtless little of which could legitimately be claimed to be that old, as constant repairs will have been needed over the intervening five centuries. Stepped paths lead up to the castle from it, through the remains of the outer fortifications. It is all exceedingly picturesque, and so is the castle from the outside, for, alas, one is not allowed to enter. It is as formidable as anything we have yet seen, even the original sheer walls of the towers were broken by window openings only in the 15th century. The view from the west of the four powerful cylindrical towers and the three tall buildings joining them, all totally devoid of ornament of any kind are forbidding and immensely impressive.

Above the castle, up on the plateau, are the interesting remains of a Roman aqueduct, which is slightly mysterious. The evidence which its method of construction provides is that it must have been built prior to the 4th century. One can see clearly where the Alans got the idea of the core of their column at Cinq-Mars from, but these remains have a higher proportion of rubble stone, which is perhaps why they have not worn as well. At the top of one of the pieces of arch, some brick is apparent, which would tell of repair work subsequent to the building of the aqueduct itself.

What is totally lacking is any idea of where the water was being carried to. There is vague reference in Gregory of Tours to the ruins 'on the heights of Maillé' of a very ancient monastery built by the first Christians in Touraine on the site of a pagan temple. Maillé was the name of this village, before a duke of Luynes gave it his own Provençal name. The traces of the priory of Saint Venant, to which the quotation referred, seem now to have disappeared in their turn, though writers of the early 19th century have claimed that it was not only possible to distinguish the Christian buildings, but also the remains of a Roman camp below them. And the Roman camp might perhaps have explained the aqueduct, where now all is surmise and speculation.

There are just 6 miles from here to Tours: time for you to find your own solution of the problem of the apparently useless aqueduct.

Leaving Saumur on the left bank of the Loire (here the south bank) there is no river-hugging road after the first 7 miles, and with few exceptions all the most interesting places are not on the Loire but on the Vienne and the Indre, and in this book dealt with in connection with those two tributaries. Nevertheless, there is still much of interest to see, and it begins about 3 miles only from Saumur, at Dampierre. In the little white Château des Morains died Marguerite of Anjou, once the all powerful queen of England, and once, long years before, the cherished little daughter of the king who ruled over the most civilized court in Europe. This daughter of the good René of Anjou and Provence, titular king of Sicily, and of Isabelle of Lorraine, was married at sixteen to Henry VI of England. She had a good share of her father's intelligence, and soon learned to manage her husband. He was always weak and sometimes near to imbecility. When the news got about that a secret clause in the wedding contract entailed the handing over of Maine and Anjou to the French, it was very easy for those who were jealous of her power over the entire realm to fan the ever-latent discontent with a foreign queen.

She was only 20 when war broke out again, in the course of which all of Normandy was lost to the English. Needless to inquire on to whose doorstep the blame was laid. The next year saw the Jack Cade insurrection. When she was 25, her husband became totally insane and Richard, duke of York, became Protector. Henry recovered, fell ill again, and the Wars of the Roses began.

Henry VI was dead, Margaret was imprisoned in the Tower of London. Louis XI could have ransomed her at any time but he, who had stripped Margaret's father of practically all his possessions, dillied and dallied for four years before finding the relatively small sum.

Friendless, homeless, unwilling for reasons of which we know nothing to join her father in Provence, she was rescued by an old servant of King René, François de la Vignolle, who allowed her to live in the château he owned at Souzay. Not long before her death (at 54), she moved into the château from which the old man took his name, the Château de la Vignolle at Dampierre. This charming manor house, partly cut into the hillside, is on close inspection altogether too charming to be true: romantics have been at work on it. Allowing for that, it must have been a not too disagreeable place for the lonely woman. Let us hope that here she died in the knowledge of the peace she never found in her world. The Château des Morains, at Souzay, has been so much altered that it is difficult to say how much of it existed in her day. It is less impressive than La Vignolle, but after four years in the Tower of London it must have seemed heaven to her. Here she spent the greater part of the four years she still had to live on her return to Anjou; there is no record of her feelings about it.

I was quoted an epitaph on Marguerite (who must have returned to the French form of her name when she came back to Anjou), but could not find out from what or where it was quoted: 'Unhappiest of mothers; unhappiest of wives; unhappiest of queens'. None of them are quite true, but few women have come so near to deserving that epitaph. And there is not much else to remember her by than the neat twin corner turrets and steeply pitched roof of La Vignolle, the narrow, lofty square tower and plain Gothic windows of Morains.

From Souzay a road leads southwards to Champigny, amidst the vineyards, Saint-Cyr-en-Bourg and Brézé, which has a remarkable château, most of which has been restored with enthusiasm and imagination and not too much regard for what was there before. What is genuine and amazing is the depth of the moats, 60 to 65 feet, cut out of solid tufa stone. The park is a joy; in it are stables, an orangery, and a round dove-cote which have not been mangled by restoration. I hope the park at least will be open to the public by the time this book appears so that it and the exterior of the château can be seen. With privately owned places these things change from year to year, and I understand that at the moment it cannot be visited.

For Montsoreau I have a very great affection. It is marvellously picturesque, seen from the river. The white, rectangular fortress rises almost from the water, with the pretty little village higgledy-piggledy beside it. Behind rise tree-covered slopes to a low horizon which allows the little spire of the château to be silhouetted against the sky. The whole picture is turned upside down in the water, sometimes with almost hypnotic effect. Often the flow of the river is imperceptible, and the water-picture is only broken by rising fish causing it to be broken by concentric, expanding circles.

Montsoreau was built almost exactly in the middle of the 14th century, but it fell into disuse and instead of the high destiny to which it seemed inevitable that it should rise, it was broken up into small groups of rooms let out to farm labourers. Piece by piece it was acquired by the *Département du Maine-et-Loire* which, with the Beaux-Arts, has just about finished the restoration as I write. Some of the rooms are magnificent now, and the Stairway of Honour brought back to the imposing appearance it must have had when it was new in 1520 (it was a later addition to the original building).

Alexandre Dumas wrote of it in *La Dame de Montsoreau*, a highly successful romantic novel in its day which had a total disregard for historical accuracy. The countess of Montsoreau seldom lived in the fortress: she much preferred the comfort of the château de la Coutancière to the frigid welcome of Montsoreau. Yet it was almost by accident that she did not have to make it her residence. There were two brothers de Chambes: Jean de Chambes was, with Bussy-d'Amboise, the principal organizer of the St Bartholomew's Day massacres in Anjou. He was engaged to Françoise de Méridor (whom Dumas turned into a *Diane*). Before the marriage could take place, Jean was assassinated. Charles de Chambes inherited the title, the château and the fiancée, and what happened then we have already seen at La Coutancière.

At Candes-Saint-Martin the Vienne joins the Loire. An amusing little ferry which can and does take cars, though one sometimes wonders just how safely it does it, enables one to cross the Vienne and continue towards Tours by the Loire-side road beyond. However, before arriving at Candes, on the very limit of Anjou, it is best to turn down N 147 in Montsoreau village and travel the few miles to Fontevrault Abbey. Now that, at long last, it has ceased to be a prison, this is one of the most evocative visits one can pay. It is one also filled with beauty: this royal abbey can now be seen without its slightly sinister prison associations. One can give oneself up to the sheer joy of the vast church, so pure in style, to the fascinating historiated capitals, to the vaulted cloisters and to the extraordinary kitchen, lovely in itself, and an example of fitness for its purpose which nothing in the centuries since it was built has exceeded and which has seldom indeed been rivalled.

To begin at the beginning, about the time the first Crusade got under way, Robert d'Arbrissel discovered that he had the gift of preaching and set out through Brittany, Anjou and Maine to bring people to the service of God. A great many decided to devote their lives to their religion and followed him through the countryside. Their very numbers grew to be an embarrassment and he decided that they must wander no more, but settle in a suitable site. This he found in a pretty, heavily wooded valley, with a natural spring which still supplies the village with good water. The spring was known as the Fontaine d'Evraud, and the earliest forms of the name of the settlement is Fonte d'Evraud.

When, in 1099, the first abbey was built, the number of his followers was said to be no less than 5,000, but this figure more probably belongs to legend. He originated a most remarkable kind of religious institution. Thanks to the generosity of noble families, and particularly of the counts of Anjou, he was able to build, within the same block of buildings but quite separate from each other, Le Grand-Moustier for nuns, Saint-Jean-l'Habit for monks, Sainte-Madeleine for fallen but repentant women, a lepers' hospital (Saint-Lazare) and a home for aged nuns which, much later, took the name of Saint-Benoît. All authority in the Order of Fontevrault (to give it its modern name) was in the hands of an abbess from the beginning to the end of its history, the monks had to obey her as completely as did the nuns. It would seem that numbers from the start were a major problem, for by the middle of the next century there were 100 or so *Fontevriste* priories in France to relieve the pressure on the mother abbey and some daughter convents in Spain and in England. At Le Grand-Moustier (Sainte-Marie-de-Fontevrault) the number of nuns seems to have varied from over 200 to about 150, and the number of monks at Saint-Jean from 70 to 50. The abbess depended directly upon the pope for spiritual guidance and instructions and directly upon the king of France for mundane matters. Until the 18th century, the abbesses were elected, but after that the king's choice was invariably accepted. The entire list of 37 abbesses of the Order is a kind of Who's Who of the aristocracy of the day. The first was Pétronille de Chemillé, and amongst the others were no fewer than fourteen princesses. Matilda of Anjou, aunt to Henry II of England, Eleanor of Brittany, granddaughter of Henry III, Louise de Bourbon, great-aunt to Mary, Queen of Scots, and Jeanne-Baptiste de Bourbon, legitimized sister to Queen Henrietta of England, were all abbesses in their turn.

If the abbesses were aristocratic, no less so were those who came here from vocation or, as in the case of Queen Eleanor of Aquitaine, to find rest after an active life. So also were the thousands of girls, including the four daughters of Louis XV, who received their education in this favoured establishment. There is one very unusual feature in the history of this combined convent, monastery and teaching establishment: despite the opportunities it provided for scandalmongers, nothing said and nothing written about it to its detriment has survived, which is so unlikely that one is tempted to believe that there was never anything of this kind to survive.

The western entrance of the abbey is a beautiful example of Romanesque purity of line and marriage of semicircular arch to vertical supports. Inside, one finds the single nave has four domes, supported in part on pendentives, in part on massive pillars flanked by columns, with historiated capitals of foliage, traceries, characters supposedly biblical and quaint monsters. It is lofty and light. Another, smaller dome covers the crossing.

The church, begun in 1104 was not completed until 1150. The chancel was formally consecrated to the Virgin Mary by Pope Calixtus II in person, in 1119. The stained glass windows, showing the arms of the Plantagenets and the counts of Toulouse who are buried in the church, are modern but not at all out of place.

It was indeed the Westminster of the Plantagenets. Henry Plantagenet married the divorced wife of Louis VII, Eleanor of Aquitaine, two years before becoming Henry II of England in 1154. His family had been the protectors of the abbey from the beginning; his aunt Matilda of Anjou was its abbess. Before his death in 1189 he recorded his wish to be buried at Fontevrault. Eleanor of Aquitaine, whose behaviour in Antioch during the second Crusade gave rise to much scandal and was the prime cause of the divorce from Louis VII, came to know it well. First, in 1194, she came to reside in the convent, but used it as a modest chancellery. Here, in 1199, messengers from her dying son Richard I sent her scurrying away to Châlus, 100 miles distant, at a speed and in a manner unfitting to a Dowager Queen of 77. She reached it 'as if borne by the wind', wrote Ralph of Coggeshall in this Chronicle, in time to receive her beloved Richard's last testament. She still had all the troubles of John's unhappy reign to face; another five years of endless misfortune until her death in 1204. One chronicler says she died at Poitiers, but Pierre de Blois states firmly that she died in the abbey of Fontevrault, where she had been received for penance at the end of her life, and that she there put on the monastic habit. The nuns of Fontevrault in their Necrology sing her praises. 'She added to the greatness of her birth by the sincerity of her life, by her moral rectitude, by the blossoming of her virtues and by her regulation of an irreproachable life, and in these excelled almost all the Queens of this world.'

Here you can see her, in the shadow and protection of the church she knew so well. In her hands she holds a little book, and who shall tell from the stone image whether it was a book of Richard's (who was as good a poet as any troubadour of his time), a book of those *sirventes* so familiar to her in the days of her Courts of Love, or a book of prayers. Close by is her dear son Richard, very regal in his beard and moustache, wearing the crown of England, the land he hardly knew. And there also of Isabella of Angoulême, wife of that other son, the problem-child and problem-man, John. And there also, head raised upon pillows, but asleep, her second husband, the passionate Henry Plantagenet, unprincipled, clear-headed, ungovernable, great institutor of legal reform, the arch-opponent of Church interference in civil matters, indirectly the murderer of Becket, and with all his enormous faults one of the very great men of his times.

The preservation of these four funeral effigies, three in stone and one in wood, when so much else was destroyed at the Revolution, is almost a miracle. They are not, perhaps, great works of art, but they are at least extremely competent for the period, and despite some results of rough handling over the centuries, moving. I find this particularly with the effigy of Eleanor of Aquitaine, the most direct link we have with the greatest woman of the middle ages, a better statesman than her able husband, a great diplomat, a good financier, a devoted mother and a woman of the highest degree of courage, a woman of amazing physical resistance to her interminable journeys, accomplished in all the discomfort of the times.

And there she is now, reading her little book. Is it not possible to assert that there is a smile on her lips? At last she, who never knew it in her turbulent lifetime, has found peace. I sometimes wonder if, having found it, her restless soul enjoys it.

There is much else to see: the chancel, with its closely-spaced, slender pillars; the cloisters, of which the southern is in the original Gothic style of the 12th century and the three others, completed in 1548, belong to the Renaissance; the 16th century refectory on the site of the 12th century predecessor, with delightful wall-paintings. There is the little church of Saint-Michel, in which the High Altar of the abbey church is now installed. It is a fine piece of work of 1621, in wood carved and gilded, with a very fine Last Supper on the bottom panel. There are many other items to be seen there which belonged to the abbey.

And, finally, there is the *Tour d'Evrault*, which really defies description. It is largely octagonal, with each side terminating in an apse which corresponds to a cooking space inside. Each has a conical roof of overlapping tiles through which passes a cylindrical chimney with eight round-topped 'windows', surmounted by a little conical roof. Inside, at this level, four great arches transform the octagon into a square, and a little higher up four more change it back again to an octagon, and behind these eight arches are the smoke ducts to twelve more chimneys of the same type as the eight lower ones, but of smaller diameter. The upper octagon is the base of an eight-sided pyramid, at the summit of which is still another of these stone cowls. This one surmounts a central chimney which picks up and evacuates the smoke and smells which may have escaped the twenty outer ones.

In this kitchen of relatively small area, the cooks suffered less from the smoke and intense heat of wood fires than does many a hotel-grill chef today. There is no very reliable record of how many meals were served from it at a time but, with nuns, monks, pupils and patients the figure could well have been around 350. It is doubtful if a cooler and fresher kitchen for large-scale cooking has yet been devised.

On the return journey from Fontevrault, a local road to the right leads straight into Candes-Saint-Martin. Here is one of the most impressive churches in the Loire valley and here also are some excellent white wines. Some of the latter after a visit to the former adds to one's enjoyment. Many traces can still be seen of the old town wall and the moats, but the principal object is the church of Saint-Martin, built in the 12th century, added to in the 13th century and fortified in the 15th century. Saint Martin of Tours was born in Hungary and brought up in Italy, as these regions are now known. It was as a young officer, and in Amiens, that occurred the episode in his life by which he is now best known, dividing his cloak in two to give a near naked beggar something to wrap round him. In or about the year 339, when he was probably 24 years of age, he became a Christian and sought his discharge from the Army; 'I am Christ's soldier; I am not allowed to fight'. After some time as a recluse, he joined Saint Hilary at Poitiers and then founded the first monastery in Gaul at Ligugé, five miles from Poitiers, where a monastery still exists. In 370 or 371, he was made first bishop of Tours and founded the near-by monastery of Marmoutier (where, again, one still exists). As an evangelizer of rural Gaul his fame spread widely in France and, as a father of monasticism, further afield. Saint Martin's in Canterbury and Saint-Martin-in-the-Fields in London bear witness to him. He was one of the first non-martyrs to be venerated as a saint.

He died peacefully in Candes in 397, and his church was built on the site of the cell in which he gave up his life to God. The Gothic nave is tall and light, with great pointed arches 'leading the eye to Heaven'. Transept and choir and semicircular apse are of exquisite symmetry and balance. Thus in the course of a few miles you may see both Romanesque and Gothic almost at their very best.

The river road passes Avoine, where France's first atomic power station is in action and may be visited. The most spectacular part of it is the great globe, 180 feet in diameter, which can be picked up by the naked eye many miles away in each direction as its shining metal surface catches the sun's rays. The plant has a frontage on the Loire, including the canal for the reactors' water supply, of over three-quarters of a mile.

This is where the Indre runs into the Loire, and Ussé really belongs to the Indre, but as the Loire-side road has for the moment petered out one has to take the very quiet and delightful one which runs along the left bank of the smaller river. Suddenly before you is the white prettiness of the castle which, it is said, Perrault used as the background to his story of The Sleeping Beauty, *La Belle au Bois Dormant*, the Beauty in the Sleeping Wood. Many of the Loire châteaux give the impression that one has stepped out of this world into the unreality of the fairy story, but none quite so strongly as Ussé. It is very easy to imagine the dark trees in the background, which now make so perfect a foil to the shining white stone of the castle, spreading round in the course of the hundred years or so and enclosing the walls and the towers and the ornamental battlements until the time ordained for Prince Charming to cut his way through and release the princess with the ransom of a kiss. Where these trees would have grown in front, between castle and the waters of the Indre, there is now the most exquisite formal garden – a blaze of scientifically controlled colour. I am looking now at a colour slide I made on my last visit. In the foreground, and at intervals along the left hand edge of the terrace above road and river, the white boxes of the orange trees, brought out from the orangery to enjoy the June sunshine. A round pool with an idle water-jet in the middle, surrounded by a deep circle of some bright yellow flowers growing close enough together to make the colour solid. Oddly-shaped beds with lines of yellow flowers, but a different yellow, which in a few days' time will make more solid masses of colour. Then a lawn, and a round bed, solid yellow in the middle of it. The terrace ends and shows another of these formal patterns at ground level below, and beyond the houses of the little village of Rigny-Ussé. A blue river, with one enormous willow silhouetted against the light blue sky, green fields, and the great curve of the horizon outlined everywhere by the thickly planted trees of the Forest of Chinon.

Suddenly, in the 15th century, the château was there. It must have been there for a long time already, but had left no historical mark. In 1462 the building of the present château began. Jacques d'Espinay bought it in 1485, and he and his son Charles completed the court-yard buildings, which were not finished until 1535. A number of owners thereafter came, and went. It passed into the hands of the Comptroller-General of the king's household, Louis Bernin de Valentinay. His son married a daughter of the great military engineer, Vauban. The magnificent terraces are therefore often ascribed to him, but in fact were created and completed by 1664, when he was only 31 and could not yet have had a daughter of marriageable age. It remained in the Valentinay family until 1780, and is now owned by the comte de Blacas, and may be visited. The visit to the Renais-sance chapel is particularly to be recommended and the Renaissance elevations and the tall keep are a joy to see.

One tiny incident from my last visit to Ussé remains in my memory and still gives me pleasure. We were talking with the gardener, and a little popular car drove up. It was driven by a lady, no longer very young, who had some small dogs with her. She and her dogs dis-appeared. '*Madame la Comtesse*,' said the gardener. Later, as we were on our way out, the same lady could be seen on the edge of one of the beds, kneeling, and carefully planting more flowers. There was something very charming and very human about the countess giving to her planting of a few flowers all the concentrated attention that the green-fingered lady of a tiny suburban house with a tiny suburban garden would give to hers.

Just beyond the village of Rigny-Ussé a road turns to the left and crosses the Indre, so that we can return to the road along the left bank of the Loire which has begun again. There are delightful views of both sides of the river, backed by trees, and all pastel coloured, until the stern walls of Langeais are in sight on the other bank. As we come to the bridge across the Loire, we have to turn right, away from the river, because the river road again comes to an end where the Cher flows into it. So we turn down to Lignières de Touraine and then left up to Villandry.

Somehow I am far less enthusiastic about Villandry than I used to be. The château itself seems more terribly fake every time I see it, and though the gardens are still remarkable, their novelty has worn off. Twice running in consecutive years nothing at all has been in flower at the time when spring is turning into summer. At no time do I like paying an extra admission fee for carrying a camera, and when in addition there are no flowers to photograph and nobody tells you so unless you specifically ask, I like it even less. If I understood the facts correctly, having done my best to isolate drops of information from a Niagara of words, it is only in July and August that there *are* any flowers, and this is the very period which those who are able to go at any other time are most careful to avoid.

These considerations may not apply to those who are seeing Villandry for the first time, and I will put all prejudices aside and give as fair and accurate an account of it as I can.

The first château was called Colombiers and was built towards the end of the 11th century. It was in this one that a treaty between Philippe-Auguste and the newly crowned Richard I of England was signed, to very little effect.

The first major rebuilding occurred at the very beginning of the 16th century when it was acquired by Henri Bohier (a name that occurs again in connection with Chenonceaux), at that time Seneschal of Lyon, a place of profit rather than of honour for he seems seldom to have resided there. Then, in 1532, it was sold to Jean-le-Breton.

Not until 1619 did it take the name of Villandry, when Balthasar-le-Breton persuaded the king to raise it to a marquisate under the more pretentious name – after all, the marquis of Dovecot would not sound all that aristocratic. The king agreed, but the bourgeois *Parlement* was not easily persuaded to register the elevation, and it took exactly twenty years to get it confirmed. Meanwhile, Balthasar had begun the next rebuilding, which was completed only much later.

This was in the 18th century, when the property came into the hands of Esprit-François-Henri, marquis de Castellane, who was to be the last seigneur with all the feudal prerogatives which were to be swept away by the Revolution. Far, far less aristocratic was the next owner, the speculator Hainguerlot who amassed a vast fortune in the

3 The gardens of Ussé

4 Château de Chenonceaux

troubled early years of the 19th century. Whatever he touched turned to gold. He, too, was filled with desire to improve his property. By 1885 it was described as 'an edifice in the taste of the 17th century', and Monsieur Hainguerlot himself was described as 'a man of taste, but first and foremost a benevolent man, whose great fortune is nobly employed'.

This would well serve as the epitaph of the next owner, the wealthy Dr Carvalho. He left the château very much as we see it today, and he started the work of restoring the Renaissance gardens which his son, the present Monsieur Carvallo (the family has simplified the original Portuguese spelling) has carried to a triumphant conclusion. The marquis de Castellane substituted the 'English park' for the formal gardens of the French Renaissance. The terraces had all gone, and a 'natural' park, with clumps of forest trees, grass-covered slopes and a carefully designed careless disorder substituted for them. All this Dr Carvalho swept away, and began to re-create the three-dimensional garden of the 16th century, mainly from the work of Du Cerceau, without whose detailed (and delightful) drawings it could not have been done.

The castle itself, as you see it now, has nothing of the fake classicism of the marquis de Castellane, but has, alas, other features which are almost as bad – the terrible change from medieval machicolations on the mainly 14th century keep to a Victorian balustrade. There are three main buildings, enclosing on three sides the formal courtyard. The gallery of the left wing has a splendid polychrome and gilt carved Hispano-Moorish wooden ceiling, so incredibly out of place that one can hardly pay it the respect it deserves. There are also a number of Spanish masterpieces, much too late for the period of the rooms, not all of which quite satisfy all art experts as to their genuineness. But the château can take care of itself – there are plenty of others and it won't matter if you give this one a miss, but there are no other gardens like this one.

The best place to see it is from the top of the keep. Immediately below is the *Jardin d'Amour*, in which the shapes of the beds are outlined by box hedges, clipped to no more than 20 inches high. They end in yew finials, so perfectly similar and evenly cut that they look artificial. *L'Amour tendre* is one, hearts and flames in a box in two shades of red flowers. *L'Amour tragique* is next, daggers in a deeper red. *L'Amour volage* is love letters and butterflies, in yellow, white and different reds. *L'Amour fou* is a crazy carnival of twelve multi-coloured hearts, arranged in no kind of logical pattern.

They are all fascinating – when there are any flowers.

On the highest section is the one thing which seems out of place, a decorative pool. The water is carried through the gardens by a canal, on the farther side of which, at the next lower level, comes the *jardin potager*, as different from the usual kitchen garden as anything can be. The patterned vegetables (no potatoes; they came much later) include peas, beans, lettuce, artichokes, spinach and onions. How do they discipline them so that they each according to their own nature grow to similar size and shape? The neat patterns of vegetables are as decorative as any other part of these gardens. The architectural motif is clear everywhere; here, verticality is given by trellis-work on which cordon pears and apples are trained, and relief from too many plane surfaces by delicious rose arbours. There is even a maze, but not an English one. This one is hornbeam, which is no substitute for yew.

The gardens are unique. They are a joy, but a joy only to be savoured at a distance. You may not tread the carefully sanded paths; you must observe from a height and a distance. This can become a little frustrating. Nevertheless, I maintain that everyone should see the Villandry gardens once. And don't miss the little village church; it is pure Romanesque (or very nearly), unpretentious and lovable.

Between Villandry and Savonnières there are some petrifying caves, and at Savonnières a bridge over the Cher takes us back to the riverside road and into Tours.

Tours is a very pleasing, provincial city, much modernized because of heavy war damage, with some good avenues and modern buildings, and delicious food almost anywhere you go to eat in it. I suppose it must be possible to eat badly in Tours, but it must also be exceedingly rare.

The cathedral is lovely without being dramatic and this may well be due to the inordinate time it took to build it. It began, naturally, with a Romanesque church. This was taken in hand in 1220 and converted to the new ogival style. But between one thing and another it did not get built, so we have the remarkable mixture of 13th century choir, 14th century transepts, mid-14th to late 15th century nave, and a flamboyant Gothic west front of the 15th and 16th century. That they hang together so well is surprising, but it would have been better if all had been of any one of the differing styles.

The front with its twin towers is delightful; above the high Gothic portail, the whole of the space between the towers is filled in with a tremendous rose-window (copied from Bourges) supported by lancet windows. It is tremendously effective from without, and within, as it fills the whole end of the nave, its effect is very lovely. Typical of the blending of styles, the harmony achieved above this height as the towers change from Gothic to end in Renaissance is a real *tour de force*.

The great street in Tours is the Rue Nationale, which used to be the Rue Royale, a name which suited it much better. It was laid out to a uniform plan in 1763 but nearly all the northern end was wiped out in the great fires of 1940. Coming down it towards the river, there is an unexpectedly good building housing the Chamber of Commerce, of first rate proportions and style, dating from 1759, and close to it the remains of what was once the town house of a famous financier, Jacques de Beaune-Semblançay, whose ruin and hanging brought down his family. At the end of the Rue Nationale are two gardens on each side of its prolongation to meet the Stone Bridge. It is now, I believe, the *Pont Wilson*, but everybody still knows it as the *Pont de Pierre*. It is a work of art, designed by Bayeux and built between 1765 and 1779. It has fifteen arches, is about 450 yards long by 16 yards wide, and is probably the finest remaining 18th century bridge in France.

There are old houses round the cathedral, and La Psalette, with admirable Renaissance cloisters and many fine old buildings around. The Fine Arts Museum is in parts very old indeed, though most of it was rebuilt in the 17th and 18th centuries. Amongst the 12th century remains is the Ecclesiastical Tribunal, part of the original Archbishops' Palace which was not taken over by the Musée des

Beaux-Arts until 1910. The hall of the Tribunal always awakens memories of the record of the confrontation of Queen Jeanne, Jeanne de France, and her unwilling husband, Louis XII, which I find extraordinarily moving.

Louis XI had a daughter, Jeanne de France who, under Salic Law, could not succeed him. The king could not bear that the throne should not pass to the direct line, and therefore married off his daughter to Louis of Orleans, then heir apparent and who, as a descendant of his grandfather's brother was not within the forbidden degree of relationship. They were married at a little country church, in Montrichard; the boy 14 years of age, pleasant of face and figure. The poor little twelve-year-old bride 'had a double hunch on her back, congenital disease of the hip, and a veritably simian appearance'.

Jeanne did all she could to please her husband, secured his release from imprisonment at one time and did no act unworthy of a wife, but on the husband's side there was physical repulsion. Then Charles VIII died, in 1498, and at last the throne belonged to Louis, and with it the chance to rid himself of Jeanne. By her marriage contract, Anne of Brittany, widow of Charles VIII, was obliged to marry the heir to the throne of France. Nobody at the time had contemplated the possibility of such an heir being already married. So Louis lost no time; claiming a forbidden degree of consanguinity, he appealed to the Pope for the right to bring a case before an ecclesiastical court for a second reason, that the marriage was never consummated. Everybody knew that the true reason was the third one – that to ensure the continued possession of Brittany, Anne must again be married to the Crown: everybody knew also that she was quite prepared to go back to her own duchy and cut its ties with France.

No lawyer could be found to defend poor Jeanne, and finally the tribunal had to nominate one Jean de Vesse, who undertook the defence only on condition that letters ordering him to do so were included in the documents of the case.

On September 13, 1498, Jeanne appeared before her ecclesiastical judges. Her interrogation was singularly unpleasant. Nobody bothered to be even superficially polite to her.

'Do you not know that Louis XI forced the duke of Orleans to marry by means of terrifying threats?'

And Jeanne answered: 'I do not believe it to be the case and I have never heard tell of it.'

'That he was to be thrown into the water and left to drown if he would not marry you?'

'I do not believe it to be so,' Jeanne replied again.

'That he never freely consented to this marriage?'

She gave the same reply.

'That after the death of Louis XI, and as soon as he felt free to do so, he testified that such a union, so violently imposed, was made without his consent?'

'I am not aware of it and I do not believe it,' Jeanne answered.

'And that that was the reason for Charles VIII being so angry with him?'

And again Jeanne answered, 'I do not believe it to be so.'

The prosecution then gave up this line of interrogation, and switched to the personal.

'Are you not aware of the fact that by accident of birth or by nature, you are full of imperfections which the majority of women do not have to suffer?'

'I am very well aware of the fact that I am not as agreeable to look at nor as beautiful of body as most women.'

'And that you are not in any way fitted for marriage?'

'I think I am as well fitted for marriage as the wife of my groom, George, who is totally deformed, but who, none the less, has borne him some very handsome children.'

The judges thought it useless to continue with the obstinate queen. They adjourned, and met again on the 19th to interrogate the king, in the comfort of his own little château of Madon, near Blois, which would be more private than the great castle of Blois.

The king's defence was very simple. Everything which had happened, everything which had been done, even to the acceptance of his wife's visits when she was instrumental in securing his release from gaol, was all done under constraint.

Then it was Jeanne's turn again. The only way to prove that the marriage had been consummated was for her to submit to searching physical examination. This Jeanne refused with scorn. She would be content that the king's word be taken on oath, in the presence of holy relics, and would abide by what he then declared.

She did not believe that the very Christian King of France would commit perjury. Neither did the courtiers. At the altar, in the presence of the holy relics, with his hand upon the Testament, he swore that everything had been done under constraint and that he had never known his wife and that everything that Jeanne and her witnesses had declared was untrue.

Sentence in favour of the king was pronounced at Amboise on December 17. As the three judges left the church after pronouncing that there had never been a marriage, a stentorian voice in the crowd called out, 'Look! There goes Caiaphas! Look! There goes Herod! Look! There goes Pontius Pilate!'

To the west-south-west of the centre of Tours is the Château du Plessis-lès-Tours ('les' or 'lès' or 'lez' in these place names means 'near') in which Jeanne was born. It has been very much restored but still gives a good idea of the favourite lodging of Louis XI. It is a very simple nobleman's manor house rather than a palace, in the Gothic manner of the end of the 15th century. Only one of the buildings remains, and some moats, and an octagonal turret enclosing a staircase. There is a little museum here, one part of it given over to that strange monarch, and another to Saint Francis of Paola, whom Louis summoned to his bedside when, distraught with superstitious terror, he felt the approach of death. The saint founded a monastery near by, of the order of the Minims (the humblest of friars), of great austerity. The remains that may still be seen are not of the original building of the 17th and 18th centuries.

The abbey that Saint Martin founded somewhere about 372 was destroyed by the Norman invaders in the 9th century, and rebuilt by the Benedictines in the 10th. This was where Pope Urban II preached the First Crusade. In 1818, as a 'National Asset' it was demolished for its stones, and only a few individual features remain of this great and historic monument. The buildings there now, which may be visited in the afternoon, date from 1847 onwards, when it was purchased by the nuns of the Holy Heart.

Also to be seen still in Tours are many delightful old houses, squeezed in between more recent buildings and a stroll around the older streets has much to recommend it.

Just about 5 miles from the centre of Tours is what remains of the old abbey of Marmoutier, founded by the town's own saint, Saint Martin, in the year 372. It survived all the wars with the English, all the wars of religion, only to be sold as national property in 1818 and wantonly destroyed. None the less, there are some interesting medieval remains: the early 13th century main gateway, the Prior's house of the 12th century, and, most curious of all, the chapel of the Seven Sleepers, carved in cruciform shape from the rock. The seven were disciples of Saint Martin; he had predicted that they would all die on the same day, and they did. But they continued to look as if they were alive, and their perfectly preserved bodies produced many miracles. It makes a fitting end to one's stay at Tours, having seen its modern attractions, to wander through this aged sanctuary.

Along the tributaries

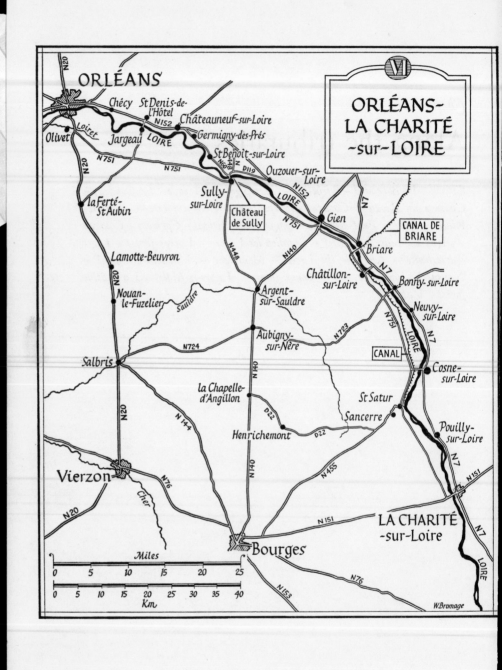

VI

ORLÉANS-
LA CHARITÉ
~sur~LOIRE

ORLÉANS

Chécy St Denis-de-l'Hôtel

Olivet Châteauneuf-sur-Loire

Loiret Jargeau Germigny-des-Prés

la Ferté-St Aubin St Benoît-sur-Loire

Sully-sur-Loire Ouzouer-sur-Loire

Château de Sully Gien

CANAL DE BRIARE

Lamotte-Beuvron Briare

Châtillon-sur-Loire Bonny-sur-Loire

Nouan-le-Fuzelier Argent-sur-Sauldre Neuvy-sur-Loire

Sauldre Aubigny-sur-Nère CANAL Cosne-sur-Loire

Salbris la Chapelle-d'Angillon St Satur

Sancerre

Henrichemont Pouilly-sur-Loire

Vierzon Cher

LA CHARITÉ-sur-Loire

Bourges

Miles

0   5   10   15   20   25

0   5   10   15   20   25   30   35   40
Km

W.Bromage

Chapter Six

Along the Tributaries

This is the place at which we call a halt to the upstream journey close to the Loire, turn back almost to Saumur, and take the left-bank affluents wherever they may lead us that is not too distant from the big river. If we did not know it beforehand, it is here that we discover that some of the finest and most interesting châteaux of the Loire are not on the Loire but on some lesser stream.

By and large, it is here also that we leave behind the wide and fast main roads, and plunge deeper than ever into the countryside. Here indeed we are going to find the 'cool, sequestred vale' and the untroubled village, the little rivers where only the *plop* of a leaping fish breaks the silence, and little towns so sleepy one prays that nothing will ever again wake them up.

The first of these lesser streams is the Vienne, which we left at Candes-Saint-Martin, and which we pick up again at Chinon. It is best, I think, to come up to Chinon from the south-west, for Chinon ought first to be seen from the river. The river bed is wide, but often there is so little water that the very fine thirteen-arch stone bridge can look quite absurd bestriding only a trickle of water. Yet there are spring days, and even autumn ones, when it is only just wide enough. It has one foot on the mid-stream island, as did the original 12th century bridge, on whose foundations the present one is built. This innocent-looking little island has just one moment of history all to itself. In 1321 the Jews of Chinon, numbering 160 men, women and children, were all driven on to the island and burnt alive, having been found 'guilty' of poisoning the town's wells. This sombre note befits an introduction to Chinon, for its whole history is of war, and death and prison.

Look up as you cross the bridge (unless you happen to be driving).

Over the grassy bank are tightly planted trees lining the main road through the town. Pleasant houses can be glimpsed between the tree-trunks. So thickly do the trees grow that none of the houses have any visible roofs. Above, and for what seems a huge length, tower and wall, tower and wall, a group of bigger buildings, more towers, more and more wall and a huge oval keep. That is the castle of Chinon.

Most remarkable is the fact that Foulques Nerra did not build this one, and never owned it, though his son did. For once, it ante-dates the great builder. It covers a good river crossing (thanks to the mid-stream island), is well up the slope and difficult to attack from the river, commands the plain above and the forest of Chinon. The Gauls had an *oppidum* there, the Romans a *castrum*. The successor to Saint Martin as Bishop of Tours, Saint Brice (*Brictio*), first built a church there, but whether before his disgrace or after his re-entry into grace does not seem very certain. He was followed by Saint Mexme, who built a second one. Clovis (465–511) made it into one of the most powerful fortresses in his kingdom. Chinon passed into the possession of the counts of Blois, who held it for two centuries, until in 1044 Count Thibault II parted with it to Geoffroi Martel, son of Foulques Nerra, count of Anjou.

Thus it became part of the possessions of Henry of Anjou, better known to history as Henry II of England. Here he died, and from here was carried to Fontevrault. This is a well-established historical fact, but the claim of the good people of Chinon that it was here also that his son Richard was carried after being mortally wounded at Châlus, and that he died here, is almost certainly false. It is by no means impossible that his body was carried here after his death, on its way to Fontevrault for burial, for as we have seen this was a good place at which to cross the river.

Chinon had a long Anglo–Angevin history. What we see of the fortress today is very largely the work of Henry II and originally consisted of two parts only, where now we can see the remains of the three. First there was the Château de Coudray, to the west, then what came later to be called the Château du Milieu, the Middle Castle. The eastern part was a late addition. Various attempts to wrest the castle from its Anglo–Angevin garrison made it clear that the river was an effective barrier against sapping, and to north and west deep ravines gave equal protection. The Middle Castle, however, was seen to be vulnerable to attacks from the east. Henry then built the new castle as an afterthought and dedicated its chapel to the patron saint of England, Saint George.

In this still new Fort of Saint George, Henry died, unlamented except, perhaps, by Queen Eleanor and cursing those undutiful sons of his who schemed and fought for their patrimony even before their father was dead. He lay in state in his new chapel, and was then carried to Fontevrault. When Richard arrived to do honour to his father's corpse, says an old wives' tale, the dead body ran blood until the undutiful son had retired from the chapel. The same tale is told of Fontevrault, but that would have been so long after death as to make it a miracle.

Richard further reinforced his castle, but Philippe-Auguste of France had marked it for his own. He dare not attack it whilst Richard was alive, but under the hapless John he undertook a siege which lasted between eight months and a year, attacking the weaker, eastern side. He tried mobile assault towers but these, as often happened, proved more dangerous to their users than those they were being used against. Sapping, however, was a different story. The walls of Saint George were sapped, and fell, and the castle surrendered. A deep moat separated it from the Middle Castle, but the French covered it over with wood and their sappers went on with their work under this cover and eventually the walls began to crack and split. This was the moment to set fire to the timber props which held the mine roof up, and the stonework began to fall.

That was the time for the mangonels to be brought into action, huge slings which hurled heavy rocks at points showing strain and weakness. The final stage was the action of battering rams, thick tree trunks swung from a triangular framework on ropes. How big the ones at the siege of Chinon were, cannot now be known, but at this time some of them were swung by at least a hundred men.

So Philippe-Auguste came into his own, and made Chinon the most considerable fortress in France, never again to be taken by siege. From the river side you can look up to the plateau nearly 300 feet above the river, and see how the steep walls of smooth rock have been made steeper and smoother by the hand of man. The castle you look at is probably 14th century, but it occupies the site of the original English castle, and there is no reason to believe it differs very widely from it.

Chinon

Once across the bridge, a parking place should be found, and the steep streets of the sleepy, prosperous little wine-town should be taken on foot. What does it matter if it gives you a good thirst; by the glass, or the bottle, the good red wine of Chinon is to be had wherever refreshments are served, which seems practically every-where. The streets and their houses are very old. If the houses seem to be leaning on each other at strange angles, like drunkards holding each other up, do not be surprised or blame the wine. Some of them look almost dangerous enough to merit being taken down, but one has the feeling that if one comes down, they all fall down.

The *Grand Carroi*, the Great Crossroads, bears the same relation to what you might expect to see bearing that name as does the cheerful Rabelais' Picrocholian War to any that we have witnessed. It is a miniature, and on it is a baker's shop which, you may well be told, is the very house to which Richard I was carried from Châlus. Once the Renaissance house which stands on the corner of the Rue de la

Lamproie was believed to be Rabelais' birthplace; the authorities changed their minds, and put up a plate on what is now no. 15 to mark the spot where his real birthplace had stood. It was turned into an inn after his death, which prospered, but has long since disappeared. Possibly it was badly built, an evil which is not unique to any one country or any one era. In any case it matters less because it now seems certain he was born at La Devinière, a little way from Chinon.

The entrance to the fortress is now by a stone bridge over the deep ditch between the Middle Castle and the Castle of Saint George and then under the clock tower. The tower is nearly 120 feet high, and only 16 feet wide, and looks slender as a needle from a little distance. In a lantern, hangs a great bell, whose formidable voice once sounded the tocsin. It now has more cheerful uses. And now one is at the Middle Castle, of which not so much more exists than of the Roman fort on whose site it was built. Most of it, within enclosing walls, is a garden. Where once royalty enjoyed the perfect views over town and river, now there is only a mass of crumbling walls.

Joan of Arc arrived at Chinon on the twelfth day of her travels from Vaucouleurs. She lodged, as she later said 'with a good woman near to the castle'. The dauphin was told of her arrival, already heralded by a letter from Sainte-Catherine-de-Fierbois in which she said she would be able to recognize him amongst many others. He sent word back that she must announce her mission. She refused. Her mission was to the dauphin, and the dauphin only. Later, the messengers came back again to assure her that they were sent by the dauphin in person and that she had no reason to withhold from them what she wanted with him. To this she agreed, and told them the King of Heaven had sent her on a double mission, first to raise the siege of Orléans, then to escort the dauphin to Reims to be anointed as king of France. After two days of hesitation, the dauphin had sent for her to come to the Château du Milieu. Little enough remains now of the *Grande Salle*, then 75 feet long and 25 feet wide . . . just a few of the steps which led up to it, and the west bay and its wide fireplace, but they remain very evocative.

The dauphin played a little trick on her, dressing very soberly and allowing himself to be outshone in gaudy apparel by many of his gentlemen. They had their own little game with Joan, pretending each in turn to be the person she was seeking. Though the hall was lit with fifty torches, at first she could not see him but none the less put aside those who were falsely claiming to be her Prince. Slowly she made her way through the 300 people present, and stood before the true one. 'Gentle Dauphin,' she said, 'I am called Joan the Maid. The King of Heaven sent me to you with the message that you shall be anointed and crowned in the city of Reims, and that you shall be the Lieutenant of the King of Heaven who is king of France.'

He denied being the dauphin, but she firmly set his disclaimer aside, and talked to him in private. All that they are supposed to have said is set down by the anonymous *Abbréviateur du Procès*, but there is no certainty that he had his information from either of the only two people who could have told. The evidence suggests that this supposed conversation is imaginary. Far from taking Joan at her own value, it is clear from the historical facts that he was still filled with doubts about her. She was virtually a prisoner in the tower, to which she had only been admitted after her sex had been confirmed by two ladies of the Court. Belief in her came much later if, indeed, it ever really came at all.

The Tour du Coudray, where she lodged for some time, cannot have looked much more cheerful in her day than it does now. Chinon indeed can have held few happy memories for her, except the day she came back having reluctantly been accepted as the last hope of saving Orléans. The Court, the dauphin, her companions in arms, all may have doubted her visions and her voices, but the people did not. Her piety, her complete confidence in herself, her good-humoured but devastating repartee, won over the people completely and for ever. Her memory still haunts the gaunt ruins of Chinon's castle.

From Chinon it is best to cross the river again and head south-east on N749 which brings one, in about 10 miles, to the little village of Tavant and a marvellous Romanesque church, built about 1150, which has a three-aisle crypt decorated with frescoes of an almost startling originality, and certainly contemporary with the church itself. Their only rivals in France are those of Saint-Savin-sur-Gartempe which is beyond the scope of this book.

These pictures belong to the school of the miniatures painted in

The charming little-visited castle of
Saint-Aignan-sur-Cher.

The trading office and residence at
Bourges of the great mediaeval merchant
banker, Jacques Coeur, is unique. It
dates from 1443 and is full of delicious
and often humorous carvings in stone.
This one portrays a fully rigged two-
masted galley of the kind which carried
the trade he financed to most parts of the
known world.

Le Clos-Lucé is the pleasant manor house in which Leonardo da Vinci spent his last years.

Lavardin is no more than a hamlet on the river Loire, but its castle, which successfully defied both Henry II and Richard I of England, covers in all more than ten acres.

the days of Charlemagne; styles and traditions die hard and one is surprised to find them in a church of (comparatively) so late a date. There is a Christ in Majesty, and a Crucifixion, which one would expect. Less expected are a Crucifixion of Saint Peter, an Adam and Eve series, David killing the Lion and David playing the harp to Saul, and a number of quite different subjects, mainly symbolic, concerning Good and Evil. These are all highly stylized, and for those not very learned in the older forms of art, at first a little difficult to digest. On going round them again there is a big difference; the eye and the mind have got accustomed to the stiffness of the stylization and the subtleness of the pictures suddenly comes home. It is a great experience which it would be a pity to miss.

Carrying on another 2 miles to L'Ile-Bouchard we find a little country town spread on both sides of the Vienne. Here there is a little jewel, a Romanesque chancel of the priory of Saint-Léonard (all that remains of it); it has, in the open air, a magnificence that perhaps it never had when the rest of the building was around it. The capitals of the powerful columns are carved with scenes of the New Testament; the little columns above which must once have supported windows have capitals with leaf designs, whilst those of the deambulatory have more leaf designs, and figures emerging from the sea (or at least from water), and monsters. The whole thing is surprisingly self-contained in its solitude, and romantic. It leaves one regretting the fall of what must have been a lofty and beautifully-designed church.

Richelieu is 10 miles south-west, on N757, and is a little like the Place Vendôme in Paris if one can imagine it reduced to the proportions of a square in a little country town, and then repeated several times over.

It all started with a little village miles from anywhere, from which Armand du Plessis took his inherited title of seigneur de Richelieu. When he achieved fame and the red hat of a cardinal, he felt that a probably rather smelly agricultural hamlet was not a possession by which his dignity would be increased, so he commissioned Jacques Le Mercier, architect of the Palais Royal in Paris, to build him a townlet there at the entrance of what he intended should be the finest modern château in France. Now Richelieu is entirely laid out on a very formal plan with everything in it built in the neo-classical style. It measures about 700 by 300 yards and where moats surrounded the town there are now gardens. Along the main street, the Grande Rue, are twenty-eight identical mansions, all richly sober. A leisurely stroll through this strange piece of town planning is very pleasant, but apt to leave one with many unanswered questions. What of *le confort moderne*, as the French term up-to-date plumbing? How are these 17th century rooms heated, or do the inhabitants have to live in the 17th century style, encased in a whole cocoon of garments? How do you deal with electric lights in a 17th century house, and how do you cook in a 17th century kitchen?

As for the château itself, for which the town was to be a sort of matching prelude, nothing remains but the rather fine park which once surrounded it. The finest of furniture went into it, hundreds of pictures by the leading artists of the time, the finest of carved woodwork, endless gilding. Nothing remains, no furniture, no hangings, no pictures, none of the treasures he poured into it, and no castle. La Fontaine sung its praises. The nobility made long excursions to see this marvel of its age. Its vaunted luxury was the talk of all the fashionable world. It is very difficult to keep track of all the cardinal's travels, but as far as I can tell he never stayed in his own château and never saw his own town completed. Too big and expensive for any ordinary person to live in, the château itself was almost totally demolished at the beginning of the 19th century, and what fragments are left are of no interest.

North of Richelieu is Champigny-sur-Veude, whose own interest is a church. This time it is not a question of Romanesque, but a beflowered gem of the Renaissance. Gone are all the Romanesque inhibitions about ornamentation, gone the severe simplicity, gone the sturdy pillars. Here everything is highly ornamented, patterned, carved, worked on, turned into a hundred different shapes and designs. From the marvellously complicated peristyle, full of pleasing detail, to the uniform series of eleven stained glass windows, all made between 1538 and 1561, which tell of the outstanding events in the life of Saint Louis, the contrast between this gay little church and the majesty of most of those which have so far been described is complete.

A few miles farther north from Champigny-sur-Veude is Le Coudray; a short distance north-east of the village is the Château du Rivau, which seems to be as good an example of châteaux of the earlier part of the 15th century as can be seen anywhere, yet appears to be very little visited. Dating from about 1430, it occupies three sides of a square which is surrounded by moats. The residential part is on three floors, the top floor having gabled windows, and all the windows being mullioned. There is a little round tower, a tall octagonal tower, and a small square tower, together with a massive square keep. To all appearances this is less rebuilt, less 'improved' and less obviously repaired than any other of its time I can remember. Nothing can make it anything but stern, but it has a quality, a kind of material honesty, to which I have not found an equal elsewhere. I am told that Coudray-Montpensier is even finer, and I have certainly admired it greatly, from a distance only, since one is not allowed to visit it.

With this we have done with the Vienne, and move farther up the Loire to the Indre. The road from Le Rivau (N174) joins N759 3 miles from Chinon, and N751 north-east from Chinon leads to Azay-le-Rideau and the Indre. It runs nearly entirely through the Forest of Chinon and from its straightness could well be a Roman road.

Any place where one has stayed and been happy automatically acquires a little golden aura. This is certainly my case with Azay-le-Rideau. The Hôtel du Grand Monarque is one of those family-run French hotels which make France still the finest country in my experience in which to travel and stay. There is no substitute for the owner-manager and his wife; you will never get the same satisfaction from a hotel under paid management; you will never get the same happy, family atmosphere elsewhere than in these owner-run places. Le Grand Monarque was only one of several in which we stayed on the last long trip before this book was really begun; they were all good. The others, though, did not offer the unusual experience of opening the bedroom door in the morning to a very large, white rabbit (straight from Alice in Wonderland) who then proceeded on a tour of inspection, ending by standing up to look at who was in bed.

There are those to whom the sight of a pair of very long white ears, pink inside, followed by a very white face with pink eyes peering through the fur, and a pink nose twitching away like mad, might not be an ideal awakening, but Jeannot was such a gentle, well-behaved creature that few could resist him. On the other hand, we did feel that there must be something deeply Freudian about his attachment to Cocotte, a very small, highly intelligent and very tame hen, but with so much to see around there was really no time to inquire thoroughly into the psychological profundities of a white rabbit (I suppose he was really a Belgian hare, but it sounds much less satisfying). Apart from our dear Jeannot, the hotel was comfortable, the atmosphere was pleasant, the food was excellent and the prices were most reasonable.

Azay-le-Rideau lives on its famous château, which, for sheer beauty, rivals Chenonceaux. Half-hidden by a curtain of trees until one is almost in it, it peeps through the foliage with a promise of grace and beauty. That promise is well kept, and never more so than during the *son-et-lumière* performance on a summer night. You can forget the words, and just let your senses be pleasantly numbed by the changing aspects of this gracious dwelling.

Some kind of a Roman village once existed along the banks of the Indre at this point. It drops out of history for a time, and then begins again with Joan's *gentil Dauphin* as a lad of only 15. The fortress, which commanded the main road from Tours to Chinon, was held by the Burgundians and there was a quarrel between them and Charles' followers. In the high words that followed, insults were hurled at Charles himself. Flaming with anger, he called his men together for an assault. His 500 men drove the Burgundians back, forced an entrance into the castle and took it. They then sacked and burnt it, and put their 350 Burgundian prisoners to the sword. After this bloody episode the castle was known for long as Azay-le-Brûlé, Azay-the-Burnt.

There is another hiatus, and history picks up the threads again exactly a century later, in 1518. I have referred before to the clan of financiers who married almost entirely between themselves and held a kind of monopoly of the senior financial posts in the lax administration of the king's government.

Gilles Berthelot was Treasurer-General of the Finances of France, he was mayor of Tours and was married to Philippa Lesbahy, who was a de Semblançay cousin. One way and another he was related to Katherine Briçonnet who built Chenonceaux, to the Beaune-Semblançay clan, to the Ruzés and the Fumées, which is to say to all the French wealth of that century.

Gilles Berthelot, then, got possession of the property and started to rebuild. It seems by now to have become Azay-le-Rideau. I have no great faith in the theory of a Ridel Azay in the 12th century being the cause of its later name. I think the fortress Charles burnt down had a 'curtain', and that the *rideau* in question was that curtain wall. There was no curtain to the new château, and all that was used of the old was the foundation in the river for, as at Chenonceaux, the new château was built on old piles. Unlike Chenonceaux, Azay-le-Rideau had a named architect, Bastien François and unlike Chenonceaux again, it was built at a single stretch, from 1518 to 1529, not a long period for the techniques of the time and the magnitude of the task. Except for outbuildings, no additions have been made since.

All the features of fortification common to the castles of the middle ages are used, but they are all used for purely decorative purposes. To them are added a wealth of decoration of the type just coming into fashion. The total effect is only a little inferior to that of the slightly younger Chenonceaux, but at Azay-le-Rideau there was no Diane de Poitiers, no Catherine de Médicis, to gild the lily.

If the analogy with Chenonceaux comes up again and again, it is because the two were so closely linked. The superintending of the work at Azay-le-Rideau fell mostly upon Philippa Lesbahy, for Gilles Berthelot was too much away from his own homes to give much time to them. Is it not virtually certain that cousin Katherine Bohier came to see it being built, admired it and used all that she had learned at Azay as a basis for her new château on an even better site at Chenonceaux? Their close similarity and the absence of an architect at the later château must have some such explanation.

You come to it over a bridge across the live moats to the courtyard, bounded on the farther side by one of the two main wings. This one incorporates the front of the main staircase, with tall wide-arched windows on each of the three floors. The other main wing is at right angles and ends in a stout round tower. The other angles of the building end in four smaller towers. All five have corbelled, decorative sentry-walks and are surmounted by tall conical roofs. The steep roofs over the wings are broken by tall, ornamented dormers springing from the line of the sentry walk.

Château d'Azay-le-Rideau]

Over the principal entrance is the Salamander of François I, but it is not clear if it was put there as a compliment to him when the building was first erected, or whether François himself added it later, and with it the initials of the proud owner, 'G B'. These devices are surrounded by complicated sculptures by an artist unknown but often compared to Jean Goujon himself.

Pilasters are used in the same manner as in some of the work at Blois which was then still new. The staircase though marks a new development carried still further at Chenonceaux. At Blois it stands proud of the building and still turns round a central pillar. At Azay it is entirely inside the front elevation, and rises straight up from landing to landing, but is not yet central. It is elegant in itself, and elaborately ornamented. There have been considerable restorations and additions of medallions of all the kings of France from Louis XI to Henri IV, of which only those on the second floor are genuine.

As, on two sides, it gives on to the waters of the Indre one cannot walk all round it, but from whatever angle you see it, from the front, from the park, the delicacy and perfection of design, the whiteness of the stone, will assuredly delight you.

Alas, they never delighted its owner. In 1522 the head of the family, the patriarchal Jacques de Semblençay, the king's Treasurer, was ordered to send a large sum of money to Marshal Lautrec in the Milanese. When Lautrec had lost the Milanese, he gave as his reason that no funds had reached him. Jacques de Semblençay was able to satisfy him that he had supplied the money. There is little possible doubt that it was Louise de Savoie, mother of the king, who had intercepted and retained it for her own purposes. Both turned upon her.

François I, for all his amiable ways, was a totally selfish, mean and revengeful man with no more morals than his immoral mother. He considered the attack upon her as an attack upon himself. Jacques de Semblençay was brought to trial. He was then 82, an extreme age for the time, and had a high reputation for integrity. He was condemned for corruption. The death penalty was invoked, and the king (who owed him much) confirmed it. He died in shame upon the scaffold.

At this, Gilles Berthelot took fright and fled the country. His books were examined, his guilt was 'proved' (to only the king's satisfaction), and François expropriated the property, and then did not know what to do with it. He had not finished with his revenge on the clan yet, though, and eventually Chenonceaux also passed into his hands without payment on his part. Gilles Berthelot soon died, and a whole succession of people lived in the château, none of any great note. Finally it was bought by the State in 1905.

It now houses a Renaissance Museum, with some excellent pieces and a fascinating kitchen, but on the whole I find it unsatisfactory. It is neither one thing nor the other. These châteaux make poor museums, neither light, nor dimensions, nor access from room to room ever being as good as in a building built for the purpose. On the other hand, the museum contents prevent one from imagining so easily what the rooms looked like when they were lived in. If they cannot be furnished in a manner which gives a picture of contemporary life in the château, then they are best left empty.

Crossing once again to the left bank of the river, D17 leads very pleasantly indeed to Saché, which gives its name to some very delightful white wines, and is well known in France for its château, in which Balzac stayed every year for many years. This 16th and 17th century building has not been much changed since he first went there in 1838, and the room in which he wrote *Le Père Goriot* has been kept exactly as it was in his day. Many of his novels, including *Le Lys dans la Vallée* were written about the immediate neighbourhood. In the château, where the furniture and tapestries have not been changed in a century, there is a small Balzac museum. But Balzac is becoming, except for examination purposes, one of the great unread and not many foreigners visit the museum.

At Pont-de-Ruan a number of water mills are still at work – an unusual sight, and the great wheels make it a charming one; as do the tile-roofed floodgate controls. Soon afterwards a rather sinister, sentry-protected property of great extent proves to be the State Gunpowder Manufactory (*La Poudrerie Nationale*), now producing rather more sophisticated explosives and it is a relief to arrive at the charmingly situated Montbazon, where one is tempted to believe that the immense keep and castle ruins are the very ones Foulques Nerra put up on ground belonging to the monks of the abbey of Cormery, which gave rise to much trouble and some compensation to them. In fact this stupendous keep (which may be visited) belongs only to the 12th century, but some parts of the foundations might just be early enough to be attributed to Foulques Nerra. Unfortunately, it was crowned in 1866 with a vast brass statue of the Virgin Mary, hideous in itself and shockingly out of place on this tall, warengendered tower. However, if you can find your way to Bazonneau, a little more than half a mile to the south-east, you will at least be able to see the *motte* Foulques built to protect his men by a wooden castle during the erection of the stone one. On then, still by the river, but after a while on the right bank, to Esvres (an old church and a not so old castle) to Cormery.

Here suddenly, in this dense countryside, we are back deep in early English history. You come to a tiny village. You find a road straddled by an ancient building making a cross between an archway and a tunnel, and a notice reading: *Abbaye de Cormery Fondée en 791 – Résidence d'Alcuin Ministre de Charlemagne.*

Here lived, here taught, towards the end of his life, Alcuin of York, known also as Albinus. Nothing is known of his background, except that by inference he must have been born at York about 735. It is known that he was a pupil at the Cloister School at York, under Archbishop Egbert and later Ethelbert. In 778, when he would then be about 43 years of age he became headmaster when Ethelbert died. By what curious fate did he become minister of Charlemagne, the great emperor of the West, the conqueror and pacifier of the Saxons, the victorious opponent of the Lombards, the man who hoped to drive the Moors of Spain back into their own kingdoms, the wiser, more sophisticated, more learned Napoleon of his age? What had this teacher in a far-off city in a far-off island in common with this towering European man of war?

It is indeed an oddment of fate, this foregathering of two such unlike figures. This schoolmaster has been called the most distinguished scholar of the 8th century, which may be true because the scholarship of the 8th century was neither plentiful nor widespread, but the books he wrote and which have survived hardly justify the description. What he certainly was could be described as 'master teacher'. He not only taught, he made his pupils lovers of learning for learning's sake. They carried his name throughout England.

He was chosen to go to Rome to fetch the *pallium* of the new archbishop of York in 781, and stopping off at Parma on his return journey, found the restless Charlemagne passing a little time there. The warrior was a great admirer of learning, spoke Latin and could read Greek. He was immensely taken by Alcuin, and offered him the post of teacher to the Imperial family. Alcuin accepted, and went to live at Aix-la-Chapelle, which was as near a capital as the peripatetic emperor ever allowed himself. It was not only the children whom

Alcuin taught, but the adult members of Charlemagne's family as well, and often the emperor himself came and at least metaphorically sat at his feet.

The great teacher spread wide the fame of Charlemagne's court. To the royal family were added the sons of the emperor's nobles, and visitors came from far to pay their respects. The spread of learning went on apace. The years passed, and Alcuin began to dream of retirement.

The emperor's pro-Chancellor, Ithier, was abbot of a Benedictine monastery and school not far from Tours, and when he died the emperor arranged for Alcuin to succeed him. That was in 796. By the time Alcuin died there in 804, the school was the most influential in the Carolingian empire, probably the largest, and the nursery for other schools elsewhere. The abbey was at Cormery.

The bell-tower, the powerful rather rudimentary bell-tower we can see as being now the tunnel through which the road passes, is the last sad remains, not of Alcuin's abbey, but the one which replaced it from about 1028 onwards. It looks even older, and perhaps there was not very much difference between this one and its predecessor. On the west side there is a very curious scalloped moulding effect and honeycomb designs, and some 11th century low-reliefs in poor condition.

The first floor of the tower is covered by the strangest form of dome, if one can use the word dome to convey an impression of a multilateral series of plane surfaces. The prior's house still exists, but is as late as the 15th century. The great refectory exists, but cannot be visited, being sub-divided into a number of private properties, which is a pity for this is a splendid 13th century building, with Gothic vaulting and wide windows. Only the remains of 14th and 15th century cloisters can still be seen.

It is, to me at least, the sturdy old bell-tower which brings back Alcuin, in his Benedictine robe, an ascetic figure no doubt, walking up and down, deep in thought, his silences respected by all. A man, from his writings, almost free of the sin of pride and perhaps to the end unaware that his teaching and his love of learning would be the greatest single civilizing influence for over a century.

There is now the choice between the fast N143 for 14 miles to Loches, or the very pretty D17 which wanders along the bends of the Indre, never very far from it, and links up with N143 for the last few miles. The latter adds very little in distance to the journey and is an exceptionally countrified and charming way to go.

Courçay, first place on it, is a riverside village with, almost inevitably, a very early church, and unusually an amusing little walk upstream between rocks pierced by cave openings, and reaching a petrifying spring. Next is Azay-sur-Indre, again picturesquely situated on the banks of the river, below a 15th century château which would have been more interesting if it had been a little less restored. The road continues through all the rich greenery of the river valley to its junction with N143. And then Loches appears.

Loches is a wayward sort of place. It is desperately difficult to drive in, and walking is really the only proper way of seeing it. That, of course, does not stop motorists from trying to get up its impossible streets and round its impossible corners. You will not regret the freedom of movement, and the freedom to stop and stare, which leaving your car in the big park by the railway station will give you, for Loches is full of lovely old buildings. Their variety makes the town unique in this part of France. Even getting into the town is a joy. For example, the Porte des Cordeliers, beautifully proportioned and of an unusual elegance with its four corner turrets, its covered sentry walk, its tall wedge-shaped roof reflected in the waters of one branch of the Indre, has all the war-like components of its older counterparts, but only for show. This is not yet the Renaissance, but what the Renaissance was just about (this was in 1497) to do with far greater exuberance.

The Porte Picoys is a little earlier and lacks the finesse of the Cordeliers, though it has much the same decorative covered sentry walk. It is very simple: a square block pierced for the road to pass through, a little austere (though there is a Renaissance niche which was very much an afterthought), and on the town side adorned only by a magnificent Gothic window.

Leaning up against the Porte Picoys is the Hôtel-de-Ville, certainly the prettiest town hall anywhere. It was built between 1535 and 1543, in the full burgeoning of the Renaissance. The difficulty is to get far enough away from it to see it. There are two wings at right angles, for the space allocated to the town to build its municipal offices was singularly small, and nothing must be done to impair the military value of the town walls. Not only was the architect forced to build it, in effect, in two parts, but he had to make it four storeys high to provide the accommodation needed. The result, as so often happens when works of art are submitted to rigid discipline in their conception, is superb. It is also probably unique in France as having been used from the day it was finished and without a single break as a Town Hall and nothing else, every day.

From one or other of the gates, one enters the old walled town itself. There is much to see, and many different ways of going round. If you enter by the Porte des Cordeliers, the tall tower is the Tour Saint-Antoine which was the bell tower of the church of that name, long since disappeared. The original church was reputedly founded by Hildegarde, wife of Foulques-Nerra, who was buried at Loches, but this tower is centuries later than that. It was begun in 1529 and is known to have been finished by 1575, and is a fine specimen of the religious architecture of a period in which churches were taking second place to private mansions and palaces. In the other direction, to your left, is the old fortified camp.

The Grande Rue rises into the Rue du Château which rises farther still. Here are enchanting Renaissance houses, particularly the Logis du Centaure, with its carvings of Hercules and the Centaur, and the Chancellerie of 1550 with the back to back 'D' symbol of Diane de Poitiers repeated here and there. You then come to the entrance of the château and its inner fortified wall. This is where you begin to be really thankful not to have a car with you for though, as the guide says, 'the circulation of automobiles is possible, but the manoeuvres are difficult,' you might be happy with a miniature car having a microscopical turning circle but you would end with deep frustrations if you drove anything else.

The castle, you find, is full of museums, but do not let that put you off a visit to the non-museum parts even if you do happen to be allergic to the educational content of such collections as the 400 landscapes of the Musée Lansyer, all by the artist of that name, or those of the folklore museum (Musée du Terroir). So pass through the gate (Porte Royale) which is a 15th century massive building flanked by 13th century towers and find the old church of Saint-Ours. It started life as 12th century Romanesque (possibly on the site of still older foundations) and you pass through a huge porch to the surprising nave. The vaults are two octagonal stone pyramids, believed

Château de Loches

to be the work of a prior who died in 1168. The effect is most remarkable and you will not see their like anywhere else. The old crypt has a quaint painting of Saint Brice, and the *Trésor* contains Our Lady's Girdle once again.

Here one enters the castle proper, which is in two parts. The older, *Le Vieux Logis*, is all turrets and battlements for defence, the other one, alongside, is essentially a dwelling place. It is known for certain that Charles VII and Louis XI lived in the one, and Charles VIII and Louis XII in the other. In the former, Joan of Arc persuaded her dauphin to go to Reims, in the latter is the charming oratory used by

Anne of Britanny. And in the ground floor area of an isolated tower is the tomb of Agnès Sorel.

It is a beautiful tomb, with a beautiful recumbent stone figure of Agnès on it. King's mistress she may have been, but her face is the face of innocence. Of all the mistresses of all the kings of France, she was the gentlest and the kindest and perhaps the loveliest. There are two lambs at her feet, *agneaux*, a pun in stone on her own name, and the gentle lambs could well have been her fitting emblem.

The king (the worthless dauphin who let Joan of Arc go to her death with no attempt to save her) was a plain man. All who recorded the period have spoken of the beauty of Agnès, and we have not only this tomb sculpture to help us to form our own judgment, but the painting *Virgin and Child* by Jean Fouquet, in the *Musée Royal des Beaux-Arts* in Antwerp. There is no possible doubt that the same original is reproduced in both picture and sculpture, and Jean Fouquet was her devoted servant and friend in her lifetime. It seems to have been a case where two artists felt no need to idealize their model, for they arrived by totally different means at similar results. The lovely girl loved her plain and uninspiring king, and lived for him, and gave him children and exercised a wholesome influence on him. She also spent his money, of whose value she had little idea, but mostly on the church.

As to her title, *Dame de Beauté*, there seems no way now of knowing whether Charles VII gave her the property at Beauté because she was already known as the Lady of Beauty, or whether it was after he gave her Beauté as a property that she became legally known as La Dame de Beauté.

Amongst the older parts of the château is the famous keep which, once again, was built on the site of an earlier one which Foulques Nerra erected. Loches, a king pin of the plan to contain the counts of Blois, controlling as it did the Indre, threatening the Cher and defending an all important road junction, was the apple of the eye of Foulques, and his successors fully appreciated its strategical importance. This vast oblong block was very beautifully built in stone at some time in the 12th century and consisted not only of the three floorless storeys we can see inside today, but also of basement cut into the rock, and semi-cylindrical buttresses outside. The walls are over 9 feet thick, and enclose a rectangular surface about 64 feet by 25 feet, and rise 120 feet from ground level. It must have been one of the most formidable fortresses in Europe, and was further strengthened by an additional bastion, another touching rectangular structure of about one quarter of the surface area of the parent building. There are many other towers around, most of which have some kind of dungeon (the keep's basement seems to have been solely for storing supplies), and one of which goes down four floors. Louis XI made Loches his State prison, and in these dungeons he is supposed to have kept the wood-and-iron cages in which the prisoner could neither stand nor lie at ease. There are also dank and tiny cells, supposedly reserved for the people who had incurred the king's particular dislike.

Both of these should be viewed with the greatest suspicion. Monsieur Jean Vallery-Radot has recalled that Philippe de Commines, in his *Mémoires* covering the reigns of Louis XI and Charles VIII, has described one as being 'a harsh prison ... with terribly big locks, some eight feet square and the height of a man plus one foot more'. This does seem compatible with Cardinal Balue (supposed to be their inventor) having been shut up in one for eight years, which could hardly be true of one in which he could neither stand nor lie down. Equally, the inaccessible cells below the level even of the moats in some cases are not so much the invention as the misunderstanding of the 19th century. They were in fact the cess-pools for the true prisoners' cells.

None the less, this is the ugly side of Loches, and it is a pleasure for most to get away from them, to look out over this town's endless assortment of roof shapes, sizes, colours and ages from the castle's higher end, or to return to the town and mingle with the shopping crowds from the rich countryside around.

Then, from the town it is interesting to turn round and look again up to the castle from what is now a boulevard at the foot of the keep, and used to be the moat. Henry II of England built most of this part of the fortifications, and it was not taken in his lifetime, but when Richard I was prisoner in Austria on his return from the crusades, Philippe-Auguste got it from John by devious intrigue.

Richard came back, somewhat unexpectedly, and one of his first thoughts on returning to his beloved Anjou (which he cared so much more for than he did England) was to retake it. His fury with Philippe-Auguste was communicated to his men, who performed the impossible: they scaled the walls and re-took the fortress in three hours. If you look up at it from that boulevard, you will find it impossible to believe that with the arms and equipment available at that time, it could have been done so quickly. However, the historical evidence is unanswerable: done it was. Thereafter it was English for ten years, and was again taken by Philippe-Auguste, but only after a siege lasting a full year. It remained a French royal fortress and prison.

About half a mile away, on the other side of the Indre, is Beaulieu-lès-Loches, where Foulques Nerra founded a famous abbey, on his return from Jerusalem. The abbey buildings, entirely rebuilt in the 18th century, are now Town Hall and schools, but the abbey church, though much damaged by the English in 1412, still has parts that Foulques knew. It was in this church that he was buried.

The abbey was founded in honour of the Trinity, the Archangels, the Cherubim and the Seraphim. The dedication was to The Holy Sepulchre, as is only to be expected, for the church was built to house a very large stone that Foulques had brought back with him, which he had torn away from Christ's Tomb with his teeth – at least, so it is recorded in the annals of Beaulieu. As Foulques had no wish to be in dispute with bishops, he did homage for Beaulieu to the pope, and it thereafter came directly under papal authority.

The fine old Romanesque church makes it clear how important this abbey was in its heyday; this can most easily be judged by the bell tower; with its tall octagonal stone spire it gives the impression of a cathedral rather than an abbey church.

It was known that Foulques had been buried in this church, but all trace of his remains and even his tomb had disappeared. In 1870 a number of local archaeologists got together to make a search for him. The last record they could find was in a manuscript of 1748 which stated that it (Foulques' tomb) 'was near the wall in which is the door of the chapter, now used as a sacristy, under the organ'. They took up the flagstones and between two and a half and three feet below them found some little columns completely hidden from view, and at their feet a single slab of tufa over seven feet long, which had been partly built over when the chapter wall was built, long after Foulques'

The marquise de
Pompadour bought the
château de Ménars.
Gabriel, the king's
architect, rebuilt it for
her.

The château de Talcy,
where Ronsard met the
blonde Italian girl whom
he immortalised in his
poetry as Cassandre.

The Loire at Beaugency. This picture sums up the landscape of much of the
Loire valley; ancient castle, ancient church, slow-moving river, miles of
meadows and woods.

Chanteloup: the pagoda, 'the grace of Versailles bearing aloft the time-
honoured silhouette of far-distant Cathay.'

time. Beneath was the coffin they hoped would prove to be his. From the very primitive coins, rings and other ornaments, they were certain it would prove to be so. They found traces of previous investigations; for example, somebody had carefully opened the coffin in the 14th century. Subsequent overbuilding probably came after the English sacked and burnt what they could of the church. Near-by pillars and walls still bear the marks of burning.

The most exciting find was the presumed skull of Foulques Nerra. It was carefully photographed before the remains were re-interred. It shows a broad forehead, high cheekbones, and a very long face from top of nose to chin. Alas, all we know from this about the mysterious race from which these fierce warriors descended is that it was related to the oldest European races, but to which one in particular is not known. One can presume him to have been tall with big limbs, deep-set eyes, a granite-hewn face (such as one still sees in Brittany), considerable intelligence and probably great firmness of character. All that is known of his history, character and ability would seem to bear out the information derived from his skull.

Continuing eastwards from Beaulieu on N 760 through the forest of Loches brings one close to the Chartreuse du Liget. This was the Charterhouse founded by Henry II in expiation of the death of Thomas Becket. It is privately owned, but the gardens may be visited, and the ruins of the 12th century church, as well as the remains of some much later cloisters. A little before coming to the Charterhouse, is the chapel of Saint John the Baptist, some 500 yards down a side turning. It is sometimes known as the *chapelle du Liget*. It is very quaint and unusual, and I have not been able to ascertain just how it came to be built this distance from the main monastery buildings with which it seems to have little or no connection. Like the monastery, it is claimed to have been built by Henry II. It is Romanesque, and good Romanesque, and it is round. I have no reason for not considering it a church of the Knights Templar, except that there is no written record that it was, but the written records of the 12th century leave many other and bigger gaps than that. The domed vaults have six contemporary frescoes of the Nativity, Presentation at the Temple, Descent from the Cross, Entombment of Christ, Death of the Virgin Mary, and the Tree of Jesse. Most people

o

would find this little additional journey well worth the time and effort.

Now N760 carries us up to Montrésor, a perfect little gem of a place, sloping up from the river and built in a kind of natural amphitheatre. Above the delicious little village, which had 554 inhabitants at the last count of which I have trace, is the castle. A double girdle of medieval fortifications follows the contours of the rocky mass which arises suddenly out of fertile land. They are really quite formidable and may well have struck terror in the hearts of attackers, but today they are so picturesque that it is quite impossible to take their towers and crenellations seriously.

The inner girdle encloses a pleasant garden, and in the middle of the garden, facing the valley of the Indre, is a most cheerful and peaceful looking château of the time of Louis XII, with mullioned windows and great dormers in the roof finished with crockets and pinnacles. The south elevation ends in two machicolated towers, and the north one in round-topped turrets.

This oblong château may be visited, and it is worth doing so less perhaps for the quite good pictures and furniture than for the pleasure of seeing so graceful a building being so gracefully lived in. Above all, one must see the delicate Renaissance church, a little marvel of restrained ornament, rightness of proportion and sense of line, with some very good stained glass and woodwork inside.

Begun – and I apologize for mentioning the fact yet once again – by Foulques Nerra, this château has much less historical interest than one would expect. It belonged to both Henry I and Henry II of England, but there is no record of their visits, if there were any. It was taken by Philippe-Auguste, and thereafter saw no more war, but passed from noble family to noble family and acquired that patina of peaceful living which marks it now.

A short run parallel to the Indrois brings one to Villeloin-Coulangé which offers little to see beyond the remains of its 15th and 16th and 18th century fortifications. Then there is a climb up the valley of a little stream called the Tourmente, though it is very difficult to see how or by what it could ever be tormented, to arrive at Nouans-les-Fontaines. Here there is a 13th century church with rare six-sided vaults. Beyond is the forest of La Tonne, and Luçay-le-Mâle, from which one can see a sturdy 15th century castle, and from there the road edges the famous forest of La Gâtine and arrives at the twin towns which make up Valençay. The little river Nahon runs through it and creates a minor ravine, with La Ville on one slope and the Bourg de l'Eglise on the other. The château is on the edge of La Ville.

Here I must admit to a prejudice or two. The château's most conspicuous owner, Talleyrand, fills me with an intense dislike of everything with which he was connected, and this affects my appreciation of what is in its way a very fine building. Also, the last time I was there the tip-cadging of the servants who are detailed as guides displeased me very much. And finally, it is vulgar and ostentatious.

Whoever built the first fortress here is difficult to trace, but it was not Foulques Nerra, and there is not much history to Valençay until Jacques d'Estampes appears on the scene about 1540. Jacques was himself of the bluest of blue blood, but he had never had any money. So, as has been known in other cases, he married it. As soon as his new wife's fortune was safely in his coffers, he bought Valençay, knocked down the castle, and started to build a home for himself. As he had a very high opinion of himself, he also saw very, very big in the matter of a house fit for him.

If it began by Jacques marrying into the formidable clan of French financiers, it went on with them. They all had money to spend, and they enlarged and embellished.

In 1719, the most extraordinary of all Scottish adventurers, His Excellency the Councillor of State and Comptroller-General of the Finances of France, John Law of Lauriston, arranged to buy it, but the deal never went through for he was swept away by the flood of inflation and bankruptcy which his *Compagnie des Indes* and new theories on banking had generated. In 1766 it came into the possession of the Villemorin-Luçay family, almost hereditary Farmers-General of Taxes.

Then came Charles Maurice Talleyrand de Périgord, the very patron of time-servers and turncoats, whose record can seldom have been equalled in any other country, and probably never.

His father was an officer in the army of Louis XV during the Seven Years' War. Early in life, Charles met with an accident which caused permanent lameness. His father, with that high degree of intelligence sometimes associated with the military, disinherited him as unfit to be his heir. It was, in his opinion, more important to have two perfect

Château de Valençay

feet than one well-filled head. Thus early the boy learned the lesson which he applied throughout his life: the only person Charles Maurice Talleyrand de Périgord can rely on to help him is Charles Maurice Talleyrand de Périgord.

He worked hard in the seminary and at the Sorbonne, was a fair scholar and acquired as he grew up a reputation as wit and rake. This was a time when much of the power of the Gallican church had got into totally immoral hands, and an agreeable young wit who could entertain a bishop's dinner guests could expect to have a good entry into a clerical career. Abbot of Saint-Denis in 1775, at the age of 21; *Agent-Général* to the French clergy in 1780; bishop of Autun, 1789 –

swift progress this for a man who, as far as is known, was a disbeliever all his life.

He was described by de Quincey as 'that rather middling Bishop but very eminent knave'. He was quite prepared to throw the Church overboard, if that was the way the times were moving. In the States General, he represented the clergy of his diocese. He was one of those who drew up the Declaration of Rights. He was the friend of any man who showed any signs of rising to the top in the confused world of the Revolution: Mirabeau, Sieyès, Lally-Tolendal. He made himself an authority on the Constitution, on finance and on education.

He took a coldly cynical delight in attacking the profession to which, officially, he still belonged. In 1789 he proposed the confiscation of the landed property of the Church; the result was what he had anticipated – the presidency of the Assembly. In 1791 he took the oath to the Constitution, consecrated two new bishops without papal authority, and publicly declared his sincere attachment to the Church, all at the same time. The Church was not appeased; Talleyrand was excommunicated.

He disliked the Terror, and got himself sent on a special mission to London as public feeling began to rise against the leaders. If he failed to bring Mr Pitt to an agreement, there is reason to believe that he allowed an open pocket to receive the pieces of gold which Mr Pitt let fall. He was proscribed in 1792 and went to Washington. In 1795 he was recalled to France at the fall of Robespierre, attached himself to Barras, and became foreign minister in 1797.

He attached himself also to Napoleon. Disgraced for a moment for taking British gold in an effort to reconcile the rebels in the American colonies with the British Government, he bounced back and gained Napoleon's good graces again by supporting his action in murdering the duc d'Enghien. 'That curséd cripple', Josephine called him over this matter; he never forgave her and worked always towards her downfall.

One day, in 1803, Napoleon said to Talleyrand, 'I want you to buy an outstanding property, in which you can receive the diplomatic corps and distinguished foreign visitors in the most brilliant manner'. How Valençay came to be chosen is not quite certain, but soon

Talleyrand was engaged in sharp bargaining with Monsieur de Villemorin-Luçay who wanted no small price for the nearly 50,000-acre estate. It would have ended by being beyond Talleyrand's means (or at least beyond what he was prepared to pay out) had not the emperor made him a present 'of the extra sum required to conclude the bargain'.

Just what Napoleon meant by 'receiving distinguished foreign visitors in the most brilliant manner' soon became apparent. Valençay was the luxurious prison of the deposed Ferdinand of Spain from 1808 to 1814.

Talleyrand was made a Prince of the Empire, Prince Bénévent, but already he foresaw Napoleon's coming doom and prepared to desert him. He had always been critical of the Spanish war, and became even more so of the war in Russia. He became the hated link, but the essential one, between the Allied Governments and the Bourbons. He was universally hated, and universally accepted. He dictated to the Senate the terms of surrender of his old master, Napoleon, and to Louis XVIII he dictated his own nomination as foreign minister. As such, he made the voice of France heard at the Congress of Vienna as perhaps no other Frenchman could have done. For the first and and only time he was caught out by events. The Hundred Days took him no less by surprise than the least well informed. Louis XVIII went into exile again, in Ghent. Talleyrand would not follow. Louis was furious at this callous desertion but under Allied pressure had to accept him as prime minister when the Hundred Days were over. His term of office was short. As soon as Allied pressure was relinquished, Talleyrand was sent packing and remained just a discontented senator until 1830. Then he became Louis-Philippe's chief adviser. When the revolution had been successful, Louis-Philippe offered him the ministry of foreign affairs, but Talleyrand preferred being ambassador in London, which at 76 might have seemed a less wearing appointment. He returned in 1834, having reconciled the British Court and parliament to Louis-Philippe. He lived until 1838. Only the good die young.

The present owner is the duchesse de Talleyrand, and whilst the property remains in the hands of the family it is unreasonable to object to so much prominence being given to the first duke. You start off on entering by being shown into a Talleyrand Museum housed in the former dependencies, in which rather minor objects, more or less directly connected with him, are displayed and explained. The 40,000 or 50,000 acres with which the estate began has shrunk since then. Even as relatively early as 1898 it had shrunk to 22,000 acres which were sold in lots in that year and 9,000 which were still attached to the château. Today either this amount or not very much less still exists. The park you visit has its flock of llamas, its herd of fallow deer, its little colony of cranes and flamingoes, some peacocks and some black swans.

The château itself after all its alterations consists mainly of two wings at right angles. On the outside of the right angle is a huge round, domed tower, totally out of proportion to anything else, rather like a child with a head still too big for its body wearing a hat too big for the head. The dual wings are much over-ornamented in places: the eighteenth century insisted on improving on the work on the sixteenth and seventeenth centuries.

Inside, the south wing is very largely decorated in Empire style, which really does not wed happily with the architecture. The whole château provides the basis for a potentially interesting study of what happens when too much money (quite well-bred money in this case) sets out to impress. And if I would find it much more interesting if the personality of *the* Talleyrand was not evoked quite so often throughout the visit, this may not strike others in the same way.

Valençay is in the *Département de l'Indre*, though the Cher is barely 9 miles to the north of it. It is to the Cher we must now go, and start again from where it runs (or more often dawdles) into the Loire.

Chapter Seven

Along the Cher and to Bourges

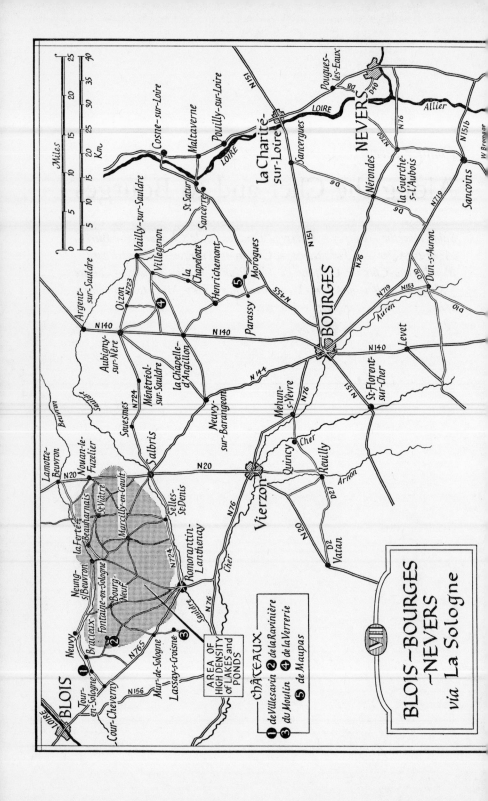

BLOIS—BOURGES
—NEVERS
via La Sologne

VIII

AREA OF
HIGH DENSITY
of LAKES and
PONDS

CHÂTEAUX
① de Villesavin ② de la Ravinière ④ de la Verrerie
③ du Moulin ⑤ de Maupas

Along the Cher and to Bourges

The Cher, as we have already seen, runs into the Loire near Villandry and then runs almost parallel to, and a little to the south of it, as it skirts Tours and begins a more generally south-east course at Saint-Avertin, much beloved of the good people of Tours who go boating and fishing and swimming there. Plantin, the celebrated 16th century printer who came to fame in Antwerp, was born in Saint-Avertin, otherwise the little town has no history separate from that of Tours.

At Larçay, for those who are interested in earlier history, is a Gallo-Roman *castellum*, about 250 feet long, built of small stones, cubes for the most part, embedded in mortar. The south side even has four engaged towers to be seen, and a similar one breaks each of the shorter sides in the centre. The walls are about 20 feet high, and as much as 13 feet thick at their base. At Véretz, or rather 2 miles to the south-east, in the Domaine de la Chavonnière (which may be visited) lived Paul-Louis Courier, a well known pamphleteer. He was murdered in mysterious circumstances between here and Larçay. There were many suspicions, many innuendos flung around, but nothing ever discovered.

The road to Bléré goes up and down the hills which form the valley of the Cher. At Azay-sur-Cher a single square tower with staircase turret marks the site of the château in which the Seigneur d'Azay once lived, and there are some very picturesque ruins of a Romanesque priory. At Bléré there is a good church of several styles, a lovely Renaissance mansion, the Hôtel du Gouverneur, and a curious grave-yard chapel of Renaissance days, with a dome. Nobody is likely to wish to spend much time on these, for Chenonceaux is now only 4 miles away.

Chenonceaux – what is there to say about it that is not already a
banality? What to describe that has not been reproduced ten thousand
times in books and postcards and the photographs visitors take? For
the moment let us leave it that it is, in my opinion, shared by countless
others better qualified than I to express it, the most beautiful dwelling
still in existence. What ancient empires, what long-forgotten artists
of the East, what unknown genius of the Americas, may have built
in times gone by we cannot know, but of all the known houses,

Château de Chenonceaux

castles and palaces which are still in being Chenonceaux must
assuredly have pride of place.

What is a little less well known is its practical nature. With
Chenonceaux the outside staircase went, for ever. With Chenonceaux,
the furious draughts which swept like murdering demons through
even a Chambord (which came 4 years later), were banished for ever.
With Chenonceaux, a more urbane domestic architecture was born.
And we owe it, as is very fit and proper, to a woman, or more
probably to two women. This is the ancestor of the modern house,
and we should never pass by without paying it our respects.

Doing just this still once again, for the purpose of this book, I was struck anew by the thought that this was an essentially feminine house, the house of a wealthy lady blessed with that rare virtue, perfect taste. I found myself thinking along identical lines with the thoughts I had had fourteen years before when I was planning a previous book,* and I did not feel that I could much improve on what I wrote then.

To begin with the château as one sees it now; the approach is up a long and dusty drive edged by enormous plane trees, leading to a forecourt. This is guarded by a brace of sphinxes, to the right of which are outbuildings. Amongst these are the stables, designed by Philibert Delorme in 1560, pleasing enough, but not particularly interesting.

From here the first view of the château comes upon you with all the shock of surprise, if you are one of those who are familiar with it only from the printed page, for you find yourself looking upon something completely unexpected for, from the front, neither the great gallery across the river nor the river itself are visible. Instead there is a decorative drawbridge leading to the rectangular terrace surrounded by a moat, that marks the site of the original château. There, too, is a splendid stalwart cylindrical keep, dating from feudal times and somewhat refashioned later in the taste of the Renaissance, which no photograph has shown you as dominating Chenonceaux. Two decorative and very formal gardens stretch right and left along the bank of the still invisible Cher. Behind drawbridge and keep, a bridge leads to the château proper, built upon the twin bank-abutments of an antique mill, linked together by a narrow arch.

It is a tremendous moment this; expecting something so familiar as to have become almost hackneyed, one discovers instead a completely unsuspected gem in stone-work, for of that well-known gallery there is still no sign. The great steep-pitched roof (half as high again as the roof of the gallery), with huge and superbly ornamented dormer windows and, above them, daring chimney groups to perfect the scheme of decoration; at the four corners of the stone-built main block are exquisite turrets so perfect in pro-

* *Châteaux of the Loire* (Putnam), 1954, now out of print).

portion that one feels an inch less or an inch more in diameter would have ruined them. They are surmounted by conical roofs. They spring from above ground level from gracefully graduated round brackets. It is impossible to convey in words the *rightness* of everything. You may look at it for hours, mentally adding and taking away, and at the end you will find there is nothing you could change to advantage. It does not even err in over-uniformity, for upstream on the eastern side a tiny chapel and a matching wing protrude to frame, at ground level, a little terrace which relieves the whole from all danger of monotony. This, indeed, of all the châteaux of the Loire, is the 'maiden most perfect, lady of light,' utterly feminine in character, without weakness yet without a single concession to troublous times beyond the domesticated keep, complete with its tall Renaissance chimney, and the ornamental drawbridge.

To see the famous gallery it is necessary to turn into one or other of the gardens as far as the Cher. There you will be able to observe that it is an extension of, and a later addition to, the southern façade. Philibert Delorme, faced with the difficulty of adding to an almost perfect building produced a masterpiece differing from, yet marrying happily with the main body of the château. It is about 200 feet long, crossing the almost full width of the Cher on five arches, rooted in cutwaters, each of which carries a semicircular turret rising to the height of the beginning of the second floor. Above this second floor, the long roof line is broken on each side by nine small dormers. At each end of the roof is a tall rectangular chimney. The gallery is unfinished on the southern bank, where it was intended to terminate in a square tower which was to provide an additional entrance to the château. Its absence is not obvious and does not detract from the appearance of the château as seen from either side.

Let us now turn back the pages of time and see how this lovely building came into being. There are somewhat vague references to the Marques family as having, in the 13th century, come from Auvergne to settle in these parts, where it held the fiefs of Bléré, Francueil and Chisseau. Guillaume de Marques presented the last to the monks of Montoussan. The first of the Marques who can be traced as seigneur of Chenonceaux was a contemporary of Charles VI. This Jean de Marques sided with the duke of Burgundy against the dauphin (Charles VII) and gave Chenonceaux its one connection with England: he admitted an English garrison into his little fortress. Nemesis was at hand. A battle between French and English took place on the plain near Chenonceaux, the French troops under Marshal Laval de Bois-Dauphin defeated the English, the fortress of Sire de Marques was taken by assault, its fortifications pulled down and its moats filled in and the trees over all the surrounding estate were hacked down 'to the height of infamy', as the phrase went in those days, to grow again as a long-lasting reminder of the treason of the owner.

The second Jean de Marques paid homage in 1431 to Charles VII for his estate at Chenonceaux and the following year was granted permission by the king to rebuild its fortifications. His son, Pierre de Marques, who succeeded him in 1460, sold the estate to Thomas Bohier, Comptroller-General of Finances for the Province of Normandy, Lieutenant-General in the King's Armies and, during the short-lived occupation of southern Italy by Charles VIII, Representative of the Viceroy of Naples, in 1496. He was also at different times Chamberlain and Counsellor of Louis XI, Charles VIII, Louis XII and François I.

Thomas Bohier, baron de Saint-Cyergue, seems to have been a man not very particular about the means he employed to get his own way. It is not very clear how he came to acquire them, but he did acquire a number of little parcels of land around Chenonceaux, through nominees. One suspects extravagance on the part of Pierre de Marques, but this part of the history of Chenonceaux is not entirely clear. The tradition, to which the known facts point but neither confirm nor deny, is that eventually no entry could be obtained to Chenonceaux without passing over Thomas Bohier's property and that this enabled him to force a sale of the castle and mill. The latter, in those days, could be a profitable investment, for under feudal laws flour could only be ground in the mills of the seigneur of the district. The Marques family denied the legality of the sale through one of the longest and most keenly fought lawsuits of the times. Not until 1512 was it settled and the purchase price fixed at 12,500 *livres*, but how much of that went in lawyers' fees we do not know.

Within the year of the end of the lawsuit, masons were already busy clearing away the old and preparing for the new. Thomas Bohier was called away to service in Italy. His wife, Katherine Briçonnet, took charge of the works. In her time no architect is mentioned in any of the still extant builders' accounts. One would like to know so very much more about her and her cousin, Philippa Lesbahy.

Under Katherine's direction, the new house was built on the piles which once supported the mill. Philippa, as we have seen, enclosed the staircase at Azay-le-Rideau. Katherine went much further. She broke away completely from the labyrinthine sequence of room and ante-room, one giving into the other, and with the draughty communicating passages of the old château. Instead, she had a large central hall, with rooms giving off it all round. The exterior spiral staircase gave way to a straight one from the hall to the upper floors.

Chenonceaux, then, was the first really sensible, modern house, designed for easier service and greater comfort and one wonders with what enormous difficulties she met and how she overcame old tradition, when the hand of every one of the builders must have been against her, and her new ideas most unwillingly put into practice. We have all seen in our own days how bitterly workmen in all trades resent any departure from the traditional. This is the most probable cause of the long delay in building, which was not over until 1521. Three years later, Thomas Bohier died in the Milanese and two years after that the châtelaine of Chenonceaux died also, mercifully before the disgrace of her family took place.

When François I lost his mother, Louise de Savoie, it was found that she had died possessed of one and a half million gold coins, which was probably the biggest fortune in France. How much of it came from the money she stole from de Semblençay we can only guess. With her death one might have expected that François' anger at the accusation against his mother (which he must have known was fully justified) would have faded. Not at all: Thomas Bohier was dead, but investigation into his financial dealings went on. Vast sums were found to be due to the king, and the son, Antoine Bohier, was stripped of everything. Finally Antoine was glad to sell Chenonceaux

5 Château d'Amboise

6 The view from Sancerre

to the king against a paper debt of 190,000 *livres*. In 1536, Constable Anne de Montmorency took possession of it in the name of the king. As with so many other possessions François acquired by dubious means, he did not know what to do with it when he came into possession of it. The work, however, now almost at an end, continued. He made only two visits to it, the first for a single day in 1538, on his return from an unfruitful meeting with the Emperor Charles V at Aigues-Mortes. François was accompanied by his wife and his mistress, and by his eldest son, who was accompanied in his turn both by Catherine de Médicis and Diane de Poitiers. The second and last was on April 14, 1545, for a day's hunting. He died on March 31, 1547. Exactly three months later, on July 1, Diane took possession.

At first there was never the money to do all she longed to do. It took 9 years to complete the gorgeous formal garden (the one on your left as you come in) with its strong pattern, not unlike the Union Jack. In the same year Philibert Delorme began that unfinished bridge across the Cher. At that time it was simply to be a bridge, making a new entrance to the palace. Diane did not design or desire the superstructure. The bridge was almost ready when Henri II was fatally injured in a friendly passage of arms. A spear penetrated his helmet and pierced eye and neck. He lingered for eleven days in agony.

The widowed Catherine de Médicis was, for the first time, genuinely queen of France. Ever since her marriage, Diane had had the greater influence on Henri II by far, had managed him and his affairs, had seen to the education of his children, had set Catherine aside. Now that Catherine had become regent and held all the power, revenge was in her hands. It says much for this often maligned woman that her revenge consisted in insisting upon the return of the Crown jewels, and the exchange of Chenonceaux for Chaumont. For those cruel days, this was an exercise in Christian charity.

Contrary to the usual belief, it was Catherine and not Diane who brought Chenonceaux to its greatest glory. She did not remake Diane's garden to her own design on the other side of the château. It was smaller, but what it lacked in size, it made up in perfection of detail. It was for her and not for Diane that the superb gallery was built on the new bridge. It was she who created the vast park, and she who filled the château with the finest of furniture, statues, ornaments and hangings brought from her native Italy. It was she who filled the library with its books.

On March 31, 1560, the king and queen made their entry. They looked a pair of happy children, which indeed they were. Little François II, was a thin and pale sixteen, Mary Stuart all of eighteen. In modern terms I suppose one would say that a whale of a party was laid on for them, and the gay young queen was never averse to enjoying herself. It was a time for the young couple to eat, drink and be merry, for there would not be much more opportunity. Nine months and five days later François II died. Soon afterwards his widow left France for ever, to face a bitter destiny as Mary, queen of Scots.

The king is dead. Long live Charles IX. Here, three years later another young king came up the drive. Sirens emerged from the little canals and sang songs of welcome, in which nymphs joined as they emerged from the shadows of the trees; then the satyrs came and nymphs and sirens ran shrieking away. Then, in resplendent costumes, the young cavaliers came galloping to the rescue and put the satyrs to flight. For four days these celebrations went on. Fireworks were brought specially from Italy for hitherto unseen displays of magnificence. The still clear waters of the Cher reflected the cannon shots' flashes, the high-pooped ships and the colourful sails of a mock naval battle. In this way was celebrated the 2 years' journey into every province in France, the longest ever made by a French king, though France derived but little benefit from it. Charles IX died at 24, eroded by remorse for Saint Bartholomew's Day and all the blood that was spilled in the name of religion. Death released him from the agony of mind which made him scream through the night like a damned soul.

Then came a last fête for still another of that unhappy race of kings, Henri III. It was held 'by the entrance to the garden at the beginning of the main avenue and by a spring which poured from out of a rock'. Henri III took his place, dressed as usual more as a woman than a man, with only his trunk hose to show which he was, his lips and cheeks painted, pearls in his ears, a pearl necklace round his uncovered throat. Below him sat his *mignons* – four of the seven soon to die – all painted up like their master, hair curled and re-curled and rising above a little velvet cap of the kind women had made fashionable, and their starched ruffs half a foot long, so that 'the head', as L'Estoile the chronicler put it, 'looked as if it were the head of Saint John being offered on a platter'. At dinner the guests were served by ladies of the Court, 'with their hair loose upon their shoulders like maenads, but for the rest dressed like men. The *maîtres d'hôtel* were all ladies of the Court also, and *maîtresses* would be a very fitting word for most, if not all, of them were the mistresses of one or other, or several of, the guests. Such a one was Madame de Sauve, a granddaughter of de Semblançay. Born Charlotte de Beaune and ending as marquise de Noirmoutier, she is described by contemporary writers as dividing her favours with rigorous impartiality between the two warring parties, sleeping one night with a Protestant and the next with a Catholic. At that particular time the two parties were respectively represented in her favours by the king of Navarre and the duc d'Anjou. It was in her bed that the duc de Guise spent his last night.

Present also was the pious Louise de Vaudemont, the reigning queen (though Catherine de Médicis made sure she had no opportunity of exercising any influence). When Catherine died, leaving enormous debts, she nevertheless managed to divide her estates between her family and her servants. Chenonceaux went to the queen, who left it in the care of Gilles de Faverolles. Only six months later, whilst she was at Tours, she learned that a fanatical monk had, the day before, stabbed and wounded Henri III at Saint-Cloud. It was a terrible shock to her, and her friends brought her to Chenonceaux to recover. It was by the cool waters of the Cher, so comforting in the summer heat, that she received a letter in the handwriting of Henri himself: '*Ma mie,* my darling, I hope that I shall be all right; pray God for me, and do not move from there.'

In their own strange way this couple were devoted to each other, and it must have been a wonderful consolation to Louise that the last letter from her beloved Henri was so affectionate and so personal, for by the time the letter was placed in her hands, he was dead. Soon all his own rooms were hung with black; his own bed, his prayer stool, his chairs were all covered in black velvet and ornamented with

silver tear-drops and lugubrious devices.* He had told her not to move
from there, and she did not. Clad always in the white robes of
royal mourning, she prayed for him by day and by night. Her ghost,
it is said, can still be seen on a moonlight night at one or other
of the windows, fingering her rosary and muttering the prayers
for the repose of her dead husband's soul of which it stood in such
dire need. She was known to all as the 'White Lady' during the
years that remained to her, those years when she was a living
ghost.

Then Chenonceaux lay abandoned and hardly lived in, until in
1733 the duc de Bourbon sold it to a certain Monsieur Dupin for
130,000 *livres*, including the fief of Civray. It is said of Monsieur
Dupin that he was of noble birth, had been a cavalry captain but had
been forced to leave the army as a result of an unfortunate affair of
honour. There is no substantial confirmation of a story possibly put
about by way of what would now be called a public relations effort.
What is quite certain is that he was a Farmer-General of Taxes and
whilst remaining a perfectly honourable gentleman ('so are they all,
all honourable men') managed by accident to accumulate a vast
fortune, which was a very good thing for Chenonceaux. He had
married twice and his second wife, Louise-Marie-Madeleine-
Guillaume Defontaine, was a most delightful, intelligent and good-
hearted person. They kept good company there, and Madame Dupin
invited Jean-Jacques Rousseau to become her secretary and to teach
the children of Monsieur Dupin's first marriage. 'We were very gay
in this lovely place,' he wrote later, 'and we ate very well; I became as
fat as a monk. Much music was played there; I composed several
pieces for three voices full of fairly strong harmony. We acted, too;
I wrote a three act play in a fortnight called *The Dangerous Engagement*
whose only merit was that it was very amusing.'

He clearly greatly enjoyed his stay there, more perhaps than anything else in his life, but he was perhaps more pleased than pleasing.
G. Touchard-Lafosse tells how, as a teenage boy, he called upon
Madame Dupin, then aged 90, and found her full of charm and
fascinating to listen to. 'There, young man,' she said as they passed a
door, 'that was the Genevan bear's den.' Reading Rousseau will give

* Some of these can be seen in the Gallery.

one no idea that he might have played the bear enough to be remembered for fifty years.

Madame Dupin lived to the age of 93. The Revolution passed her by. Was it the memory of Rousseau which protected her? Far more probably it was her endless kindness and charity to all around her which fenced her in with a barrier impenetrable by the hot heads of the Revolution.

She was succeeded at Chenonceaux by Monsieur Dupin de Francueil, who left it to his son-in-law by a daughter of his first marriage, the comte de Villeneuve, who managed also to be a grand-nephew of Madame Dupin and cousin-german of George Sand (Aurore Dupin, Baronne Dudevant) and, like her, descended also from Marshal de Saxe and in a left-handed fashion from Louis XV.

Madame Pelouze, who bought it in 1864, happily did not share the current taste for Gothic ruins, but knew and loved the true Renaissance architecture. Under her, a return was made to as near the original Bohier design as could be traced. Now the château is in the expert hands of the Menier family, to whom every visitor to Chenonceaux owes a great debt. What it has cost to maintain it in its present state of perfection one cannot learn, but the sum must be vast. The same good taste which has guided the maintenance of the exterior for the more than half-century the château has been in the hands of this family, is visible also in the interior. Chenonceaux is one of the châteaux best worth visiting in full.

On the ground floor, four rooms (as we have seen) open on to the vaulted vestibule, and from this unusual beginning the visit is a constant joy. I have no intention of making a detailed list of all the lovely things to see, but will just pick out haphazard a few items which particularly struck me: the majolica-ware flooring of the great Guard Room, the dainty chapel, the carved oak ceiling of the library in the spur across the Cher, the Louis XIII and Louis XIV furniture in the big drawing room and, generally, the very fine tapestries.

More and more it seems to me, as the years go by, that the unique quality of Chenonceaux is its serenity – serenity and gaiety. It is as brilliantly white and cheerful in dull weather as in bright. It evokes none of the dark, depressing days it has known in its long history. It

seems impregnated with irresistible tranquillity, this other 'foster-
child of silence and slow time'.

There is nothing else along the Cher to compare with the combined
interest and beauty of Chenonceaux – perhaps nothing else in all
Touraine, where only Chambord with its very different fascination
can bear direct comparison – but for those who want a lovely drive
from old village to old village through green and heavily wooded
country, with little traffic on the roads, this is a splendid opportunity
for a restful experience. It will lead away from the Loire, but only to
bring you by a fairly straight road across the great bend of the river,
as far (if you like) as Nevers. For most it will be a journey of discovery, for the tourist seldom wanders in these parts.

First along the right bank of the Cher comes Chissay-en-Touraine
and on the way there the road runs at the foot of slopes honeycombed
with caves, many of which have been made into troglodyte dwellings
– warm in winter, cool in summer, and dry as a bone, I have been
told, which is more than can be said for many houses. Chissay is
dominated by the white mass of its château, very impressive from
below. The keep and the turrets are splendid, and if the rest shows all
too strongly what the 19th century did to an old château, the general
effect is nevertheless very agreeable. One cannot visit the château,
which is perhaps just as well for I believe the inside was completely
transformed in the nineteenth century into something more suitable
for contemporaries to live in. Only 2 or 3 miles on and one arrives at
the western suburb of Montrichard, Nanteuil. There is a very beautiful church here, with 12th century transepts and a 13th century nave.
The corbels of the vaults of the nave are carved with the heads of
kings and bishops, and in themselves make the visit worthwhile. The
Lady Chapel extends over two storeys and is said to be, in part, a work
of piety by Louis XI. The great, fierce castle looms overhead –
Foulques Nerra again, overlaid by later work of the time of Philippe-
Auguste and again much later, by Louis XI, and then dismantled by
Henri IV. The outer ramparts belong to the 13th and 15th centuries.

Much, much less impressive but infinitely moving to those who
know the story, told in previous pages, of Jeanne de France is the
parish church of The Holy Cross. In this tiny church poor Jeanne was

married. One looks in amazement at the little nave. How could it have held the great crowds of princes and nobles attending a royal wedding? It couldn't, and it didn't. They were not there, only the immediate family, and as few as possible of those. There could have been many advantages in this: the bride's misshapen body and twisted face could well be considered to demand a private ceremony. What probably endeared the idea to Louis XI was the wonderful saving in expense.

Keeping to the right bank, though in fact D 17 on the left bank is at this point a prettier road than N 76 on the right, a turning off to the left at 6 miles from Montrichard leads through the village of Monthou-sur-Cher to the 16th century Château de Gué-Péan. Two fine Renaissance pavilions mark the entrance to the courtyard, and in front of them two round towers, one taller and fatter than the other, and a little like the stout tower of Valençay when one comes to think of it, which is not entirely a recommendation. One might do better to cut this castle out and spend a little longer amongst the old houses and streets of Montrichard.

A 5-mile leap now to Saint-Aignan, and to the Cher which the road avoids after Thésée. Beam-and-plaster houses distinguish it, and the tall early Gothic church with mural paintings and a Renaissance château. A gross of stone steps leads up to the château, making a kind of monumental entrance to it which the castle itself does not quite live up to. There is a splendid view from the terrace.

This quite improbably pretty village has two industries particular to itself. First, in the infinite caves in the hills of tufa stone is used an adaptation of the Champagne process to the white wines of Touraine: here they sleep their quiet winters through, all fermentation tamed, and in the spring come to sparkling life with the second fermentation and the captivity of this bubbling life until the customer draws the cork. Unless of course the cork gets blown out from within. This plopping of the occasional cork and the consequent wastage of good Champagne I have always thought to be one of the sadder sounds in life. The second industry is the knapping of flints, which was given up for dead in 1935 but, refusing to stay dead, sprang to life again in 1962. There is a museum at Meusnes, 10 miles away by D 17, on the road to Selles-sur-Cher, where the whole art and craft is explained.

It is a little nearer to Selles by N76, to reach it one has to cross the river again, but D17 is quieter and pleasanter. At Selles there are two châteaux which may be viewed, one medieval and the other Renaissance, with some good furniture and decoration. There is also a fine old church, once the church of the abbey which honoured Saint Eusice, a hermit believed to have died in 542 on this then remote site.

Villefranche-sur-Cher need not detain you, but Mennetou-sur-Cher (it is on both Cher and the Canal du Berry) demands a little time. It is a marvellous little sleepy place, still partly contained within the surrounding wall of 1212, which you enter through one of the three town gates, each pierced in a square tower. In the steep and winding streets are houses from the 13th century onwards, and the whole little town might belong to a film set, were not everything one sees and touches so very solid and so very real.

Château de la Ferté-Saint-Aubin

Next, Vierzon, on the top of a hill which puts it 400 feet above sea-level. It still has a town gate with a belfry above, and some lovely old houses which look on the green banks of the Yèvre where it runs into the Cher. A curious mixture, this town of 30,000 inhabitants which in so unlikely a place is a substantial industrial town, making porcelain and glassware and agricultural machinery, a river and canal port (Canal du Berry), and yet boasts so much that is old and river banks which are quite lovely.

It can also be reached from Orléans down the fast N 20 through the upper part of the Sologne: this is a magnificent run through the wood-lands and past the meres. It also runs through the delightful La Ferté-Saint-Aubin, where the château was rebuilt to great effect between 1635 and 1660 to the plans of François Mansart. The river Cosson flows through the broad water moats, which are lined by balustrades of typical 17th century elegance. Though the domain was sold off in parcels in 1863, the château is still surrounded by a large and agreeable park. Lamotte-Beuvron and Nouan-le-Fuzelier through which one also passes are not nearly so attractive, but Salbris, last place on the way to Vierzon, has the most charming brick and stone church, part 12th, part 15th and part 16th century.

For the time being we leave the valley of the Cher to the west; our road is nearer the valley of the Yèvre and reaches Mehun-sur-Yèvre in 10 miles. Of the once very famous 14th century castle of Jean de Berry only two towers still stand. One of them is a gaunt skeleton reaching up into the sky, the other has been restored and houses a little museum. One thing does remain, though, of this 14th century town, the town gate, surmounted by a clock, and very evocative it is.

From here it is a quick run of no more than 20 miles to Bourges, one of the most interesting towns in France and one well worth a long journey to see it. It is also one of the most exasperating for the motorist, but it would lack all its charm if it were not. The street pattern has changed little since the days when Joan of Arc's dauphin was 'King of Bourges'. The Hôtel-de-Ville is just alongside the cathedral; in it is the Syndicat d'Initiatives (Tourist Information Office). I cannot too strongly recommend that you follow the plenti-ful direction panels to the cathedral, park the car and get the free street map of the town. It saves hours, enough to make it possible to leave the car in the cathedral park and see Bourges by foot, which it merits. It also saves one's temper. First, the cathedral.

Bourges has the widest Gothic cathedral in France and, I believe, in the world. The five tremendous portals on the west front set the scale for the rest. Inside one realizes its vastness even more easily than from outside. One steps in, and catches one's breath. The unity of the interior is as striking as its size. Everything belongs together and no ornamentation distracts the eye. There are no transepts. One looks straight down along nave and choir, and the end of the apse seems light-years away. The line of columns is unbroken; a whole forest of columns runs with mathematical exactitude of place to the far, far end. They look slim, but the effect is produced by brilliant use of colonettes which distract attention from their real girth. They make five aisles, each differing in height from its neighbour. This entails three different heights for the windows, the great and glorious and effulgent stained glass windows which must be bracketed with those of Chartres. This indeed is the glory of light and colour being dedicated to the greater glory of God. This first sight of Saint-Etienne at Bourges is a great religious and emotional experience, felt as deeply by the unbeliever as by the believer.

The facts about it are simple. Like Chartres it was built in a single, though protracted, burst of enthusiasm between 1200 and 1260. It is 387 feet long and the nave is 121 feet high. Everywhere it has the uniformity of a masterpiece. Even where repairs have been necessary (as when the north tower fell down in the early 16th century) the repair work has been most carefully matched.

After her divorce, Jeanne de France chose Bourges as her retreat and came often to pray in this cathedral, and in it she was buried. The Revolution destroyed her tomb but, as she was canonized after her death in 1505, one of the chapels bears the name of Sainte-Jeanne-de-Valois.

Another of the chapels is called after Jacques Coeur, and is recognized by the rich ornamentation. It does not house his body, for he died in unjustified disgrace, but the standing and importance of the man can be judged by the Hôtel Jacques-Coeur, which is the finest specimen of Gothic domestic architecture in France.

Jacques Coeur, the man who financed the ungrateful dauphin, lived from 1400 to 1456. He was one of the very greatest merchant-bankers of the middle ages. His *hôtel* was both a rich man's comfortable dwelling house, and a wealthy banker's counting house. The disposition of the rooms, the amusing blank windows in the façade (with a stone carving of a man one side and a woman the other looking out, servants perhaps looking out for their master's return), the strong room to hold his treasures, the two chimney pieces in the gallery carved to illustrate a comic tournament and the assault on a castle, and the decoration in the courtyard entirely derived from the exercise of his business, are all unexpected and captivating. One thing at least is certain – this financier had a great sense of fun.

And then, at intervals throughout these winding streets, the most lovely old town houses. And I have left to the last one of my best loved features of this very lovable town, the gardens next to the cathedral, so beautifully kept, so quiet, and fresh, and restful.

It is 42 miles by N76 from here to the Loire again at Nevers, far beyond Orléans.

Chapter Eight

To Orléans by the Loir and by the Northern Bank of the Loire

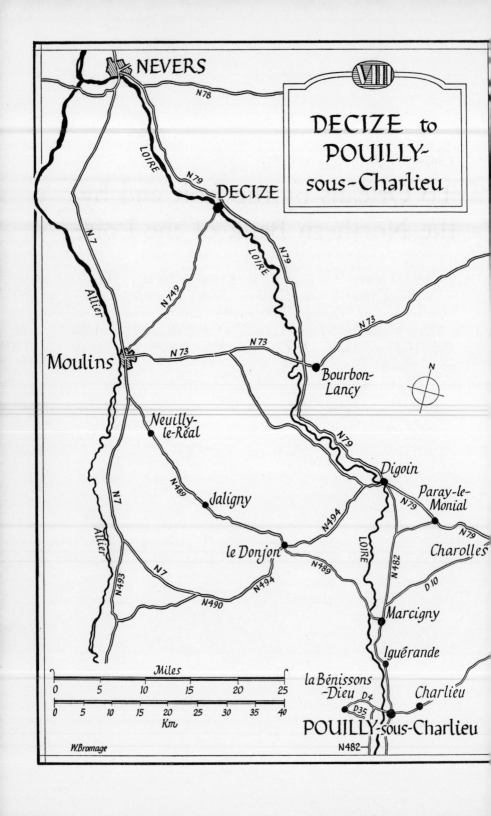

NEVERS

N 78

VIII

DECIZE to
POUILLY-
sous-Charlieu

LOIRE

N 79

DECIZE

LOIRE

N 79

N 7

Allier

N 749

N 73

N 73

N 73

Moulins

LOIRE

N 79

Bourbon-
Lancy

N

Neuilly-
le-Réal

N 489

Jaligny

N 79

Digoin

Paray-le-
Monial

N 79

N 7

Allier

N 493

N 7

le Donjon

N 494

N 489

LOIRE

N 482

Charolles

D 10

N 490

N 494

Marcigny

Iguérande

Miles

0   5   10   15   20   25

0   5   10   15   20   25   30   35   40
Km

la Bénissons
-Dieu

D 4

Charlieu

D 35

POUILLY-sous-Charlieu

W.Bromage

N 482

To Orléans by the Loir and by the Northern Bank of the Loire

If you already know the Loire between Tours and Blois, which is the most frequented section of the river, or if you wish to get away from the traffic along it at a peak holiday period, there is a northern road which is interesting and usually almost traffic-free. Although in interest it has nothing to compare with Amboise and Chaumont, it does have Vendôme and some smaller and quite delightful towns along the Loir. The Loir, it must be remembered, was for long the moat round the outer walls which defended the Loire from attacks from the north. It is a very quiet and pretty river, winding its slow course between prosperous valley slopes as it reaches out towards Châteaudun and Chartres.

Take the road northwards from Tours (N158) and 4 miles out take the left fork on to N159. For 22 miles, almost without a single bend, this road runs through the countryside, now along the edge of green fields, now through thick woods or by the side of copses, and sometimes giving glimpses of the huge pools which are a feature of this flat country. Château-la-Vallière is itself on the river Fare and is a cheerful little country town with nothing particular to distinguish it except its situation. It stands above the *étang de Val-Joyeux*. This word *étang* is very difficult to translate accurately. It can be as small as a pond or as big as a lake. It is defined, in French, as 'a stretch of shallow water in an inland situation'. Even this gives little real idea of what an *étang* can look like, and in this area and in the area between Orléans and the Cher, does look like. Certainly the Val-Joyeux *étang*, well over a mile wide at this point, betrays its shallowness only by its reeded edges, and its stagnation not at all. It is a true lake, well over a mile wide, hemmed in by thicknesses of massive trees.

A one-mile each way excursion to the west to the Château de Marcilly at the hamlet of Marcilly-sur-Maulne is worth-while, but only on Mondays and Thursdays, its sole opening days. It was re-built in 1608 and subsequent years. A bridge over the wet moat leads into the courtyard, open on this site and closed on the three others by well designed if rather stern buildings, in which one can see memen-toes and portraits of a family long attached to the countryside around and devoted to hunting, together with the uniforms and decorations of the members who distinguished themselves in the public service. Altogether a rather touching display of family pride in ancestors none of whom were really famous.

The road is usually close to the Loir for many miles after Château-du-Loir. In many cases these old riverside fortresses were destroyed during the Hundred Years War; with the final defeat of the English, their need had passed. Only the 'château' in the name recalls the warlike past of this peaceful river. It is 6 miles from there to La Chartre-sur-le-Loir and another 4 to Poncé-sur-le-Loir, where there is a lovely italianate Renaissance château, the exact date of which is not known. It has been ascribed to the time of François I, but one would expect it to be amongst the early non-royal works of the Italians Charles VIII brought back with him, or who followed him, if one went solely by decoration. Yet it follows the 'French School' of Azay-le-Rideau and Chenonceaux in its straight-up staircase and very tall roofs. Its unique feature is the staircase in six flights whose coffered vaults are decorated with mythological and allegorical sculptures. Its capitals serve also as consoles for arched beams. They are decorated with heads of cupids of differing designs. The second floor coffers and those of the third floor are lavishly adorned with flowers and animals and even whole sculptured scenes. Outside, this château differs from Azay and Chenonceaux in having discarded the round tower with pepperpot roof for a square pavilion.

The château is not the only reason for lingering in Poncé. The church is also most interesting. The mural paintings are of the year 1180, a date which seems well authenticated, and though they are much faded they are worth the trouble of poring over them. On the

7 The church of Germigny-des-Prés

8 Polignac (Haute-Loire)

north wall there is one in particular which brings a very odd fact to mind. It is the scene of a battle, in which Muslims are fighting Christians, and was undoubtedly in some way related to the Crusades. The odd thing is that the Crusades, a dominant interest in Europe for nearly two centuries, gave rise to hardly any illustrations and this is an extremely rare example of a battle between Moor and European.

A little farther upstream, beyond Couture-sur-Loir, D57 turns off southwards to the Château de la Possonnière, 3 miles away. This is a lovely little Renaissance château, barely more than a manor house, built by Ronsard's father. Here Pierre de Ronsard was born, and never was a poet born in more suitable surroundings. Latin tags, engraved on stone, are everywhere. On the garden elevation it is *Veritas filia Temporis* ('Truth, daughter of Time'), on one of the turrets *Voluptati et Gratiis*, an invocation to sensual enjoyment and seduction by beauty. Against which one must set what is presumably its ending on the first window of the great room, *Avant partir*, before dying, a classical variation on 'Let us eat, drink and be merry, for tomorrow we die'. There are also some religious ones, as a counterblast to the pagan: *Domi*(ni) *oculus longe specu*(latur), 'The eye of God ranges far), and *Domine conserva me . . . Respice finem . . . Avant partir*. This strange mixture of paganism and Christianity runs through all the work of the son. Well might he say, as in that inscription, 'The Lord preserve me . . . Think of the end . . . Before departing'. All who know only his verse might well believe he was the Don Juan of his times. Both he and his friend, Joachim du Bellay, wrote as though the pleasure of the flesh and the senses were all they lived for. Yet both, for the times, led lives morally and materially quite austere. I can no longer trace the quotation, but it is a very apt one: 'They wrote like Epicures and lived like Anchorites'.

This rambling house, extending into caves in the rock, quite literally *caves de vin*, seems much more liveable in than many more magnificent ones. The Ronsards were obviously companionable people, with a great sense of humour. One of the wine cellars intended for 'foreign' wines – that is to say, any not grown within a radius of 10 miles, is cheerfully labelled 'Barbarian Wines'. The entrance to another one is marked with the warning *Sustine et abstine*,

Q

which it might not be unfair to translate as 'take a grip on yourself and don't drink too much'.

Everything is delightfully unpretentious, even the Great Room with its splendid fireplace adorned with the arms of the Ronsards. After all these years, it radiates happiness: for a house still more medieval than Renaissance, it is quite astonishing.

No road quite follows the Loir at this point, and it is best to take a little country road from La Possonnière (D10) and then turn up left on D8 towards Saint-Jacques-des-Guérets. Here again there are wall paintings on a 12th century church, and very good ones, much larger than those of Poncé. One of them, The Descent into Hell, is a particularly fine piece of work, and the largest of all.

One then crosses the river to Trôo, notable for the fine remains of its ancient fortifications. These in the main belong to the 11th century; others are reminders of a rebuilding of the town's defences in the 13th century. A single 12th century wall is what remains of a once famous Lazar-house, of a size to make one grateful that leprosy, this scourge of medieval Europe, is no longer with us. Up the Rue Haute is a considerable colony of troglodyte dwellings, some with arched porches cut out of the rock, and flowers growing in pots on the balustrade of an excavated terrace. Most of them have useful chimneys and the view from above of this colony after climbing up the steep stairs of the Escalier Saint-Gabriel is made highly remarkable by the appearance of these chimneys which overtop the rocks and are, to the eye, connected with nothing. One can go on up and up, ending on the top of a grand tumulus, and look from what seems a great height down a great length of the valley of the Loir, and the picturesque ruins of the once formidable castles of Lavardin and Montoire-sur-le-Loir.

On the road towards Montoire, to the left, one can see the 16th and 17th century Château de Chalay, very decorative. So soon after La Possonnière it will not seem very exciting.

Montoire-sur-le-Loir, to my generation, is associated with the unhappy memory of October 24, 1940, when Marshal Pétain met Adolf Hitler at the railway station, and sold France for an illusory peace. Not at heart a bad man, Marshal Pétain, but a bitter and disappointed one, and cursed with the same philosophy as Talleyrand: 'it doesn't matter what I do, for everything I do is for the ultimate good of France'. Both were men consumed by vanity and both in their generation did untold harm with the best intentions.

The ruins of the once majestic castle are on the top of a hill above the south bank of the Loir. The square keep belongs to the 12th century, and most of the fortifications around it in a very irregular pattern are of the 14th and even the 15th. On the way up to it is the Chapelle-Saint-Gilles, which was part of a priory once held as a benefice *in commendam* by Ronsard. In it there are some very famous murals, many of which are undoubtedly from the first quarter of the 12th century. They include a magnificent Christ sitting in Judgment, with all the apocalyptic detail, and a most interesting pentecostal scene with red rays coming from Christ's hands to touch the heads of the apostles. This apparently is the Palestinian tradition; it is to be seen on the tympanum at Vézelay.

Lavardin, which is only just a step up the river, is very tiny (about 250 inhabitants) and very picturesque. It is also very old, and happily some of the buildings have managed to survive two sackings by the troops of the Plantagenets. The church of Saint-Genest is mainly very early Romanesque and must originally have been part of a 9th century priory. The porch and bell tower show some 11th century low reliefs, but it is above all for its mural paintings that the little place is visited. These are undoubtedly the finest in the region and are being well cared for by the Beaux-Arts. There are both frescoes and distemper work, and they cover the centuries from the 12th to the 15th.

Second only to the church in interest is the castle, which makes the most romantic of ruins. It belongs to the 11th and 12th centuries, and proudly resisted attack by both Henry II of England and Richard I. It covers some 10 to 12 acres, and was triple-walled, with each circle of walls rising a little farther above the hill. The square keep rises 85 feet, and there is a magnificent view for those who care to climb the ladders provided for reaching the sentry walk. From there one can appreciate to the full the powerful position it occupies on the top of this hill and on this bend of the river.

We pick up N817 again north of Montoire. At Les Roches-sur-Loir is the most extraordinary of all the troglodyte colonies. This time there were not enough caves to go round, so those who desired to benefit by all the advantages of a fine, modern, warm cave dug their own out of the rock. This is, I think, the only place where the 'artificial cave dwelling' exists. The direct road cuts out Rochambeau, but it matters little for the château closely connected with Jean-Baptiste Donatien de Vimeur, marquis de Rochambeau, may not be visited. This is very disappointing and I trust only temporary, for I understand there are many interesting records there of this leader of the French forces and hero of the American War of Independence. Instead the road takes one straight to Vendôme.

This is an agreeable and interesting town of about 15,000 inhabitants, well situated on the banks of the Loir, with some fine old buildings. It is also a place which I remember particularly for its very rigorous observance of the sanctity of the French lunch break. Do not expect to be able to do anything except eat and drink between midday and 2 p.m., and it is safer to allow a quarter of an hour either side. No doubt the rapid Americanization of French towns will one day bring in its train lunch-time opening of shops but, at the moment of writing, a great silence falls at noon and lasts the full two hours.

The ancient Gauls had a town of some kind here. Then there was a Gallo-Roman town. In the 10th century it became the capital of an independent county. It is a wonderful thought that this somnolent little place sent an expedition to help throw the Moors out of Oporto, in Portugal.

In 1361, the English came and pillaged it. In 1375 it passed by inheritance to the House of Bourbon. Henri IV inherited it but had to fight for his heritage. He hanged the Catholic governor and dismantled the fortress. His son by Gabrielle d'Estrées, César de Vendôme, was given the town. The last of the Vendôme family died in 1712, and it passed back into royal ownership. It was in the front line for a time during the Franco-Prussian war of 1870, and in 1940 an air attack wiped out one of its central districts.

The church of the Trinity offers, says the guide book, 'a happy succession of styles from the middle of the 11th to the beginning of the 16th century'. 'Happy' is not the adjective I would have chosen. This was an abbey church, and it has one very splendid part, isolated from the rest, a magnificent 12th century campanile, which served both as bell-tower and as a keep in times of danger. Square at the base, it ends at the top in a very graceful octagon, and its stone spire carries a 13-foot high iron cross. With this, its total height is over 260 feet. I think it is a masterpiece of its time and know of no true rival to it. The capitals on the four remaining Romanesque columns of the transept pillars; the 12th century stained glass window in the third of the absidial chapels (Virgin and Child); the 15th century choir stalls and their quaint carvings; these are some of the delightful details I remember of this fine old church.

Then there is the Hôtel de Ville, part of the 14th century town gate of Saint-Georges, defended by two towers, and all the machicolations and crenellations decorated by Marie de Luxembourg at the beginning of the 16th century with Renaissance medallions and designs – absurd, but quite delightful. And there are the quaintest old houses, and the more serious neo-classical brick-and-stone monastery buildings of the 17th and 18th centuries, now forming part of the Lycée Ronsard. It is a small town, Vendôme, and easy to walk round. The walk is really rewarding.

Twenty miles of straight road N 157 and you are back on the Loire again, at Blois. And now we must go back to Tours and see what happens by the shorter and more orthodox routes north or south of the river.

Leaving Tours by the right bank (in this case, the north bank), first comes Vouvray, a prosperous wine town at the foot of the slopes where 'the finest white wines in Touraine' come from. (I quote a wine grower of Vouvray). They are good wines and though I prefer them still to sparkling, the latter also are very drinkable. And having a glass as a refresher is really the best reason there is for being in Vouvray, for it is not an exciting town in its own right. There is really little else to look at for the next 15 miles upstream until Amboise comes into sight.

Although Amboise is bisected by the river, it is not in two equal parts, but it would be absurd, because the bigger and more important part is on the left rather than the right, not to describe it at this point.

Despite the passage of the centuries, the bombing of all the Loire crossings in 1940, the disappearance of the lovely gardens which, like those of Blois, were designed *à l'Italienne*, by Pacello, and the loss of something like half the castle, Amboise remains one of the most evocative of the royal châteaux of the Loire. The royal châteaux work on the imagination with their long histories of war and lust, and intrigue, and violence and gaiety, more than any which remained in private hands.

Certainly also of the royal châteaux Amboise is the oldest. There is a long island in the middle of the river, which makes the Loire easy to cross at this point. Here King Clovis met Alaric II and his Visigoths. This island was made the boundary between their kingdoms. On it they swore eternal peace and friendship. Eternity proved not to be a very long time: in a few years Clovis fought Alain II, and slew him with his own hand, and swallowed his kingdom. The Ile-d'Or, for that is the name of the island, proved in the long run a truly golden isle for Clovis.

To move forward from the 6th century, the little plateau on which the present castle stands has always known a camp or fort of some kind. Certainly there was a Gallo-Roman fortress there. In the 11th century there were two different forts on the plateau, and one in the town, each one a pawn in family feuds which were put into cold storage when a common enemy appeared. Then the counts of Amboise held the town. Then the Crown confiscated it, and Charles VII gave it to his wife, Charlotte of Savoy, as a residence.

Its modern history began when Charles VIII, who came to the throne at 13 and soon threw off the tutelage of his sister, really became king, and a headstrong one, with his marriage to Anne of Brittany. In 1492 he began to rebuild the castle. Two years later he set off to conquer Italy.

Ultimately defeated by the combination of the pope and the emperor, Spain, Venice and Milan, he returned nevertheless weighed down by the booty – furniture, textiles, paintings and silverware, all carried out with the impassioned energy of the Italian Renaissance. With him came the men who would teach their French counterparts, those men who were equally great as craftsmen and as artists. They taught so well, they found in France such receptive minds, which the last phases of French Gothic illustrate, that in a handful of years the French pupils had created a Renaissance of their own, deriving from the Italian, but suited to the light, the countryside and the character of France.

The unique part of Amboise, or at least of the half of Amboise which remains intact, are the two broad towers down to the Loire. One must never forget that the river was, until well into the 19th century, the most comfortable and useful means of travel. Roads were appalling, coaches virtually unsprung, and progress at the rate of a heavy horse, not more than three miles an hour. Wherever the river was wide and deep enough, very comfortable barges going downstream with the current could average a much better speed, and even upstream against the current were no slower, and they did not rock and heel and bump and jolt. It is therefore a little surprising that the Tour des Minimes with its broad spiral ramp up which men could ride, and carts and sledges could be horse-drawn, as they came straight off a river boat, would seem to be the only one of its kind. It was also some sort of fortress, being of a solidity equal to that of the average keep.

Today one enters the castle from a little street between the Town Hall and the church and a tiny square. A ramp leads up to the castle entrance. What one can visit of the castle is the Logis du Roi, pre-Renaissance, a Renaissance building at right angles, the Saint-Hubert chapel. The Logis du Roi was begun in 1491, before the Italian adventure, which is clearly shown by it to have developed but not created the king's artistic imagination and his good taste. See how light and delicate is the gallery of the upper floor, under the roof. See, too, the dormers absolutely bristling with pinnacles which always remind me of porcupines throwing out their quills. These are firm indications of a mind already resenting Gothic discipline and seeking new forms of artistic expression.

The famous chapel is a tiny work of absolute perfection, a jewel by Benvenuto Cellini magnified to the size of a small building would not be more perfect. Completed in 1493, at a time when the Renaissance was knocking at the door. The front faces the gardens, but the east end projects over the rampart and is supported by a massive buttress. There were doubtless at the time excellent reasons for it to bestride the wall, but now it seems just a piece of virtuosity. It has stood already for the better part of 500 years, remarkable in itself. What is

even more astonishing is that in 1940 a shell exploded on a main
cross-beam, yet still the chapel stands in its precarious position.
Further damage was done in 1944, but was less potentially dangerous
to the structure.

Outside the lintel is graced by, on the left, a high relief of Saint
Christopher bearing the Infant Jesus, headless, alas, after a shell

Château d'Amboise

burst, and on the right the Vision of Saint Hubert. This comes from
one originally told of Saint Eustace who, a Roman General under
Trajan, was converted to Christianity by a vision of a stag carrying a
luminous crucifix between its antlers. Unlike Eustace, Hubert had
a real existence. He was the patron of the hunters and trappers of the
forests of the Ardennes in what is now Belgium, most of whom were
still pagans when he set out to convert the region in the 8th century.

On the tympanum above, the Virgin is supported by Charles VIII
and Anne of Brittany, a very beautiful and rather mysterious piece of
work. There is no French artist known to be living at that time who
would seem capable of work of such extreme delicacy and depth of
feeling. On the other hand, it is certainly not in the contemporary
Italian style. It has been suggested that Charles brought artists from

Flanders to decorate his chapel, but no record of this exists. Perhaps it does not matter very much. It does not affect the result, which is that Amboise gives us one of the most lovely doorways of all time, and if one saw nothing else of Amboise, this exquisite piece of work would amply reward one for the visit.

Inside, too, the carvings are immensely rich. The keystones of the vaults have pierced carvings of great intricacy and delicacy. From the terrace one can see Le Clos-Lucé, where Leonardo da Vinci spent the last days of his life, and in this chapel a flagstone tells of his bones resting underneath. Unfortunately this seems most doubtful. François I, who had brought the great man from Italy, given him a pension and the use of Le Clos-Lucé in which he died three years later, seldom came to Amboise after Leonardo's death, but that he had been greatly influenced by Leonardo's ideas is obvious at Chambord.

He did, however, come once, to receive the Emperor Charles V in the Tour des Minimes, which certainly surprised the emperor and nearly frightened him to death. It was all hung with tapestries, and torchbearers stood every few yards of the spiralling ramp. Charles was riding his white horse, and was half way up when one of the torches set fire to one of the hangings and very soon the whole tower was filled with smoke. Some of the soldiers tried to urge the horse upwards towards safety; others thought it would be quicker to descend to the outer air and between the two the bewildered horse just stood still. Eventually all was well, buckets of water put the fire out, the smouldering hangings were pulled down and stamped on, and the emperor, even then not quite sure that this was not an attempt on his life, emerged coughing and spluttering into the fresh air at the top of the tower.

To return to the Logis du Roi, below the gallery is the Salle des Etats which was made into a prison for Abd-el-Kader, the Arab Emir who fought the French in North Africa for fifteen years from 1832 to 1847 in an attempt to make an Arab Empire of his own, and failed. The Salle des Etats was ruined by being cut up into smaller rooms. In them Abd-el-Kader might have been imprisoned for ever, if the newly declared Emperor Napoleon III had not chanced to visit Amboise and to feel a duty to see the Emir. In an emotional interview, Napoleon III promised his prisoner he would set him free, and kept his word. By so doing he made of the bitter enemy of France one of the best friends that country was ever to have in North Africa.

The windows of the rebuilt Salle des Etats (1906) give on to the Balcony of the Conspirators, supposedly the grandstand of the royal family and the Guise clan to watch and rejoice over the terrible deaths of La Renaudie and his Protestant hotheads. It is a horrible story with all the shedding of blood, the treachery, the cruelty and the heroism of Shakespearian tragedy.

Catherine de Médicis was at Amboise, with the boy-king her son, François II, and his little girl wife Mary, the future queen of Scots. And with them were the all-powerful François 'Scarface', duc de Guise, and his brother Charles, cardinal de Lorraine. Corroded by their limitless ambition, successful through their great intelligence and, in the case of Scarface, great physical courage, they made the Catholic party their own, and spurred it on to horrible excesses, though neither of them had a single ounce of true religious feeling. Catherine de Médicis, who saw herself as the mediator between Protestant and Catholic, was at this time entirely in their power. She knew she was unloved in France, she knew she was despised by these princes of the House of Lorraine who were hardly more French than she.

Still further persecution of the Protestants led to an ill-designed and worse managed conspiracy by a man from Périgord, La Renaudie, which may have been secretly but was not openly supported by the Protestant prince de Condé. The conspirators (who were to come in small numbers, unperceived, and join together at Amboise) were betrayed to Scarface.

They were trapped and chased and exterminated in a campaign which lasted a month. They were hung, they were drowned, they were decapitated. Most of this bloody revenge was accomplished at Amboise. Accomplished, too, in the presence of the royal family. Some were hung from this balcony and the convulsions observed in detail from other windows. From this balcony the pleasing sight was offered of others, broken on the wheel, being put into sacks and tossed into the Loire, which on occasion was temporarily choked with corpses.

The carnage went on for days, during which the royal family came out after dinner, 'despite the stench of decaying corpses, to see the grimaces and contortions of those who were still hanging alive from the battlements'. A more partial chronicler, Régnier de la Planche is even more specific. 'In order the better to see the prisoners who had been given over to the cruellest torments, some still booted and spurred, some with body and limbs already broken on the wheel, some decapitated, the gentlemen in their silks and their velvets came and arranged themselves at the windows, with their ladies, as if it were some theatrical performance, without any sign of pity or compassion that was not feigned.'

> Monarchs, terror-stricken, paled and let fall
> From their trembling hands these blood-dyed ghosts . . .

wrote Théodore-Agrippa d'Aubigné, poet, companion in Arms of Henry of Navarre, and ardent Calvinist, who as a boy witnessed part of the proceedings. And one last quotation, the forebodings of the duchesse de Guise which were so soon to begin to be fulfilled. To the queen-mother she said, weeping, 'Madame, Madame, what vengeance is here being got ready for the future . . . blood calls for blood . . . May God save your sons, the princes, and their children'. God did not save them. The sickly little king was already in the last months of his life. Charles IX, after a constantly blood-stained reign, died in convulsions of terror and remorse. Henri III was assassinated. Mary Stuart died under the headsman's axe.

Poor Mary. I think her ghost still haunts Amboise. She was, Brantôme wrote, 'in great dolour (after the death of François II) in the white mourning which became her so well. The pallor of her face vied with the whiteness of her veil, whose artificial bleaching could not compete with the natural snow-white of her countenance'. And as she left France, she wept, crying out *Adieu, France, adieu*, and the new little king, Charles IX, wept with her, regretting, he said that 'I am too young to marry you myself'. And perhaps even her own long imprisonment and grim death were better and easier to bear than to have been queen of France during that sickening reign of the little boy who loved the gay, pretty, pleasure-loving girl.

About half a mile from the château, by the Rue Victor-Hugo, is the Clos-Lucé, where for three gentle years Leonardo da Vinci lived and dreamed and doodled. At the time of writing a great deal of work is being done there: over the years the Beaux-Arts have removed a great deal of later work, have uncovered at least one painting, The Heavenly Choir, which belongs to the school if not to the master and, I believe are on the verge of further disclosures. Rose-red brick framed in white stone, sharply pointed slated roof, square turret – that is the charming manor house of Le Clos-Lucé. In it is the little oratory which Anne of Brittany built for Charles VIII, the work-room and the bedroom of Leonardo and some frescoes and tapestries of the 16th century. There are independent exhibitions concerning the man and his work: models of the machines which he designed, amazingly modern; reproductions of some of his drawings, and X-Ray photographs of some of his paintings taken by the Laboratory of the Louvre Museum. A visit here is to be recommended before visiting Chambord.

On the left bank, 1¼ miles upstream and therefore near enough to be considered as part of Amboise is a very unusual hotel-restaurant, the Château de Pray. It is one of a group entitled 'Châteaux-Hôtels de France' to which is added the formidable sub-title *Gentilhommières, Manoirs et Vieilles Demeures transformés en hôtels-restaurants*, which can be rendered as 'Country seats, Manors and old Residences converted into restaurant-hotels'. This one is an old manor house, with a rectangular centre block ending in two fat round towers, complete with conical roofs, with views of the Loire at the end of a large garden. It has a small number of rooms available for guests and serves a very good table. I will not pretend that you cannot eat as well elsewhere for somewhat less, but the setting is worth the difference in price. If you wish to spend a night or two in a place which though being a hotel has none of the feeling of one, if the idea of sleeping and eating in a small château appeals to you, this is the place for you.

However, we have to be across the river, on the right bank, speed-ing towards Blois by a road which keeps close to the river for most of the way and with very little to distract one from the fine views across it. There is Limeray, with a much rebuilt church which has some fine old statues, beginning with the 14th century, and that is about all worth stopping for on the 21-mile run into Blois.

Blois is situated mainly on the north (right) bank, of which the best view is from the centre of the hump-backed bridge across the Loire. It was built by Jacques-Ange Gabriel and was completed as late as 1724. I find it hard to understand how still in the sophisticated 18th century engineers and architects (Gabriel was an outstanding architect) could believe that if a long bridge were not arched in the middle it would collapse. Another quarter of a century passed before Perronnet found people ready to believe him when he assured them that his flat bridges would be no weaker in any way and stronger in some ways. However, this is not a good place for appreciating the castle which is almost alone in not facing the river but northwards. It is an extraordinary jumble of styles of the 13th, 15th, 16th and 17th centuries arranged as a rough rectangle around an inner courtyard, but in no kind of order of time scale. In one corner is the 13th century Tour de Foix, joined to the next one by the Gaston d'Orléans wing of the 17th century. The next wing, at right angles, is that of François I of the early 16th century. On its far corner is the 13th century *Salle des États*. At right angles to it again is the early 16th and late 15th century Louis XII wing, and we come back to where we started with Charles d'Orléans' gallery of the mid-15th century, and the Saint-Calais chapel again of the late 15th and early 16th centuries.

Its story will help us a little to disentangle this chronological muddle. What, and exactly where, the original fortress was is not known. It was certainly very early indeed, perhaps Merovingian. The famous (or infamous) Thibault the Trickster may or may not have built the first one of which there is any kind of proper historical record: certainly he could have done. The Châtillon family took over, knocked down Thibault's fortress and went on building for the next century a dark medieval fortress of great military strength and no comfort at all. The Tour du Foix, in the far left-hand corner as you enter from the Place du Château remains from this era, and the early part of the Salle des États, which for long was France's equivalent of Westminster Hall.

In a most dishonest and rather novelettish manner Blois passed from the Châtillon family to that of Orléans. It seems to have been the regular thing in nearly every act of the long drama of the French monarchy that the villain of the piece would be an Orléans though, as we shall see, there were one or two exceptions. At this time the comte de Châtillon had married a young wife with a very pretty face, a face which came to be admired by a younger man than the husband, a veritable prince charming, the duke of Orléans, brother of the king. Orléans, always pleading poverty, extracted large sums of money from his mistress, which she in her own way wheedled out of her husband. Eventually there was no more ready money in the Châtillon coffers. There was nothing for it but to sell the château. Then the wife discovered that Orléans never had needed the money, but had tucked it all away with the bankers and was able to produce it to buy the château. It did him little enough good. He died from the hand of an assassin.

His son, Charles, was the loser at Agincourt. He was taken prisoner and lived a quarter of a century in England, by no means unhappy and writing some very sweet and wistful poetry. Finding himself a widower, he decided to marry again. His bride was Mary of Cleves, who had, like Juliet, reached the mature age of fourteen. There was, of course, some discrepancy in age – a slight matter of 36 years. The marriage completely rejuvenated him and he set about demolishing a good part of the fortress and building for his young wife and himself something more approaching a suitable love nest. Of this more delicate building, only a simple but immensely pleasing gallery remains, near the chapel site on which his son was to build.

All things come to him who waits long enough. He had wanted a son, and after 21 years, when he was 71, he got it. What bawdy tales were in circulation concerning this late birth one can imagine, but it seems they troubled the proud father not at all. They gave the boy the royal name of Louis, and in due course he became Louis XII, after the death of his cousin Charles VIII.

Louis XII's equestrian statue surmounts the gate by which you enter, which is fitting enough, for this was his wing, of which the external elevations are in stone and brick. The ground-floor is an open gallery; the pillars are decorated with the fleur-de-lys, and alternate with columns delicately arabesqued.

Whatever we may think of the behaviour of Louis XII towards the unfortunate Jeanne de France, it is impossible to deny that he was a good king for the times. Anne of Brittany was a sobering influence, and she proved a businesslike helper in the affairs of State. France knew a period of peace, and suddenly the arts flourished, and the

Château de Blois

very cradle of the Renaissance was Blois. Louis' natural good taste had much to do with it. For example, in 1499 he brought Mercogliano from Italy to design new gardens for the château, which were three-dimensional of the kind that can still be seen at Villandry, but on a much larger scale. They have not existed for many centuries now, having been built on to make new streets, with the unhappy result that the justification for Louis' new home turning its back on the river cannot be properly appraised: it was done for the sake of the gardens which were the marvel of Europe as seen, northwards from the château.

To such an extent had the new ideas triumphed that the François I
wing, built only twelve years after his father's, belongs to an exciting
new world. The richness and inventiveness of decoration baffles
description. This was a time when the creative genius of France rose
to its highest level. If Italy had supplied the foundations, France
built gloriously on them. Everything is made to look so easy, however involved the pattern, however unusual the design and the
medium. I believe that such must have been the case: this decoration
was an outpouring of a country's artistic feelings which endless war
had suppressed for a hundred years. The monumental fireplaces, the
ingenious decorative use of emblems some of which, on the face of it,
would in any other age have presented the gravest problems of
satisfactory use as elements of decoration, and above all the stupendous staircases, repay and more all the time you can spare in studying
them. Of all the staircases, Blois remains the public's favourite. It
was a pioneer, to be much copied. Instead of the staircase being
contained within a cylindrical tower, as the spiral ones were,
this one has an octagonal cage, three sides of which are recessed
into the building whilst the remaining five project on to the courtyard. The cage is an openwork one, with walls cut away to leave
what are in effect pillars at each exterior angle so that stairs and
balustrade slope up from pillar to pillar. At all times, with the king
in residence, there must have been endless coming and going on it,
and when there were games or jousting in the courtyard it was an
excellent grandstand, and on ceremonial occasion gave room for
an impressive number of guards to stand and light it with their
torches.

At Blois, one meets another tragic bride, Anne of Brittany's now
motherless daughter Claude: one more step in building the indis-
soluble tie with Brittany which was the desire of each succeeding
king. The young Claude was duly married at Saint-Germain-en-Laye
to the young king François I. There was no wedding feast, for as soon
as the ceremony was over, the bridegroom changed into hunting
dress and was off after the forest deer. A few days later, the plain and
sad-faced bride arrived at Blois. She returned to her old home ('her
face spoiled with weeping') with a solitary wagon containing all her
personal effects and wedding gifts. The gift from the bridegroom was

not some priceless stone, some jewel-set crown, but 'a four-post bed, and a counterpane'.

In financial affairs François maintained a strict neutrality; as long as someone supplied all the money he needed, he did not in the least care who it was. Spending lavishly, he attracted to his Court artists, musicians and poets and made the corps of Maids of Honour, very strictly disciplined under Anne of Brittany, a new power in the land. From his reign to the end of the French monarchy, women were all-powerful at Court. François spent other people's money with a free hand. It was claimed that when the Court was in residence at Blois, it supported, directly and indirectly, about 15,000 people.

Henri II came to the throne. Also the unfortunate Catherine de Médicis, sneered at by the high French nobility as 'a Tradesman's daughter', from the commercial origins of the Medici. She was an artful and scheming woman, with a great deal of native Italian subtlety. For this she was greatly disliked by ordinary people. She tried to keep peace in France and was, for considerable periods, more successful than most people care to remember. She suffered in her family to an extent which might well have driven a lesser woman out of her mind. She had little defence against the Guise clan, who could at any time have raised the rabble against her if she had not to some extent fallen in with their plans.

Small wonder then that she took to astrology. Her own private astrologer, Ruggieri, seems to have been as big a fake as any other. Her Cabinet at Blois has walls covered in carved wood, 237 panels in all, four of them being beautifully disguised doors to cupboards, whose workmanship is a joy to see. Inevitably, these were supposed to be her 'poison cupboards'. There is not one iota of historical support for this, nor any reason at all to believe that, directly or indirectly, she ever poisoned or attempted to poison anybody. As every kind of virus disease, apoplexy and heart attack was supposed to be the result of poison, we surely have a most exaggerated idea of the numbers who died this way. As Catherine had brought from Italy the fashion for beauty products, unguents, face paints and face powder, it was probably these she hid in the four marvellously concealed cupboards.

On the second floor, just above Catherine's Cabinet, reached by a

R

staircase still known as the *Escalier des Quarante-cinq*, are the apartments of Henri III, which were the scene of the assassination of the duc de Guise. So little have they changed that it is possible still to re-enact it almost perfectly. It took eight men of the forty-five to kill an unprepared man, whilst the king watched from a hiding place until he was sure that his rival was dead. He leaned down and slapped the face of the corpse. 'God!', he said aloud, 'how big he is. He seems even bigger dead than he did when he was living'. He hurried below to tell his mother: 'I have no companion to share with now,' he said gaily, 'for the king of Paris is dead'.

The more dangerous Guise was dead, but there remained one living Guise still. The king gave the word, and armed men fetched the cardinal de Lorraine and took him to a cell. The next day – it was Christmas Eve in the season of Peace and Goodwill – he was murdered. Their bodies were burned on a fire, and what was left was thrown into the Loire.

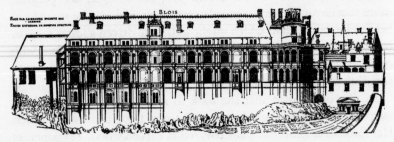

Château de Blois – garden elevation

Came the feast of Christmas, and Henri was happy. The too powerful Protestants had been taken care of by the massacre of Saint Bartholomew. The too powerful Guise brothers had been taken care of by treachery and assassination. Henri could rule in peace. He could rule in peace, but only for a year, when he would be assassinated in his turn by a monk, a fanatical supporter of the Catholic League through which the Guise clan had won power.

He was succeeded by the king of Navarre, King Henri IV of France for whom Paris was well worth a Mass. The royal connection with Blois was all but over.

There still remains to account for the neo-classical wing, the wing of Gaston d'Orléans, count of Blois, brother to Louis XIII. To keep him interested in something other than his perpetual conspiring, Louis encouraged him to rebuild his château of Blois. Gaston set to work to create something that would have been the size of Versailles had it ever been finished. With Mansart to design it and speed the work on, the huge wing was built in just three years, including destruction of so much of the old that the loss still hurts. It was all to be very elegant, and very classical, and to look out on gardens stretching away to a false horizon, as was done at Versailles, because Gaston was sure he would make it a royal palace as soon as he came to the throne. He never did: when all hope for an heir had been given up, the future Louis XIV was born. Gaston gave up, and stopped the building. In his old age he could not bear to live in what was to have been his kingly palace, and with more sense than he had shown for most of his life, he went on living in what was left of the Renaissance wing.

When he died, the royal connection was broken. And today? Today Blois is unique in the opportunity it gives to study in a single place three periods of architecture, with good specimens of each. I find myself equally attracted by its architecture and its history, and repelled by its vast empty spaces. It is always possible to people such places in one's mind, but I find both more and more difficult to do as I get older.

Five miles up from Blois, between the main road and the river, with delightful gardens running down to the water's edge, is the Château de Ménars. We can run rapidly through its not very exciting history.

At the very beginning, Ménars was a little house owned probably by some middling rich man. This house, whatever it was, came up for sale in 1637 and was bought by Guillaume Charron, a maker of wine casks and a wine merchant. Basically, today's great house was his, with the exception of the two additional wings which detract rather than add to its appearance. He went on adding acres to the property, until it was so magnificent that in 1654 Louis XIV authorized its carrying with it the rank of vicomte. A nephew inherited in 1669, one Jean-Jacques Charron, who had a sister, Marie. Marie was at this time, and had been for 21 years, the wife of Jean-Baptiste Colbert, who shone with much of the reflected glory of Louis XIV, whose minister he became. Jean-Jacques Charron went on adding, and improving, and making the gardens a little paradise, so Louis agreed to increase its rank, and it now carried with it the title of marquis. Finally there came the day when the Charron of his generation ceased to have any interest in it, and sold it, with the title, to a lady born Antoinette Poisson, better known to us all as the marquise de Pompadour. By that time its value had risen to 880,000 *livres*.

She used to come down to it for a few days every quarter, and watch over the gardens and the rebuilding which was in the hands of Gabriel, architect to the king. As far as is known, Louis XV never visited this possession of hers, which she owned only for four years before her death.

It was her brother, the marquis de Marigny who inherited and went on embellishing. Much of what he created in the way of the final disposition of the grounds has lasted to the present day.

The exterior of Ménars, which is very uniform, very widespread, very plain and altogether in the simplest version of neo-classical, is to my mind rendered disproportionate by the extreme length of its façade; imposing, yes; beautiful, no. But all the little buildings and those delightful gardens are a pleasure to visit. So, too, is the interior, every detail of which is perfect. With just enough furniture to give it an atmosphere, it is not impossible to see La Pompadour, with her quick, bright eyes, taking in every detail, advising on the colour of a wall, the covering of a chair, the placing of a table. But it is above all in the gardens, still ornamented with some of the urns and vases and busts which she must have known – in the garden to which she gave as much time as she could, and which she loved, that one most easily feels the presence of this, the last of magnificent mistresses of kings, the cleverest, the most artistic, the most successful of them all. I quote from an unknown 19th century author: 'The descent from her reign of grace and decorum to the boisterous vulgarities of Dubarry was profound . . . She secured her reign to the last hour – no sooner had she closed her eyes than she was forgotten'.

If one feels that this thought is a sad one with which to leave Ménars, I would like to suggest a more cheerful one. Ménars belongs to the Compagnie de Saint-Gobain. What it costs the company to keep this lovely château and these magnificent gardens, I have no idea, but I do find so heartening that a great industrial concern should serve the community in this way, without any attempt to get any kind of advertisement for their action.

A short distance away, at the far end of the great park of Ménars is Cour-sur-Loire, where one can spend a few very pleasant minutes at the 15th and 16th century church, which has some very fine 16th century stained glass. Then speed on to Mer, and turn left there to Talcy.

This is another of the unpretentious treasures of the Loire. Why it stands on this not very exciting plain when the lovely river flows only 6 miles away is not easy to understand, unless one considers that the peace of the countryside compensates for loss of views. It is very tranquil here, and must always have been so. Seen from the outside it is a little forbidding, with its keep and its crenellations and machicolations. A door leads one through the keep; the other side, on the right, one can see the delightful residential wing, with an arcaded gallery on the ground floor. The upper floor carries two pointed gables whose sloping edges are adorned with crockets. It is simple and delicious, as, on the kitchen-garden side, is the immense dove-cote, most successfully out of proportion with the house, and very old wine press, under the walnut trees. Has the wine press really served for 500 years? I think with repair work done each year, that probably it has.

One now realises that the frown on the outside is a mask intended to keep unfriendly people from coming nearer and that the true visage of Talcy is the smiling one behind the mask. For sheer charm, I would give this precedence over all others mentioned in this book, but then I am influenced by sentiment, and not just architectural achievement. Once I believed the generally accepted statement that it was built by Bernard Salviati, cousin of Catherine de Médicis, about 1520, but with further study of the internal evidence I am certain that it was no more than a rebuilding, chiefly inside, and that the structure is at least a generation earlier.

Bernard Salviati had a daughter living with him in this château, a little fifteen-year-old Italian blonde. Staying with him he had a poet,

Pierre de Ronsard. To little Cassandre, Pierre wrote some very beautiful poems. I do not think he loved her in the ordinary sense; a certain distance kept alive a purer passion. Did she love him? If so, not for long. He was older than she, and deaf, but she must have been wonderfully flattered by the poems he made of her and for her.

In these quiet and lovely surroundings I find it easy to imagine the deaf poet just catching the tapping of her shoes as she comes hurrying down the pre-Renaissance spiral staircase, and seeing the blush of pleasure flushing her face as he steps forward to offer her a new tribute from his pen. This is how, at least poetically, he saw her:

> The childish beauty of her fifteen years,
> Her golden locks rippling into many a curl,
> A rose-pink brow, a fair youth's soft-hued cheeks,
> A smile that lifts my soul towards the stars;
> A virtue worthy of her beauty,
> A snow white neck, a snow white throat,
> A heart mature within courageous breast,
> A very human lady, her beauty near divine;
> An eye so bright it turns the night to day,
> A hand so soft it smoothes away my cares
> And in its fingers holds my very life;
> By a song sweetly sung,
> By a smile, or a sigh –
> By such enchantments
> Are my senses enslaved.

The great dove-cote, with its 1500 pigeon-holes, provided many comparisons for his poems. His room overlooked it, and from it one imagines came the germ of that fragile ode beginning:

> My little lady dove,
> My dear, dear little beauty,
> Joy of my eyes, come, kiss me!

And as the autumn evenings drew in, and the two sat in the great room and watched Cassandre's mother spinning, whilst she talked, or read by candlelight, the germ of one of his most famous poems doubtless began to sprout.

Quand vous serez bien vieille, au soir, à la chandelle,
Assise auprès du feu, dévidant et filant,
Direz, lisant mes vers en vous émerveillant:
Ronsard me célébrait, du temps que j'étais belle!
... n'attendez à demain;
Cueillez dès aujourd'hui les roses de la vie.

When you are very old, at dusk, by candlelight,
Close to the fire, talking and spinning,
You will say, as in wonderment you recall my verse,
'Ronsard sang my praises in the days when I was fair.'
... Wait not for the morrow:
Life offers you its roses; begin to pluck them now.

In 1562 Catherine de Médicis, in one of her many efforts to reconcile Catholics and Protestants (which historians prefer to forget), brought together in this gentle setting the Guise clan, representing the Catholic Church Militant, and the Condé clan, representing the Protestant factions, though where they all put themselves is difficult to imagine. Nothing came of the effort, of course. To the Guise family, the Protestants were a formidable barrier to the realization of their ambitions. To the Condé supporters, the Guise clan were blood-stained oppressors. Catholics never admitted Catholic atrocities, Protestants never admitted Protestant atrocities. When two sides in a dispute are equally determined that the other is not to be trusted in any peaceful solution, it takes more than even a queen of France can offer to bring their quarrel to a close.

Another 8 miles upstream is the busy and pleasant town of Beaugency. It has a remarkable bridge across the Loire, 1,444 feet long, and 22 arches, which at first sight are all of very different designs. A second look corrects this impression, though the bridge always remains a quaint oddity. Many of the arches, but not the six 16th century centre arches, had to be rebuilt after 1940 to the original design. On the fourth arch there used to be a tiny chapel for the pilgrims to Saint James of Compostela. English pilgrims crossing to northern France and Normandy; pilgrims from the Low Countries and Germany; French pilgrims from the north, the east and the Paris region, all met in Tours to cross the Loire, and continue on towards the Pyrenees and the roads of northern Spain, but they by no means all crossed at Tours. If they were going to take a road farther inland, through the fat lands of the Périgord, they crossed at Beaugency.

The *Tour de César* had nothing to do with Caesar, but is a fine rectangular keep of the late 11th century. Once a covered way led from it to the rest of the castle. The present castle is 15th century in the main, with some earlier parts, and may be visited. The church is, as is usual in this part of the world, quite interesting but not outstanding. The Hôtel de Ville, on the other hand, although rather heavily restored in 1893 – a bad period for restoration – has not unduly suffered, and remains a very pretty Renaissance building. In the Rue du Puits-de-l'Ange (which was presumably a fountain surmounted by the figure of an angel, rather than one at which an angel appeared) is a most rare and interesting example of a fine town house in the Romanesque style, of which nearly all were rebuilt in a Gothic style; this Maison des Templiers is well worth looking at, even if the Knights Templar were once again given the credit for something they did not build.

Meung, 4 miles on, used to be the residence of the bishops of Orléans, and although their château can be glimpsed near to the church, it cannot be visited. The church itself is partly 11th century, partly 12th and mainly 13th: it is interesting but again not outstanding.

And 11 miles up from Meung, we arrive in Orléans.

Chapter Nine

By the South Bank of the Loire to Orléans. By La Sologne to the Loire above Nevers

Mountlouis-sur-Loire – Château de la Bourdaisière – Amboise forest – Chanteloup pagoda – Chaumont-sur-Loire – Château de Beauregard – Celettes – Cheverny – Chambord – Saint-Laurent-des-Eaux atomic station – Cléry-Saint-André – Château de la Source – The Loiret – Orléans – Germigny-des-Prés – Chécy – Jargeau – Châteauneuf-sur-Loire – Saint-Benoît-sur-Loire – Sully-sur-Loire – Gien – Cosne-sur-Loire – Argent-sur-Sauldre – Aubigny-sur-Nère – La Verrerie – Morogues – Villegenon – Parassay – Château de Maupas – Sancerre – Saint-Satur – Pouilly-sur-Loire – La Charité-sur-Loire – Nevers – Bracieux – Fontaine-en-Sologne – Mur-de-Sologne – Lassay-sur-Croisne – Château du Moulin – Salbris – Romorantin – Quincy – Reuilly – Issoudun – Ardente – Nohant – La Châtre – Châteaumeillant – Culan – Saint-Amand-Montrond – Bruère-Allichamps – Meillant – Charenton – Ainay-le-Château – Tronçais forest – Meaulne – Bourbon-l'Archambault – Moulins – Dompierre-sur-Besbre – Digoin – Charolles – Baugy.

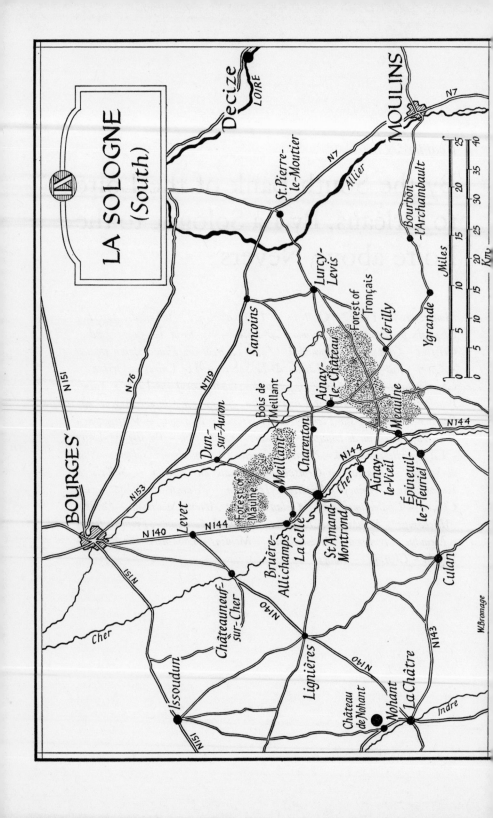

LA SOLOGNE
(South)

IX

Decize
LOIRE
MOULINS
N7
Allier
N7
St-Pierre-le-Moutier
Bourbon-l'Archambault
Lurcy-Levis
Forest of Tronçais
Cérilly
Ygrande
Sancoins
N151
N76
N719
Bois de Meillant
Ainay-le-Château
Méaulne
N144
BOURGES
Dun-sur-Auron
Meillant
Charenton
N153
Cher
N144
Ainay-le-Vieil
Épineuil-le-Fleuriel
Levet
N140
N144
Forest of Maulne
Bruère-Allichamps
La Celle
St-Amand-Montrond
Châteauneuf-sur-Cher
N140
Culan
N15
Cher
N140
Lignières
N143
Issoudun
N15
Château de Nohant
Nohant
La Châtre
Indre

Miles
Km.

W.Bromage

By the South Bank of the Loire to Orléans. By La Sologne to the Loire above Nevers

Coming out of Tours on the left (south) bank of the Loire the first place one comes to in just under 8 miles is Montlouis-sur-Loire, on a slope of a hill in which a number of dwellings have been excavated. It is the centre of a small wine-growing district, whose wines have a good reputation. A mile and a half away to the south-east is the Château de la Bourdaisière, in which Gabrielle d'Estrées may have been born in 1565. The present château is no more than a reconstruction of the 16th century style, with the exception of a few remaining parts of the original château built in 1520 by Philibert Babou, another of the great financiers of the time of François I.

Continuing along N751, one comes at the very outskirts of Amboise to a right turn on to a little side road which runs through the Forest of Amboise and takes one to the Chanteloup pagoda. It is one of the oddest sights imaginable to find this Europeanized, full-size pagoda standing upright in the middle of a French forest. For an explanation of this very expensive joke we have to go back to the days of Louis XV. In the early days of Louis' life, the château of Chanteloup was built for Jean d'Aubigny, but nearly all trace of this massive building has now disappeared. Choiseul bought it at the time when he was the trusted minister of Louis XV. It is probably to his credit rather than otherwise that he fell foul of Madame du Barry, who gave the king no peace until he agreed to exile Choiseul to his estate at Chanteloup. No term was fixed for the exile, which lasted for four years.

The duc de Choiseul was a man who made friends, and kept them. Even whilst the king was frowning on him Choiseul's friends kept him company, and there were those who found this rival Court at Chanteloup preferable to the king's at Versailles.

When Choiseul's exile was over, in memory of the kind friends who had risked a king's anger to come to him, he decided to build a pagoda, on the same pattern as the one that had been put up in Kew Gardens in 1762. Those, at any rate, were the instructions given to architect Le Camus, but what went up (taking three years to build) was something on a much bigger scale, about 125 feet high, with six floors diminishing in size to make a rough pyramid. To make this *Chinoiserie* even less Chinese in appearance, the whole thing stood on a circular peristyle, with sixteen each of pillars and columns. It was, it seems to me, a conscious parody by Le Camus of the temporary fashion for things supposedly Chinese.

And there it is, 'the grace of Versailles bearing aloft the time-honoured silhouette of far distant Cathay', the only pagoda in the world with a classical colonnade, four wrought-iron balconies and Louis XVI style decoration throughout.

It is a fantastic place to visit, with the circular room of which each floor consists diminishing in size as one mounts by means of the inward staircase. The ornamental wrought-iron hand rail carries at frequent intervals the 'C' of Choiseul. The marble tops of the round tables on the first floor had, so the tale goes, hurriedly to be turned upside down, as on them there were the names of all those who had visited Choiseul during his exile, and these would be too handy a guide to the Revolutionaries for their proscriptions if they were left visible.

The view from the top of the pagoda is magnificent. The whole splendid sweep of the Loire from Tours to Blois is unfolded, with all its forests and woods and fields and parks and châteaux. This view is unique.

Up the little road to Amboise, then along by the river again for the 11 miles to Chaumont-sur-Loire, another of the really famous castles.

With its great round towers it is a most satisfying sight, everything
that a formidable castle ought to be, commanding the most splendid
views of the Loire, and shining white as if it were the subject of an
illuminated miniature.

There is no point in going into the quarrel between Louis XI and
the House of Amboise which led to the original fortress being totally

Château de Chaumont

dismantled in 1465. His quarrel with Pierre d'Amboise did not last,
and the estate was handed back. Immediately the construction of a
new castle was begun. Pierre died before it was completed, but the
work was carried on by his eldest son, Charles I of Amboise. On the
latter's death, his son, Charles II of Amboise, continued with it and
completed it in 1510.

When Henri II died in that unfortunate joust in 1559, Catherine de
Médicis began to be a real queen instead of trailing along behind
Diane de Poitiers, who even took the children's education out of her

hands and, seeing what happened to them, made a thoroughly bad job of it. The next year, the queen bought Chaumont. Meanwhile, Diane had thought it discreet to retire to Chenonceaux. Then came the wronged queen's only act of revenge. She enforced the exchange of Chenonceaux for Chaumont.

As far as I can trace the course of events, Catherine never stayed at Chaumont. She had bought it for the exclusive purpose of exchanging it for Chenonceaux. It is therefore not a little surprising to be shown 'Queen Catherine's bedroom' in the east wing, complete with canopied bed and furniture and tapestries of the time of Louis XIII. Even more remarkable is the cold and uncomfortable room in a corner tower which was, we are told, 'Ruggieri's room'. It has its own interest, for in it hang a portrait of the astrologer and two of the queen, but it hardly seems possible that he was ever there.

Chaumont was once a square built round a big courtyard, but in the 18th century the north side, which commands the view over the Loire, was knocked down. One enters over a drawbridge, between the two great round towers of the south-east corner. Above the doorway are the arms of France, and the initials of Louis (XII) and Anne (of Brittany). At the foot of the sentry walk, the double 'D' of Diane de Poitiers. Under the porch is a mosaic of a wild boar, a tribute to Diane as the Huntress. There is nothing at all to remind one of Catherine, which strengthens the belief that she never lived there, or intended to. On coming into the courtyard, one can see that the western (that is the left hand) building has been left very much as it was built, but that the other two were substantially altered in the 19th century. Here, too, are the memories of Diane. Her room was in this eastern wing, the room in which, often awake through the night, she dreamed of her strange past and lived again, perhaps, through some of the great days. If she was Henri's mistress, she was also his business manager, and a very sound one. She was more a mother than a mistress to him, and he had a deep need of mothering. In their love there can have been little passion. She was in her way a very great woman and once she laid down the effective reins of government nothing went right for France or France's kings.

There is no very direct route from Chaumont to Cheverny and it is

best to continue upstream by N751, and in Blois itself turn down to
the right on to N765/156. The two separate a mile or so down, where
it is necessary to follow N156, even though N765 is to be rejoined
later. Another mile or so down, by a little road to the left, one reaches
the Château de Beauregard. This admirable property was bought in
1550 by Jean du Thier, one of the four secretaries of Henri II. This
highly cultivated man was the friend of Ronsard, who sang his
praises in his verses. The first château was built on the foundations
of what had been a hunting lodge of the Bastard of Savoy. The great
Italian painters and woodworkers of Fontainebleau decorated the
interior. A financier once again, Paul Ardier, bought it in 1631 and
between that date and 1638 added the return wing. At the beginning
of the 19th century, Madame de Gaucourt decided to modernize it,
during the course of which disastrous attempt the chapel which
Nicolo del Abbate had decorated with frescoes was pulled down.
Most of the damage was happily put right in our own times by the
present owner.

The most interesting thing in Beauregard is Paul Ardier's gallery
of portraits, real and imaginary, of 363 of France's most notable men,
many of which have been copied to hang in Versailles, but the whole
house is full of delightful things.

Then back down the little road to the village of Celettes (the very
ancient, probably Merovingian, carved bone reliquary of Saint
Mondry in the village church is interesting) then across again to
N765, and down it to Cheverny.

This is a château not like any other we have yet seen. It is situated
in a great park, and looks out on such splendid trees that I do not
know where one could go to find more beautiful ones. The same
family has been in possession, with a few breaks, since the present
château was completed in 1634. Before that it belonged to the elder
branch of the same family. Raoul Hurault was a secretary to Louis
XII, and built the first château in 1510, where the outbuildings are
today. In some way that is not yet clear – for the discovery is quite
recent – Diane de Poitiers bought the property through or from her
estate manager at Chenonceaux in 1551; during her ownership three
small pavilions were added to the outbuildings and were the work of
the same master-mason whom the architect, Philibert Delorme, had

employed at Chenonceaux. She sold it back to the Hurault family, to Philippe Hurault. In 1582 it was raised to the honour of carrying with it the title of comte. In 1634 Henri Hurault, comte de Cheverny,

Château de Cheverny

started to rebuild it entirely, in the style of the period. In 1755, through lack of a direct heir to the elder branch of the family, it was acquired by the comte d'Harcourt, in 1764 by the comte de Saint-Leu and in 1795 one of the Revolutionary Clubs put forward a proposal for its demolition, which fortunately did not take place. In 1825, the cadet branch of the Hurault family, in the person of the Marquis Hurault de Vibraye, was able to buy it back. Today it belongs to the Marquis Philippe de Vibraye.

It is very imposing, all of one piece, very serious and without a single frivolous touch – a narrow centre piece, an identical wing each side, two identical corner pavilions, the various elements having roofs at differing heights which break any monotony without destroying the pattern.

In its furniture it is unique, as it is in its pure 17th century decoration. Because it is lived in and fully furnished with the right period furniture, it gives an impression of wealth and aristocratic living which we have not seen elsewhere. The rooms are fascinating, from the simple majesty of the Guard Room on the first floor to the ornate luxury of the King's bedroom.

As no king ever slept here, the latter needs a word of explanation. When the king gave permission for it to be built, he retained the *droit de gîte*. This meant that when he wanted to spend the night there (if, for example, his hunting in the forest of Cheverny had gone on later than he expected) he had the right to call for shelter and bed without warning. The king's bedroom must always be kept fully prepared for his arrival. And Cheverny is still waiting for him to come. The superb bed is entirely covered in white Persian silk of the 15th century, embroidered with once magnificent but now faded flowers. The king from his bed could follow, through a series of 17th century tapestries, the fortunes and misfortunes of Ulysses. If that bored him he had only to look up to the ceiling to study the painted story of Perseus and Medusa. Then there are thirty painted panels telling a complicated story from ancient Greece about a princess of Ethiopia, abandoned at birth by her mother, adopted by a High Priest, herself made a priestess of Diana at Delphi, then secretly affianced to a Thessalonian youngster, whom she follows on board a Phoenician ship headed for Egypt. They are captured by pirates, and separated. Then the chances of a war bring them into the possession of the king of Ethiopia where they, 'making full circle of their banishment, amazed meet'. The princess's real identity is disclosed, the young Thessalonian is proved to be a powerful prince in disguise, they marry, and all is gas and gaiters. I can guarantee that working that story out from the thirty painted panels is an incomparably better sleep-maker than counting sheep jumping a stile, the sheer improbability of which worries one enough to banish sleep.

s

There is a Cheverny pack, for this is hunting country, and a very pretty sight the huntsmen make in their uniforms, if you have the chance to see them. The hounds you may see in their kennels, but in my opinion it would be better to do so when a heavy cold prevented the proper functioning of your organ of smell, unless, of course, like some fear-filled travellers, you never journey without a clothes-peg.

This is a noble château, nobly maintained. There is no exact parallel to it elsewhere in France.

It is 10 miles across the forests to Chambord, the phenomenal Chambord. It stands in an enormous park of nearly 14,000 acres (now a game reserve), surrounded by a wall which measures over 20 miles in length. The château itself is a huge oblong, measuring 170 yards in length and 120 in depth. It is claimed to have 440 rooms, but I have lost my note on the fantastic number of windows. There are six round towers, sixty feet in diameter, which make other round towers one has seen look like rickety children. As one approaches it, all the lower part appears to be of simple and perfectly ordered uniformity of design. The whole, however, is surmounted by a roof on which all the architectural flowers of the Renaissance have blossomed at the same time and in the same place.

There is a stupendous lantern, apparently infinite turrets, and dormers, there are 365 chimneys (a figure one has to take on trust), there are stone bells, and cupolas and little steeples, and carvings and decorative details rich in invention and lavish in execution. It is, to repeat a phrase I first used many years ago, 'the skyline of Constantinople on a single roof'.

And how did all this come about? The main lines of the story are well enough known, but the bare bones do not build up into a very satisfactory skeleton. It began, of course, with the sport of kings, hunting. This huge forest, not then separated from its neighbours as it is today, was a wooded heath rather than the unbroken woods which the term 'forest' has since come to imply. It was very rich in game and lent itself admirably to hawking. This part of the vaster forest was a long way from Blois, at least 12 miles from the nearest point on the perimeter of the present park, and when the counts of Blois were late in running down a deer, and the daylight began to fade, the long return over rough ground was not welcome. The first building here, then, was a simple hunting lodge where the counts and their huntsmen could spend the night.

In 1519, François I, a passionate devotee of hunting and owner of the domain, had the hunting lodge knocked down and plans prepared for a more formal residence. Nothing fully explains why that

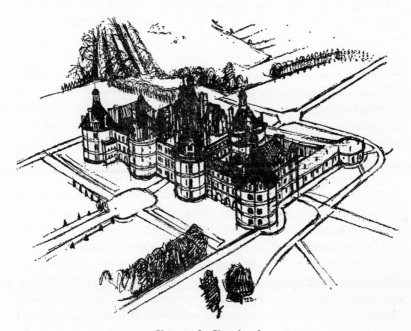

Château de Chambord

residence had to be a real palace, situated in a damp and inaccessible part of the forest, with no views other than of the forest itself, and far from any possibility of water transport or properly made up road.

Romantically-minded historians have told of a love affair with some near-by châtelaine. From all that is known of François, this is not impossible, except for the total absence of any near-by châteaux which might have had pretty young châtelaines. If such were the sole reason, why a palace when he was perpetually short of money? And who was the lady? There is no historical record of her, and none of those who tell the story give her a name. This explanation, then, can be discarded.

Human beings are complex creatures. It does seem possible therefore that several different reasons led François to this extraordinary choice of site. The very unsuitability of the site was a challenge. Out of the wilderness he would create a paradise. Versailles gives us a later example of just this desire. He wanted a palace free from the centuries of other historical tradition of which Blois and Amboise were all too well supplied for so vain a man. Here *he* would be the tradition; there would be no past glorious figures connected with it to diminish the lustre of his own glory. He wanted a palace for which all the credit would go to him, not just improvements on or additions to other men's creations. He wanted a place where, when he desired solitude, he could find it. At the same time it must be fit to receive the ladies of the Court, and it seems probable that he himself laid down the requirement that the flat roof could be used for the ladies of the Court to watch for his return from hunting expeditions.

Who the architect was is another mystery. Names come and go in the building records over fifteen years. Dominici de Cortone is now often put forward as the probable architect; he was one of the architects of the Hôtel de Ville in Paris (the one burnt down at the time of the Commune). French names occur, Pierre Neveu or Nepveu, Denis Sourdeau, Jean Gobereau and, as General Superintendent of the work, François de Pontbriant, governor of Loches and Blois. There is indeed a whole succession of names, as if masons came and masons went, but that the unity of design did not suffer from the change. The only name that remained constant throughout is that of François himself.

The more I consider this problem, the more firmly I come to the conclusion that the answer is there: there was, properly speaking, no architect other than François himself. He had the technical help of men such as de Cortone, and local men such as Pierre Nepveu, but he, in his own mind, held the master-plan. He also had the help of a much greater man, living not too far away, at Le Clos-Lucé – Leonardo da Vinci.

The moment that this thought comes into mind, so many things fall into place. Now that the da Vinci notebooks and sketch books have been published, 'the skyline of Constantinople' can be seen in them over and over again. He had a period of doodling, when his mind ran on oriental skylines with towers and minarets crowding in on one another. The contrast between the apparent mathematical regularity of the lower stories and the Arabian Nights effect of the ornamented roof is something that would have appealed to the

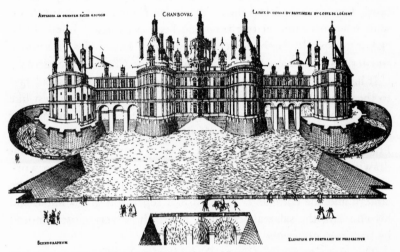

Château de Chambord – front elevation

old maestro. The way his mind worked would lead to something of the sort. And when we come to the staircase, his combination of mathematical knowledge and vivid imagination is needed to explain it.

Behind the façade which greets the arriving visitor is the courtyard and in the courtyard is the square keep, and in the very centre of the square keep is the most famous of all staircases, the Chambord double spiral. It rises straight up to the lantern, which itself rises another 108 feet above the top floor of the building. It is so arranged that the person on one spiral can see and call out to a person on the other, but the two can meet only on the ground floor or the top. It is very beautifully executed and decorated, but remains an architectural and (for the times) mathematical *tour de force* rather than a practical addition to the palace. It must have been little more than a show-place; after all, there are another 62 staircases for day to day use!

Here again, the Leonardo da Vinci sketch books give the strongest clue to its designer, for it must not be forgotten that this was the very first of its kind and the work of a brilliant innovator who must have been heard of again, who must have designed others of its kind, had he lived. But this year, when actual work had started on Chambord, Leonardo da Vinci died. And in his sketchbooks you can see with what his mind at one time had been occupied – spiral shells, elaborate spirals, both dexter and sinister. Lay a dexter upon a sinister, and you have the double spiral of the Chambord Staircase.

It has been said before that the roof looks as if François had said to the assembled masons, do, each of you, that which you best like to do. If there was no architectural overlord other than François that might be getting towards the truth, though I can more easily visualize François calling them together and showing them a da Vinci general drawing of the finished roof and getting them on the spot to work out where everything could go in relation to the fixed ones – the lantern and the chimneys. The constant repetition of his initial and his emblem, the salamander, show clearly how very closely indeed he had been associated with it.

The work went on. François' children were left unransomed in Madrid because he had not the money to pay the ransom – his own ransom, for which the captivity of his children was the guarantee – but money for Chambord could always be found. This I think is a further pointer to the predominant place Chambord occupied in his mind; such obsession is more easily explained if he were indeed personally responsible for its creation and its design. He even proposed to alter the course of the Loire to fill its moats, a scheme which Leonardo da Vinci would have loved to plan for him. Chambord was near enough finished in 1539 for him to receive the Emperor Charles V there. He had guaranteed the safety of the emperor and his troops who wished to cross France in order to put down a rebellion in the Low Countries. The emperor had hinted that if François agreed, it might be possible to come to some arrangement about the Milanese, source of conflict between them. Nothing came of it, and French historians have waxed very indignant at the emperor's conduct in breaking his word, but though he may have hinted, nowhere is it on record that he actually promised; if he did, François was not in a position to complain of other people's broken promises. Whether it was just the architecture and the furnishings, or whether it was his greeting on arrival 'by a swarm of young women dressed as Greek goddesses who ran in front of his horse and strewed his

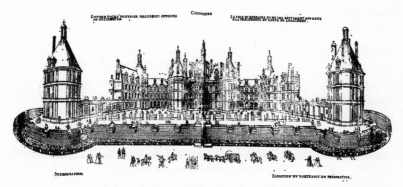

Château de Chambord – rear elevation

path with flowers' which also inclined him towards praise-giving, the emperor pronounced Chambord to be 'the epitome of human industry'.

No doubt he was taken to admire the roof terrace with all its wealth of carving and design, and to admire its suitability as a grandstand to watch some military events, and tilting and displays of horsemanship below, which was one of its major purposes. And surely something else will not have escaped that sharp, cold eye of his: a dainty cupid chasing a salamander, in a niche of the staircase – a perfect summing up of the king's life. And before that life was over, the wreck of what had been the handsome, graceful, daring young king is claimed to have cut upon a pane of glass with the diamond in his ring, *souvent femme varie, fol qui s'y fie*, woman is fickle, 'tis folly to trust her. The basis of this legend would appear to be quite different. Brantôme is the only writer who claims to have seen anything of the sort: the other chroniclers are repeating hearsay only. He tells how he went to the empty Chambord one day and was well received by the caretaker, who remembered him and his family, and took him round to see it.

"Having taken me to the king's room," Brantôme writes, "he showed me something written by the side of the window. 'There, Monsieur' he said, 'if you have never seen my Master's writing, there it is.' And, reading it, I saw that there were these words, written in big letters: *Toute femme varie*, all women are fickle." So it seems a case of saying good-bye to the diamond, the pane of glass, the direct reference to the duchesse d'Etampes who supposedly had just been caught deceiving him.

There always remains something unfinished in a place the size of Chambord, and Henri II went gently on with it. It has few enough associations with him, the principal being when he there received the German princes for the signing of a treaty which brought Metz and Toul and Verdun into France.

François II and Charles IX came to Chambord, and with all the ebullient youth at Court, the double staircase came into its own for little love games of greater and lesser innocence. The next king to come was Louis XIII, but he soon passed it to his brother, the Gaston d'Orléans whom we have already met at Blois. His little daughter, *La Grande Mademoiselle*, used the staircase for games with her father of the same kind as the innocent ones of the loving couples of earlier reigns, but a more pleasant aspect of a most unpleasant man.

Louis XIV loved his Chambord; in it we can see the germ of Versailles, another palace built in the midst of a wilderness, another case of fantastic efforts to bring water to it from long distances (only this time at the cost of many millions and many lives) and another case of overwhelming size.

The theatre came too, when the king was there. Molière presented *Monsieur de Pourceaugnac* for the first time, and the king was not amused, which meant that nobody else dared to be. Lulli the composer was taking part, and to save the day jumped off the stage, feet together, on to the orchestral harpsichord, which he went right through. The king laughed, so the Court laughed. The king went on laughing during the rest of the play, but whether at Molière's wit or at the memory of Lulli's clowning we do not know. It was much the same with *Le Bourgeois Gentilhomme*; a morose king hardly laughed at the first performance, but at supper told Molière in a loud voice that he had enjoyed it. Then the courtiers remembered that they, too, had enjoyed it, and the second performance was a great success.

Versailles was now in, Chambord was now out. Louis XV had no further use for the latter, and presented it to his father-in-law, Stanislas Leczinski, until recently king of Poland. He lived in it from 1725 to 1733, and turned the King's Cabinet of the days of François I into his oratory, and had the moats filled in.

Next came, in 1748, Maurice, comte de Saxe, then 52 years of age and still a great but unrepentant sinner. He was the hero of the Pyrrhic victory at Fontenoy and, ironically, a bastard son of Augustus of Poland who had driven poor Stanislas Leczinski off his throne.

The marshal lived in state with six of the cannon he had taken from the enemy and two regiments of cavalry, formed from a tough selection of Cossacks, Tartars and Wallachians, together with a handful of Martinique Negroes, and a tougher collection of hard-bitten soldiers can seldom have been known. Their ponies from the Ukraine were just about as tough as their riders. They ran free in, and fed themselves on, the forest, but came at a trumpet call.

The marshal's affairs with actresses were notorious and disgraceful. Already, twenty years before, he was generally believed to have been responsible for the sudden and horrible death from poison of Adrienne Lecouvreur, the supreme actress of the Comédie Française. She was refused Christian burial, for the uncharitable maintained that she had taken her own life, but this was never proved. She had to be buried without benefit of Church at the end of her own garden, and later the city authorities took over part of the garden for street widening and, all unknowingly, made a road over her pathetic grave. Not until 1952 did workmen digging down to the foundations of a Paris street find her skeleton.

At Chambord his victim, La Favart, was blackmailed by his monstrous bullying of her actor-manager husband to appear on the stage where Molière played. The marshal was powerful enough to see that the poor man was not employed by any other theatre. He gave in, came to Chambord to produce and act, and to see his wife carried off to the decrepit marshal's bed.

In two years the old marshal was dead (some said in a duel which was hushed up) and the great days of Chambord were over. It was gutted at the Revolution. Napoleon gave it to Berthier, who sold most of the hardwood timber and never lived in it. In 1826 it was bought by public subscription and presented to the infant duc de Bordeaux. He was the *enfant du miracle*, the posthumous son of the murdered duc de Berry, second son of Charles X, last of the legitimate French Kings. In 1830, when Charles X was driven out of France by his own folly, Louis-Philippe solemnly undertook to be regent for the little duc de Bordeaux, but kept the Crown for himself. The Duke might have been king of France, but refused to serve under any but the white flag of Joan of Arc and so, like his grandfather, threw away his chance of reigning. Eventually the State bought his château.

The furnishings of Chambord are dull and shabby and give no idea of what it was like in its heyday. Better nothing at all than these scattered remains of a past glory. The decorations in stone are marvellous and are not improved by a miserable handful of pictures, some of doubtful authenticity, and the playthings of the little duc de Bordeaux. The staircase, of course, must be seen. And when you have finished admiring it, ponder for a moment on how unpractical even genius can be. It was built to rise without break to the top, and nobody stopped to think of the inevitable consequence – the world's coldest and most violent draught! So floors and ceilings had to be put in to keep down the draught, but that completely spoiled the artistic end, the unbroken view of this elegant and complex structure from base to top.

As you walk away, have another look at the outside, for one particular thought may not have struck you. It is in every respect a marvellous piece of assymetry which manages to retain a general but false impression of symmetry. It is obviously quite deliberate. And that brings me back to Leonardo da Vinci. Who else in that time and place could or would have thought of that piece of whimsy, or had the knowledge to make an overall plan which the master-masons could freely follow? And who else had authority enough to get the king to accept it? I rather think that François I enjoyed the joke.

· · · ·

From Chambord, D112 leads across a corner of the forest back to
N751 again, and for the next 15 miles there is nothing of outstanding
interest except perhaps a glance at the atomic power station on the
Loire near Saint-Laurent-des-Eaux. Cléry-Saint-André is worth
stopping at to see a relative rarity for this part of the world, a vast
flamboyant Gothic church, with strong historical connections.

The basilica of Notre-Dame was rebuilt entirely during the 15th
century by Charles VII, by Dunois, the companion in arms of Joan of
Arc and principally by Louis XI (the result of a vow taken during the
siege of Dieppe in 1443). The tomb of Louis XI, destroyed during the
Revolution, has been re-created from original designs which fortunately still existed. To it has been added the very fine statue of Louis
by Michel Bourdin, of the early 17th century. The white marble
kneeling figure is a masterpiece. So is the Chapel of Saint James,
florid in design, but remarkable in its workmanship. This was the
offering of two brothers, Dean Gilles de Pontbriant, and François de
Pontbriant who, the next year after the completion of the chapel, was
put in charge of the works at Chambord.

After Cléry comes Orléans, 8 miles away, but before going into the
city it is a good idea to turn off to the right on D13 which goes
curving round to the source of the river Loiret. This is in the grounds
of the Château de la Source, and is quite a phenomenon. The river,
which is only 7½ miles long, springs into life fully grown, and very
much the same width as it is when it flows into the Loire. It begins in
a circular basin about 250 feet across. Immediately it forms a quite
reasonably sized river. This must be considered *the* source. About
140 yards down the nascent river one finds a second source, emerging
from a hole in the very bed of the river. The whole is phenomenal and
one is not surprised to learn that the temperature of the water never
goes above 60°F, it also never freezes. What regulates it is the subject
of much learned argument. Many believe that the little river is fed
by an underground stream deriving from the Loire itself.

The park in which all this takes place is the Parc Floral de la
Source, which is quite beautiful, and open from April 15 to the end
of October. A quarter of a million bulbs are in flower from the
opening into May, then come 50,000 irises and similar flowers until
September; from June to September 100,000 rose trees bloom; from

July to October there is a display of 150,000 annuals, and 15,000 each of begonia and dahlia, and all this against a background, all the year round, of over 5,000 conifers and decorative bushes. This is a truly marvellous display, and though the charge for admittance is a little high, it is certainly worth every penny of it.

The short journey to Orléans is through Olivet, a pleasing suburb with at least one very agreeable hotel, and a number of restaurants just above river level, but way down from road level.

Orléans is a spacious and agreeable place, very modern in large part after suffering very heavily indeed from bombing during the 1939–1945 war, but with some interesting old houses and churches nevertheless still remaining, and its cathedral. This cathedral is most astonishing as it is in effect a pastiche work which has taken centuries to complete. A Gothic church, to replace an earlier Romanesque work which was threatening to fall down, was begun in 1287 and still not complete in 1586. In that year:

> Protestants in a state of frenzy broke into the cathedral during the night, loosened the base stones of the four pillars of the transept, pushed in hollowed logs carrying a charge of gunpowder for temporary support, attached to the transept spire long ropes which they threw down to men waiting below, and laid a train to the gunpowder. When the signal was given, the train was lit, the cables were attached to teams of horses and pulled also by crowds of Protestants. When the train reached the hollowed logs, the gunpowder blew up, the crossing collapsed, the spire came hurtling down, and nave and transept crashed with them.

This incredible account seems nevertheless to be true.

Each monarch, from Henri IV to Louis XVI played some part in the restoration of the cathedral, but the whole of the rebuilding was done in the same style as the parts that were spared of the Gothic building. Nave and choir are 17th century, the transept a little later, the aisles nearest to the towers early 18th century, the towers and the façade late 18th century. The way that they all marry happily is a source of endless astonishment when one thinks of so many other cathedrals, which in a single building incorporate five or six different styles. Orléans is unique. It is very light and handsome inside, and one that should be visited.

Orléans is full of Joan of Arc, with celebrations every year, and many shops selling Joan of Arc souvenirs, but the sad thing is there is nothing left to remember her by. The nearest one can find is little more than a name, the Quai du Fort-des-Tourelles, the place where Joan was wounded by an arrow. You cross the river by the fine new bridge, the Pont Georges-V, and turn sharply left. A commemorative plaque on the parapet marks the medieval bridgehead, and in exceedingly dry summers when the river has shrunk almost to nothing, it is possible to see the foundations of the ancient bridge. In 1949, in record low water, coins and other ancient objects were recovered, but with more recent flow control this may never happen again.

In a grand slow bend, the Loire just beyond Orléans has reached its most northerly point, and begins the south-easterly part of its long journey towards its source. It passes by Chécy and Jargeau, where Joan of Arc fought the English and, 11 miles from Orléans, reaches Châteauneuf-sur-Loire. The château is no more, but in its place a modern building housing the town's administration. Around it is a pleasant park, open to all, spread over something like 100 acres, where at the end of May and beginning of June the rhododendrons are a splendour. From here one takes a little local road, close to the river, which the main road has left, to Germigny-des-Prés.

Here is a very early Romanesque church, much restored, but with features as old as any known in France, and therefore perhaps the most genuinely old of all. From the decorative tamarisks which mask the south side to the solid square bell-tower, it presents a combination of strength and beauty rarely so well achieved. It began in the year 806, when Theodulphus was bishop of Orléans as well as abbot of the near-by Saint-Benoît-sur-Loire. It was built in the shape of a Greek cross, with four apses. A nave was added in the 15th century, but it has not yet lost the air of newness due to a well-intentioned but rather too drastic restoration in 1865–1869. However, one must remember that if this particular restoration had not taken place, there would be no church here at all today. What is so magnificent is the ancient yet perfect mosaic in the semidome of the east apse. It was unearthed at the beginning of the 19th century from under endless coats of whitewash and very carefully cleaned and replaced in the 1840s. It shows the Ark of the Covenant of the Lord, complete with angels and cherubim. The experts believe it to have been brought from Ravenna, and it might have been amongst those which Charlemagne was authorized to remove from that city, when he took it from the Lombards in 774, to decorate his palace at Aix-la-Chapelle. There are something approaching 130,000 tiny glass cubes, coloured gold and silver (the mark of Ravenna mosaics) and green and purple. The art is Armenian, but how the artist was found and brought to this remote hamlet to mount it is a mystery.

D60 leads straight down to Saint-Benoît-sur-Loire, whose 1,300 inhabitants compare pitifully with the 15,000 who once lived here as dependants of the great abbey, known at first as the Abbaye de Fleury. Fleury was a very holy place in the time of the Druids. It was about the year 650 that Leodebod of Orléans founded the Benedictine monastery, which grew immensely in power and wealth and popularity after one of the monks went to Monte Cassino (then in ruins after sacking by the Lombards) and returned with the body of Saint Benedict.

Fleury became a renowned educational centre under Charlemagne and Charles the Bald, having up to 5,000 pupils. A number of the monks became able illuminators and copyists, so that it held an exceedingly rich and precious collection of manuscripts. After the Normans had inflicted great damage, fortifications were built round it.

It adopted the Cluniac rule, and continued to prosper. It grew so rich that Louis VII was able to borrow from it the money he needed for the Crusade. Its abbots became commendatory. Odet de Coligny was one, and Richelieu another. Unfortunately for the abbey, Odet turned Protestant (he was the elder brother of Admiral Coligny, the Protestant leader) and retired from the scene accompanied by a very large part of the abbey's treasure.

In 1792 it was declared National Property, and all but the church was destroyed. Monks of the Benedictine rule returned to rebuild the abbey in 1944, and in 1959 it officially became one again.

It is the church with which we are concerned, as a magnificent example of Romanesque. It is in the unusual shape of an archiepis-copal cross, reserved for the churches of mother-abbeys. One enters through a porch-tower of the beginning of the 11th century into the big nave (1150–1220). The transept is 12th century, and beyond it is the funerary monument to Philip I who died in 1108. The chancel is pure Romanesque (1070–1110), which marries well with the pointed arches of the nave. Particularly interesting is the central pillar, the axis on which all else turns.

The relics of Saint Benedict are in the crypt (about 1070) which communicates with the chapel of Saint-Mommole, earlier probably by at least another century.

For a man who has exercised such enormous influence, very little is known about Saint Benedict. He was born at Norcia, in Umbria, about 480. He died at Monte Cassino in 547. After some unsuccessful attempts to establish the kind of rule he desired in other monasteries, he established the very famous one at Monte Cassino. Here he drew up his own monastic rule, which he described as 'a school of the Lord's service, in which nothing harsh or rigorous should enter'.

This marvellous church retains all the atmosphere one might expect from a place which has known a thousand years of prayers and supplications. Perhaps it is good for all of us from time to time to enter these ancient places of worship and to feel their atmosphere and to remember that a thousand years ago men could build to last, to the greater glory of God.

The charming village of Sully suffered heavily from bomb damage in 1940 and again in 1945, but it has been well rebuilt and is a cheerful place – one, incidentally, in which the little Hôtel de la Poste provides magnificent food in homely surroundings and creates a pleasant atmosphere which makes one sorry to leave it. Its château is, in a way, the very last one that belongs to the Loire valley.

It is a medieval fortress, as seen from the outside, but once within its outer walls there is a very pretty Renaissance dwelling, Le Petit Château, which makes a delightful contrast to the dark and heavy fortress. They both stand within broad and deep moats, by the side of a river spanned by a long and graceful suspension bridge. The old castle has sturdy round towers and corbelled sentry walks, which can have seen little change since Joan of Arc was here. Inside, on the first floor is a dark room where the king received, and next to it an immense hall which served as an ante-chamber. Above them both is another huge room with perhaps the most splendid chestnut rafterwork the Middle Ages have left us. Perhaps here, but probably in the

Château de Sully-sur-Loire

one below, Joan had her interviews with the king who had the inimical de la Trémoïlle at his elbow. The first time she was fresh from her triumphs in the field, and carried the day against the king's favourite. They set out from Sully for Reims, Joan radiant that her dauphin was at least really on the way to be made king like his predecessors in the cathedral there, but de la Trémoïlle out of temper, and the king, as usual, petulant and vacillating. However, he was crowned and anointed, and Joan went forward in an attempt to seize Paris. It failed, and when fighting weather began again next spring, she returned to the king at Sully.

This time there was no aura of success. All through the month of March 1430, she was kept hanging about there, waiting for Charles to make up his mind, virtually a prisoner. In April she was allowed to go, and doubtless with thanks in her heart and on her lips, she rode again down the green banks of the Loire. Only a single month ahead of her was capture by the Burgundians, and less than a year ahead trial, condemnation, the stake.

If the old château is all Joan, the new one is all Sully. Maximilien de Béthune, future duc de Sully, bought the property from the de la Trémoille family in 1602. First of the great line of able statesmen who made France a major world power, he was also an able soldier, leading the Protestant forces of his master, Henry of Navarre, to victory at Coutras and at Ivry. He was no less successful as a financier. When he took over, less than half the taxes raised reached the king's exchequer. In thirteen years he raised the State's income from nine to twenty millions. In 1590, there was not a penny in the chest. In 1609 there was a float of twenty millions.

Subsequent members of the Sully family had no such greatness. The young Voltaire fled there from Paris, when he was expelled for insulting the Regent. Here he wrote comedies, and flirted with the young women. The duc de Sully of that time amused himself by turning Le Petit Château upside down, making study into dining-room and bedroom into salon, at which his ancestor must have turned in his grave.

On the whole I think that the old château, with its evocations of Joan of Arc, is the one that lives in the memory. It is a fitting one to be the end really of the castles of the Loire Valley. What is still to come belongs to another Loire region altogether, different in climate, in appearance, and in people.

We still follow N751 along the left bank of the Loire. The river is seldom visible along this stretch and we only meet it again at Gien, 14 miles from Sully. As one crosses the hump-backed bridge, there is an excellent view of this agreeable town, much of it still looking new after the rebuilding. The church, new and most successful example of modern ecclesiastical architecture, and the château, stand out above the new houses to make a wonderful scenic composition. The church is new, except for the imposing square tower, all that remains of the original church built by Anne de Beaujeu, eldest daughter of Louis XI, in the 15th century. She adopted Gien, and gave it the present castle and bridge, and made it the town it is.

The church which had to be rebuilt entirely, save for that grand

T

square tower, is now in reinforced concrete entirely brick clad, including the round pillars and the splendid vaults. It is very warm-looking and light inside with some remarkable modern stained glass which, with the capitals of the pillars, may well be what sightseers come first to see in the generations yet to come. These capitals are quite extraordinary. Those of nave and chancel were the work of Henri Navarre, those of the side aisles of Georges Muguet, who between them have made architectural history, for these rivals to the old Romanesque carvings in stone are equally explicitly historiated, but in terracotta. They tell of the life of Joan of Arc, the story of the creation of the world, of the evangelists and the patriarchs, the prophets and the apostles, of Eden and the Paradise that was lost and of the crafts of this part of the country. Indeed, in a very different way, they have recreated the entire medieval tradition of the historiated capital.

The castle was built by Anne de Beaujeu in 1484. It is one of the most handsome of all those which adorn the banks of the Loire; it is entirely in brick with slated roofs, and no longer belongs to Touraine or the lower Loire. This marks the transition point; it would not look out of place in Burgundy, towards which the Loire is now steadily turning. Saint-Sauveur-en-Puisaye, in the Yonne, is well under 30 miles away as the crow flies, and Auxerre no more than 45. So the walls of the castle reflect two separate styles: their sole decoration is the geometrical pattern of black bricks on the red bricks – looking, as it were, towards Burgundy – and the occasional use of a contrasting white stone – looking towards the style of the Touraine.

The castle today is given over to a large, well-arranged hunting museum, of which I am unable to give a useful account. However, those who know better than I, say that it is very well carried out.

The 25 miles or so from Gien to Cosne-sur-Loire, up the right bank of the river, are not very interesting, except where, at Briare, the canal is carried over the river on a bridge and from river level it is quite excitingly unusual to see a barge floating above one's head.

Infinitely more rewarding is to re-cross the river at Gien and speed away on the flat, straight, fast N140 the 12 miles to Argent-sur-Sauldre, a delightful little bucolic town, having a château once associated with the duc de Sully, of which the grounds are open,

and a 15th century church, and an attractive setting on the meander-
ings of the Grande Sauldre, which is very much smaller than its name
might lead one to suppose.

Our main destination, though, is 5 miles south of here, the delicious
little Aubigny-sur-Nère, so rich in its associations with the Stuarts
that I am surprised more Scots on their way south by N7 do not
make this little detour. Its street pattern still shows clearly how once
it was a little circular, walled town, with the houses clinging to
church and castle. It can be traced to Gallo-Roman days, as Albinia-
cum, then disappears from history to reappear in the early middle
ages as belonging to the Chapter of the Abbey of Saint Martin of
Tours. The interesting Gothic church is named after Saint Martin,
and it is of a transitional Gothic architecture very rare in these parts.
The people, however, felt that the abbey was neglecting them, and
appealed first to Louis VII and later to Philippe-Auguste to take over
the town. The dynamic Philippe-Auguste was the one to act on
their request: in 1189, Aubigny was taken into the royal domain.
He soon built ramparts and gave the town a new and prosperous
life.

It was then a royal town when Charles VII, who had called on
Scottish help against the English they both so much detested, made
his constable, John Stuart of Darnley, the gift of Aubigny and the
surrounding countryside as an expression of his thanks for the
brilliant service he had rendered the French Crown. That was in
1423; by 1425 John Stuart was in residence, and the Stuart dynasty of
Aubigny had begun its reign. This continued until the town was
taken back in 1672, after the death of the last male heir of the Stuarts
of Aubigny. There were distinguished issues of this family, for
following John Stuart who was the first commander of a Regiment
of Scots Guards in France, there was his successor who became a
lieutenant-general in the forces of Charles VII. This Berold Stuart
was not only Captain of the Scots Guard, but commanded the French
forces in Italy. Robert Stuart was both marshal and ambassador.
Edmé Stuart, duke of Lennox, who had much influence on James VI,
the future James I of England, was one of those who conspired to
free Mary, queen of Scots and restore her to her throne. Ludovic
Stuart of Aubigny, son of the duke of Lennox and Richmond, was a

pupil at Port-Royal, became a canon of Notre-Dame in Paris, and Grand Almoner to the Queen.

Louis XIV, the year after he took Aubigny back into the royal domain, attached a dukedom to it, and gave it to Louise de Penan-coët de Kéroual, better known on this side of the Channel as 'Madame Carwell', or Louise de Keroualle, or duchess of Portsmouth, the subtle, baby-faced Bretonne who was so deeply involved, as the mistress of Charles II, in all kinds of pro-French plots. She was the mother of Charles Lennox, duke of Richmond. She took up residence in Aubigny at the death of Charles II and lived in it, and improved it, until her own death in 1734.

On her death, the property passed to the duke of Richmond, and his successors held it until 1834 when his cousins brought a most involved law suit which, had they been successful, would have lost him four-fifths of the value of the property. So he sold it, lock, stock and barrel, with all its rights and appurtenances, and closed all further British contact with Aubigny. He won his case, but had no wish to enjoy a French title or a French property.

It was not only Stuarts who settled in Aubigny, for many more humble Scottish families also came. They put up the glassworks and cloth mills which gave Aubigny its prosperity for many generations.

The castle built by Robert Stuart in the 16th century, now houses the Town Hall, but may be visited with the permission of the mayor (and a tip to the concierge). It has been much altered, but the entrance with its pretty corbelled turrets is of his time, and the keystone of its arch carries the arms of the Stuarts. The house which was once that of Charles VII has in its corner post a recess in which the 'B' of Berold and the 'A' of Anne Stuart can be traced in the complicated pattern of arabesques. This house is now called La Maison du Bailli. And the Stuart arms are again to be seen on the vault of the part of the church which was destroyed by fire and rebuilt by Robert Stuart in the 16th century.

There are further memories of the Stuarts not many miles away, at the Château de la Verrerie. This was the summer residence, and went with the town of Aubigny. To reach it, take D7 south-east from Aubigny for 7 miles, then turn right on to a local road (D89) which leads to the castle. It is the prettiest of mainly 15th century châteaux, decorated anew in the 16th. It went with Aubigny to the duchess of Portsmouth, and was sold in 1841 by the duke of Richmond to the marquis de Vogüé, whose descendants hold it to the present day.

The main building is the earliest and has in the middle a hexagonal turret holding the spiral staircase. It is closed at one end by the chapel, which has a turreted porch, and at the other by an outer protective wall ending in a square tower. A later building is in brick and white stone and is on very well designed arcades. The whole, with chapel, and square tower, and round tower, and water to set it off, is very lovely. It may be visited on Sundays and public holidays from Easter, and from Whitsun every day between 2 and 7 p.m.

Because the distance involved is not very great, I think it worth continuing to Morogues before turning away to regain the banks of the Loire. For this, one takes D 89 eastwards to Villegenon, then D 7 and D 11 southwards through the pleasant hills to Henrichement, then D 12 from Henrichment to Parassay, where D 59 turns up to the left to the Château de Maupas at Morogues.

I have the happiest memory of my one visit to Morogues and the Château de Maupas, which still belongs to a marquis de Maupas. It is a much restored 14th century building, with a great round keep and rectangular wings. It stands in its medieval strength amidst the most formal and feminine French-style gardens. It is the true residence of the Maupas family, and one is received with old-world courtesy by an old-world butler, who explains the house to you with such delightfully good manners that if there were nothing at all to see inside it to visit it would still be a real pleasure. The Louis XV restorations (one should really call them rebuildings) make for good rooms inside, which are well furnished. There are many mementoes of the duc de Bordeaux (or comte de Chambord, after the château was acquired by the public for him) and his mother, the little Neapolitan Princess Carolina who became duchesse de Berry, set the fashion for sea-bathing at Dieppe and for climbing the Pyrenees (to the horror of high society), and who set up a one-woman revolt against Louis-Philippe, the usurper of her son's throne. She was rather silly, highly emotional and extraordinarily courageous, and one might say of her as Napoleon said of her grandmother, 'the only man in the family'.

An odd feature of Maupas is the vast number of plates which cover the walls adjoining the staircase, plates from many countries, from many eras, and of infinitely differing patterns. Their positioning involves certain problems. If one gets up to the height of the top layers in order to examine them properly, one is laterally too far removed to see them. If one gets close enough laterally to see them in detail, one is then too low down. Binoculars are suggested.

Through Morogues and along the 4 miles of local road to join N 455 and then a very pretty 16-mile run north-east to Sancerre and the Loire.

Sancerre is as delicious as the wine which takes its name, and that is saying a very great deal. It is a walled town on a peak, with very narrow and very steep streets, very badly paved because heavy rains wash the surface away, there is an old Catholic church, a Protestant church which began in the 16th century, a wonderful separate belfry of about 1500 and endless enchanting little houses whose age really doesn't matter. And when you get to the top, and to the terrace planted with lime trees which smell heavenly in the hot sun, you get such a view over the plain and the Loire – and a viaduct with a beautiful curve – as you will remember to the end of your days.

Below is Saint-Satur, which is recorded as being old in the 11th century, and has a 14th century church, and even older houses, as is the case with Sancerre. From Saint-Satur one crosses the river and rejoins N 7 5 miles above Cosne-sur-Loire. Another 4 miles upstream, and one is in Pouilly-sur-Loire.

The Pouilly-Fumé of the Loire is not to be confused with the Pouilly-Fuissé of Burgundy. It is a very good wine in its own right, but it does not age so gracefully, nor have so full a flavour as the Burgundy, but it is, I feel, just that little superior to the Sancerre wines. On the other hand, those of Sancerre are better than the plain Pouilly-sur-Loire wines, which are simply not comparable with the true Pouilly-Fumé.

Another 8 miles up N 7, amidst the cars hurrying along towards the Côte-d'Azur, to La Charité-sur-Loire and the old Sainte-Croix abbey church, a vast Romanesque building whose nave, alas, was totally ruined during the Wars of Religion. It is interesting, for here we feel that we really are not along the Loire at all, but somewhere in Burgundy, for this grandiose building was the perfect example of Burgundian Romanesque. It has some very good capitals.

The road deserts the river now for the last 15 miles into Nevers, through Pougues, which I do not find the most exciting of French spas. I hope my memory serves me well and that it was indeed upon the very last stretch of our Loire-side journey on N7 that I saw a quite unforgettable sight. It was pouring with rain, one of the heavy downpours that the mountains of the *Massif Central* which are now close at hand precipitate suddenly upon this part, but not so heavily that I could not distinguish, with horror, the products of a roadside factory, on the right, stretched out for public approval along a great length of grass. In a long, long line there were perhaps hundreds of identical plastic terriers, each with leg cocked, watering his unfortunate neighbour – very realistically in that rain! The thought of these horrors being no more than representative of the thousands more that could be produced in that factory, the thought that soon every garden in France would boast one of its own, made a lasting impression.

Then the towers and spires of Nevers were before us. Nevers belongs to all appearances to Auvergne. It has nothing in common with the other cities of the Loire we have so far seen. It is in many respects already a town of the Midi, in everything but climate. It is a pity that so many just rush through it, in order to rejoin N7 on the south side and go racing away towards the sunshine and the Mediterranean, for there is much there to see and admire.

It starts off right, taking you under an 18th century town gate as you arrive on the Paris road. Turn left at Saint-Pierre down the Rue des Francs-Bourgeois as far as the Rue Saint-Etienne, where you will find the church of that name, and a very exceptional church it is. It was built all at one go, between 1063 and 1097, and the style is mainly that of the severe Auvergne Romanesque, but there is a timid addition of some Burgundian decoration. It has never been materially changed in 900 years.

Back in the centre of the town the 15th and 16th century Ducal Palace, now the Palais de Justice, is undecided whether to belong to the Gothic age or to the Renaissance. It is well preserved, and a fine building. The cathedral is more impressive than one would expect from a mixture of 11th, 12th, 13th, 14th and 16th centuries. It too belongs to Auvergne. And in the convent chapel of Saint-Gildard you may see the reliquary in which lies the body of Saint Bernadette of Lourdes.

From the Place de la République there is a tremendous view of another great curve of the Loire as it bends out towards the mountainous journey to its source.

Arrival at Nevers along the river entails missing the lower part of the Sologne which provides a short cut, for those who wish to save time, from Blois to Moulins and Moulins across to the Loire again at La Bénissons-Dieu. This is largely exploration of the deepest and least frequented countryside where a car with a foreign number plate is an exceptional sight.

Infinite variations of the route are possible, but an interesting way of seeing a great deal without going too far off the direct route is to take N765 from Blois to Cheverny, up to Bracieux (see the pretty Château de Villesavin, with its 16th century dove-cote with 1600 pigeon-holes), and from there on D120 through the heart of the Sologne to Fontaine-en-Sologne (Château de la Ravinière, also 16th century, but not so fine) and D20 to Mur-de-Sologne and, near Lassay-sur-Croisne, to the Château du Moulin. This entirely charming early château, built between 1480 and 1502, is really a manor house of the times in the happiest combination of brick and stone, with an outer surrounding wall, making a square, and moats fed with water from the river Croisne – the whole thing on a very small scale but very lovely. From there, by D20 and D59, one reaches Romorantin which, with its 8,000 inhabitants is the biggest town in the Sologne. Very pleasantly situated on the banks of the Sauldre, it has some fine old buildings: the remains of a 15th-16th century royal château (where François I was brought up), and a number of fine old houses of the same age.

From here one can continue through the green heart of the Sologne, plentifully supplied with pools, to Salbris where one turns southwards on N20 to Vierzon and from there on N76 to Mehun-sur-Yèvre.

Two or three miles westwards on D 20 begin the vineyards of Quincy, and this really very elegant white wine, light and refreshing and of good flavour, deserves being tasted on the spot. Reuilly and its vineyards are another 10 miles along D 20: less elegant than the Quincy wines, they are nevertheless well worth sampling. It is another 10 miles by N 718 from Reuilly to Issoudun. The wooded Sologne here changes into a wide and dull plain, but Issoudun itself is still quite interesting, despite local industry. Its show piece is the Tour Blanche, called after Blanche of Castille, built on an artificial mound, a true *motte*, and dating from about the year 1200. It is a fine round tower, nearly 90 feet high. At its foot is the Town Hall, an elegant building of the early 18th century.

From Issoudun, it is about 17 miles by D 19 to Ardentes on the Indre, where, taken to the left, N 143 leads to Nohant. Before reaching there, a short detour takes one to the isolated little Mare au Diable, which gave George Sand the title for one of her more sociological novels.

Her little château at Nohant is rather moving. She passed all her childhood here and returned to it all her life when she needed periods of rest. Here Chopin let his fingers play over the keyboard on a soft summer's night, and a Nocturne was born. Despite his family's accusations that she contributed to his decline, it is clear beyond doubt that the exact opposite is true. She cared for him, nursed him, encouraged him, and restrained him, where a less scrupulous woman might well have let him give unrestricted effect to a passion which might well have brought him earlier to his grave. She loved many men, and those she loved best were the ones on whom she could in some degree exercise her maternal instinct.

Here is an extract from Chopin's *Journal*, dated October 12, 1839. They tell me I'm getting better. The cough and the pain have gone. But deep within myself I feel something is wrong. Aurora's eyes are veiled (*Aurora one of George Sand's own names*). They shine only when I play. My fingers wander gently across the keyboard as her pen flies across the paper. She can write whilst listening to music. Music from above, music from all around, gentle music, Chopin music, clear as a spoken declaration of love. For you,

Aurora, I would crawl on the ground. Nothing would be too much for me; I would give you everything for a look, a caress, a smile from you when I'm tired. I want to live for you alone; I want to play sweet melody for your ear alone.

It was the musician George Sand loved, the musician who was also a dependent invalid. Here is an extract from her *Impressions et Souvenirs*; for the sake of the feeling of immediacy, I have kept the French original's historic present.

Chopin is at the piano, quite unaware that we are all listening to him. He goes on improvising, apparently quite haphazardly. Then he stops.

'Come,' says Delacroix, 'that's no way to end it.'

'I've never really begun it. Nothing's come to me, nothing but pale reflections, shadows and contrasts. I'm looking for colour, but I can't even find a pattern for it.'

'You'll not find the one without the other,' continues Delacroix, 'and you'll end by finding them both.'

'And if all I find is nothing but moonshine?'

'Then you'll have found the reflection of a reflection!'

This idea pleases the great musician. Without giving the impression of beginning it again, he glides into his improvisation. Little by little our eyes are filled with soft colours, the counterpart of the gentle melodies our ears are hearing. Then . . . he strikes the blue note, and we are in the blue of a transparent night. Diaphanous clouds take on fantastic shapes; they fill the sky and crowd round the moon which throws great opal discs into them and awakens the sleeping colour. We dream of a summer night, we await the song of the nightingale.

That was the summer of the Sonata in B flat minor, of the second Nocturne and of three Mazurkas.

The table is set in the dining room, waiting for the return of Liszt, or Balzac, or Delacroix, or Flaubert, or Dumas the Younger, or of her poor husband, the Baron Dudevant, who used to sit at it and get drunk because he couldn't understand the erudite conversation going on about him. The little theatre still shows the scenery of the last play to be given in it, in 1864. And the theatre, too, seems to be waiting, perhaps for Solange, the shockingly spoiled little beauty who was once its leading actress before she married a mad sculptor and became the bane of her mother's life. George Sand's boudoir and study are preserved as they were when she died in the château in 1876, recognized by all as one of the most remarkable women in all the history of literature.

Beyond Nohant, N 143 turns more directly eastwards as it runs through La Châtre, an agreeable but unremarkable little town, and in 10 miles reaches Châteaumeillant. There is a rather remarkable Romanesque church here, having six absidial chapels; another old Romanesque church has become the Hôtel de Ville, and a 16th century castle has been turned into the headquarters for the Gendarmerie. The river Arnon runs through very lovely country as it reaches Culan, where we turn left on N 697 for 15 miles to reach Saint-Amand-Montrond, which is a large place for this part of the world, and very old. The Romanesque church, the mound on which once stood the castle (Mont-Rond, it is sometimes written 'the round hill', gave the place its name) and the pleasant and relatively rich local museum should be seen. Five miles northwards on N 144 is Bruère-Allichamps, just above the Cher, quaint and old, surrounded still by ramparts. If ever you thought of making a journey to the official centre of France (and a lot of people do odd things such as this), this would be your target. In this sleepy old town you are equidistant from the four corners of France.

About 4 miles to the west (D 92) is Meillant. This was a Roman military station, and later became a fief under the Franks, when the first castle was built. In 1127 it was rebuilt and then in the 16th century, at the time it belonged to Charles d'Amboise, it was refurbished by Jocondo, who had worked with Michelangelo, with the remarkable result that the interior is that of a medieval fortress, but the outside is highly decorated with emblems and coats of arms and cyphers. There is a *son-et-lumière*, which has an interesting basis in the long history of the château.

Leaving Meillant, D 37 takes one through the woods to Charenton and on to Ainay-le-Château which, like Meillant, is a *Demeure Historique* and has a *son-et-lumière* performance. It is a magnificent example of an original medieval fortress and Renaissance dwelling. The medieval castle was octagonal, stern and symmetrical, but somehow made more human by round towers at the corners, and protected by water moats. Inside this strong box is set the jewel, the

Château de Meillant

Renaissance house which is all smiles and welcome, and set about by cheerful statues.

The D 28, in about 9 miles, after cutting across a corner of the great Tronçais forest, returns us to the Cher at Meaulnes. From this little place, between forest and river, Alain-Fournier took the name of the hero of that modern classic, *Le Grand Meaulnes*. Everything round here will remind those who know and love the novel (the two could well be synonymous) will remind them of it. At Bourges, to the north, the tall young Meaulnes first made the acquaintance of Valentine, the fiancée of Frantz de Galais. The Ferté-d'Angillon of the novel is the real La Chapelle-d'Angillon, where the hero of the book lived with his mother.

The mysterious Domaine des Sablières is partly the old abbey of Loroy, between Bourges and La Chapelle-d'Angillon and partly the castle in the latter place. The all-important Sainte-Agathe of the novel you reach from Meaulne by crossing the Cher and taking D 4 to Epineuil-le-Fleuriel. Perfectly recognizable still is the school, the Café Daniel, the Place de l'Église, the Quartier des Petits-Coins – although the book was written as long ago as 1913. As for the water-logged land, the remoteness, the indifferent country roads, the attraction of the river, well, you can soon see for yourself how accurate the sensitive build-up of atmosphere was in the book. The motor car has made a difference; that is inevitable, but what is so remarkable in these parts where the only tourists are admirers of this little masterpiece is that it has so obviously remained basically unchanged.

What I have not succeeded in tracing is the original of the 'Maison de Frantz', though I have been told it exists. Lovers of the book will remember this passage:

> They were now on an open path, and a little farther on they could see where the guests were crowding round an isolated house standing in full countryside.
>
> 'That's Frantz' house,' the girl said, 'and now I must leave you ...' She hesitated, looked at him for a moment, smiling, and added: 'My name? ... I'm Mademoiselle Yvonne de Galais.'
>
> And she went quickly away.

At Epineuil-le-Fleuriel, near the church with the bulbous tower, is the school. In the school, where Alain-Fournier himself used to sleep, is a very humble and deeply moving miniature museum given over to the relics of the young man whose death in the first World War was a great loss to world literature.

Now we can push on literally to fresh woods and pastures new, first going back up D 28 to see something more impressive of the Tronçais forest where this road meets N 478 and turning right along the latter. Here one can appreciate that this is France's finest oak and beech forest, in which not many years ago the last of Colbert's trees were cut down. For the actual trees, the forest of Fontainebleau has nothing comparable to offer, though it is admittedly more varied and picturesque. Here the whole process of forestry, as designed three hundred years ago, is followed precisely as it was. The life cycle of oak and beech is fixed at 225 years, with intermediate cuts to give room for the selected long-term trees to expand. I find it the most cheerful thing in the world that nine generations from now the last of the saplings planted this year will be felled, and that the men of *Eaux et Forêts* are happy to work for so distant a future, despite atom bombs, hydrogen bombs, flying saucers and all other modern improvements which threaten the very existence of the human race.

Just beyond the little mid-forest village of Tronçais, N153 cuts across N478. Turn right down it; follow it through its right angle bend at Ygrande and it will lead you through Bourbon-l'Archambault (a spa extolled by Vitruvius, and frequented by Louis XIV, and Henrietta of England and many other historical characters) to Moulins. A cathedral town, and one time capital of the duchy of

Moulins

Bourbon, Moulins has very many interesting remains: a 15th and 19th century cathedral, with interesting late 15th century stained glass, the Renaissance Pavillon d'Anne de Beaujeu, and many old houses near by. Leave by D 1 2 for Dompierre-sur-Besbre from which 3 miles of N 480 will bring you on to N 488 and to the Loire at Digoin. Here you can cross the Loire, to find that the fat lands of the Bourbonnais are continued on the other bank. N 79, as described elsewhere, leads to Paray-le-Monial, and it is a temptation to push on another 8 miles through the cattle-bearing pastures to Charolles, which gives its name to the world-famous breed of cattle. This dull little town (the prosperous and the picturesque seldom go together) is nearly a thousand feet up and dominates the rich countryside for miles around. A minor road, D 10, very pretty in parts carries you again to the Loire at Baugy, only 8 miles distant.

This highly condensed suggestion will not be to everybody's taste. Only at Bourbon-l'Archambault and Moulins will you be likely to see the usual *Bar américain* signs frequent in places where tourists gather, and as for trying to explain to other people afterwards where you have been, my advice is give up before you start and show them on a map.

From Nevers to Le Monastier

Decize – Bourbon-Lancy – Digoin – Paray-le-Monial – Roanne – Balbigny – The Loire Gorges (i) – Montrond-les-Bains – Saint-Rambert-sur-Loire – The Loire Gorges (ii) – Le Pertuiset – Monistrol-sur-Loire – Yssingeaux – Retournac – The Loire Gorges (iii) – Vorey – Lavoûte-sur-Loire – Le Pur-en-Velay – Duguesclin – Saint-Vidal – Bouzols – Polignac – Chavaniac-Lafayette – Iguerande – Pouilly-sous-Charlieu – La Bénissons-Dieu – Lavoûte-sur-Loire – Peyredeyre gorges – Le Monastier-sur-Gazeille – Les Estables – Mont-Mézenc – Bonnefoi Charterhouse – Sainte-Eulalie – Salettes – Arlempdes – Pradelles – Pont-de-Labaune – Auberge de Peyrebeilhe.

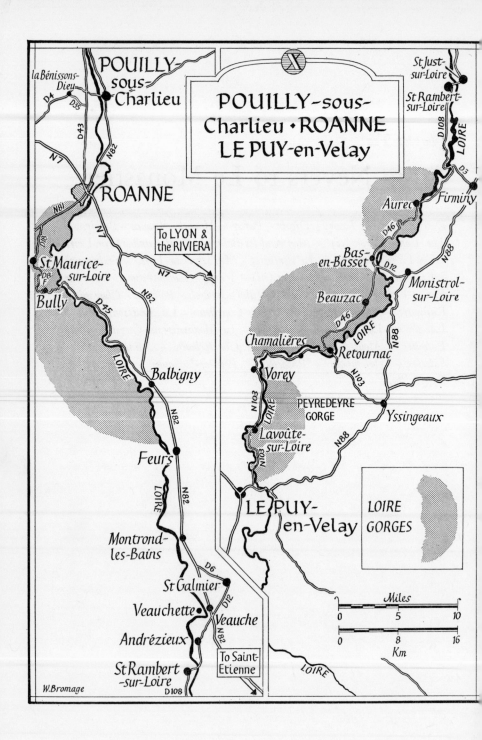

POUILLY-sous-Charlieu • ROANNE LE PUY-en-Velay

X

POUILLY-sous-Charlieu

la Bénissons-Dieu

St Just-sur-Loire

St Rambert-sur-Loire

ROANNE

Aurec

Firminy

To LYON & the RIVIERA

Bas-en-Basset

St Maurice-sur-Loire

Monistrol-sur-Loire

Bully

Beauzac

Chamalières

Retournac

Balbigny

Vorey

PEYREDEYRE GORGE

Yssingeaux

Lavoûte-sur-Loire

Feurs

LE PUY-en-Velay

LOIRE GORGES

Montrond-les-Bains

St Galmier

Miles

0   5   10

Veauchette

Veauche

Andrézieux

To Saint-Etienne

0   8   16
Km

St Rambert-sur-Loire

W.Bromage

From Nevers to Le Monastier

It is impossible to leave Nevers without looking back with some regret on its faded red roofs and ancient towers. Behind one are the fat lands, and the splendid food, and the open, amiable and gentle people. Ahead are mountain pastures and cold stone villages, a people living in poverty and in isolation, with no historical background of luxurious living in gracious châteaux. Ahead are hill-top fortresses, mostly ruined, and a whole long history of civil wars, of wars against the independent Companies left behind at the end of the Hundred Years War to live on what they could steal by force, of wars waged in the name of religion, with both sides claiming to be doing the will of the same merciful God. Ahead are twisting mountain roads, with villages only at long intervals, and little enough traffic to give the feeling of being in company.

All this does not happen straight away. The road out beside the Loire (N 79) follows the river fairly closely along a plain as far as Decize, a little old town on an island in the river, above which, on a rocky knoll, are the remains of a castle that was once the pride of the counts of Nevers. There is also a quaint church with Romanesque choir and pre-Romanesque crypt. In fact you have to turn off N 79 in order to see it, which few motorists ever do, much as it deserves a visit. The same is true of the next place down, Bourbon-Lancy, a cheerful spa standing on a height from which there are picturesque views over the Loire (2 miles distant) and its valley, and over the fertile Bourbonnais plain to Moulins on the Allier, only 20 miles or less away. Then another 20 miles to the south-east brings one to Digoin.

Digoin is a water town, occupying a pleasing position on the right bank of the Loire and between the two branches of the Canal du

Centre which links the Loire (for barge traffic) with the mines and industries to its east. The canals, in fact, are the most interesting things in this industrial townlet, for the one that comes from Roanne is linked to the one that goes north-eastwards towards Montceaux-les-Mines by a fly-over, and it is really an extraordinary sight to see barges, as at Briare, sailing gaily away overhead on a broad aqueduct which is supported by fifteen magnificent arches.

Only 8 miles to the east is Paray-le-Monial, a pretty little town in a pleasant valley which used to bear a name straight out of some medieval romance, Orval, The Golden Valley.

Paray-le-Monial is now famous as the place of origin of that modern festival of the Roman Catholic church, the Feast of the Sacred Heart of Jesus. This arose from a vision granted in the 17th century to a French nun of the Order of Visitation, Marguerite-Marie Alocoque. This particular devotion was approved by Pope Clement XIII in 1765, but was particular to Paray-le-Monial until 1856, when it was extended to the whole church. In 1864, Sister Marguerite-Marie was beatified.

There is an abbey church in pretty little Paray-le-Monial, a most interesting Burgundian-Romanesque building dating back to the 12th century, and based on the one at Cluny. This was proclaimed basilica, that is to say officially a pilgrimage church, in 1856. The cult took on such proportions that when, as a symbol of France unconquered and free, a vast synthetic Romanesque basilica was built on the hill of Montmartre, dominating Paris, it was dedicated to the Sacred Heart of Jesus, and more or less copied from this delightful old basilica. Next to the basilica, the town's most precious building is a luxurious Renaissance town house, built between 1525 and 1528 for a rich local merchant, which has now become the Town Hall. The wide front is decorated with medallions and charming little pieces of sculpture, as is the gallery which forms the vestibule. And this is almost the last we shall see of Renaissance architecture on this long journey.

The river road south from Digoin is no longer N 79 (which is the one to Paray-le-Monial) but N 482, which does not run very close to the river. It is not a very interesting part of the journey, and industrial Roanne is not exciting, except for the amount of barge traffic on canal and Loire – a reminder that a very high percentage of France's heavy materials, such as coal, iron ore, building sand and bulk oil fuel is still water-borne.

We are now approaching the point where the river itself becomes a centre of interest again. By leaving Roanne on N7 (which crosses the town from north-west to south-east on its way to the Côte-d'Azur) and then taking the right-hand bend on N82 towards Balbigny and Montrond-les-Bains, one comes to the first of the Loire gorges. These are not really all that impressive, and certainly bear no comparison with those of the Tarn, but they are interesting to see for the first time.

Overlooked by splendidly romantic ruins of a 14th and 16th century castle on a hill top, Montrond-les-Bains is an attractive little spa standing on the right bank of the Loire. Its waters are strictly medicinal and are not indicated nor sold for drinking with meals, being highly mineralized. As a spa, it specializes in the treatment of stomach ailments and liver complaints, arthritis, anaemia and obesity, and perhaps hypochondria, by means of hot springs which deliver their waters at a temperature of 26°C (just on 80°F).

It is best to cross the river here, rather than to go on down N82 as far as Saint-Etienne, a large industrial town conspicuous for its lack of charm. A local road to the left soon after the river crossing goes back to the Loire at Saint-Rambert-sur-Loire and, as D108, continued by D46 and D47, leads you to the next set of gorges after having taken you across the river again at Le Pertuiset. There are plenty more to come, so it is best to carry straight on down D47 when it leaves the river in order to reach Monistrol-sur-Loire. You will be just on 2,000 feet up here and the views over the winding Loire valley are remarkable, as is the Romanesque church and the two splendid round towers which remain of the 15th century stalwart castle of the bishops of Le Velay, which seem to indicate that they belonged very much to the Church Militant.

You can, from here, continue down N88 to Yssingeaux, crossing the Lignon on the way, then over the Col du Pertuis and down to river level again at Le Puy-en-Velay. If you have not had your fill of gorges (there is a dreadful joke to be made here, but in charity I will abstain) take D12 from Monistrol-sur-Loire – one wonders at the

name, for it is three and a half miles to the Loire – over the river to
D 42, taking the left turn on to it, and continuing on D 46 and D 9 as
far as Retournac. Here, through Vorey and Lavoûte-sur-Loire the

Monistrol

road follows the winding gorges to where a short road to the right
leads into that wonderfully unlikely town, Le Puy-en-Velay.

You can visit Le Puy time and time again, and be just as astonished
by it as the first time. There is the very southern cathedral, unique in
plan. Beyond it is the Rocher Corneille, a pinnacle of rock on which
is uncomfortably perched a gigantic statue of the Virgin Mary made
(one would have thought most singularly inappropriately) from 213
of the Russian cannon taken during the Crimean War at the siege of
Sebastopol. It was cast in 1860. The Rocher Corneille on which it

stands rears its thin rocky head to a height of 2,484 feet above sea level, so as to ensure that this stupendous and hideous statue can be seen from vast distances.

At a little greater distance from the cathedral is something even more remarkable to look at, and a great deal more pleasant to look upon. This is the Rocher-d'Aiguilhe, a straight-up narrow pinnacle of rock, 280 feet high, on which stands an old and very beautiful oratory, Saint-Michel-d'Aiguilhe.

Often forgotten when people talk of the beauty of Le Puy is the startling contrast between it and the green and pleasant little river valley coming up from the south. Le Puy is three miles nearly from the Loire, but this is the valley of La Borne, one of its tiniest tributaries. Look up from it towards the mountains through which your way will lie if you are going to the source of the Loire, and see how grey and cheerless and forbidding they look after its gentle greenery.

There are a hundred spots from which one can get views showing how the original town clustered round the first cathedral. It reminds me irresistibly of Marcel Proust's description of Combray (which is, in fact, the little town of Illiers, near Châteaudun). 'Combray could be seen to be keeping the grey and woolly backs of the packed houses as near as possible to its own long, black cloak, as the shepherd in the open country does to his ewes to gain protection against the wind.'

Many claims have been made for the antiquity of Le Puy and certainly there are many Gallo-Roman remains. As, however, these are in museums, nothing absolutely proves that they originated in Le Puy, for there are many Roman villas and villages at no great distance, from which they might easily have been brought to it. Better proof, perhaps, is to be found in the top step of the sixty leading up to the cathedral. It is enormous, and of the size and shape of those one has seen as part of dolmens. This is known as 'the fever stone'. An inscription, in terms of history quite modern, declares that the sick who stretch themselves upon this stone and there go to sleep, wake cured (*plebs hac rupe sita fit sana sopore si quearas quare virtus abscribitur area*). It is known that from the early Middle Ages, miracles were attributed to the stone. One claim was that the Virgin had been seen to stand upon it. It is difficult to resist the temptation to see in this a continuation of a Druidical or earlier rite well into Christian times.

Such thoughts are supported by the discoveries made just over a hundred years ago in the cathedral nave, including a large animal frieze. It was a bas-relief and consisted of four large blocks of stone encased in the eastern wall of the present nave, and of eight other and similar ones now to be seen at the Musée Crozatier. The total frieze would have been 33 feet long and 3 feet high, dating in all probability from the 1st century of the present era, and certainly not later than the 2nd, so that it may well have had its place in some earlier and non-Christian shrine. It is a most interesting work, and well merits the double journey to cathedral and Museum.

The question of the antiquity of Le Puy will probably never be satisfactorily solved. Again, nothing proves that this frieze of deer and boars and lions was not brought to the cathedral site from some other place when the first church was built here. Modern students think that Christianity in the Velay could well date from the 3rd century, but not earlier than that.

What is certain is that at least two other churches preceded the 12th century Romanesque church we see today, and it is probable that the first of them was built on the site of a pagan temple, for the Romans usually built where the Druids had worshipped, and all over France churches have been found to stand upon the remains of Roman temples.

The first certain proof of a Christian church on the site is dated 493: there is then a long break in the record, for the next church of which remains have been found was built as comparatively late as the 11th century.

The present remarkable building has the famous flight of sixty steps leading to a very fine triple porch set in a polychrome façade. The doors of the side chapels are in carved cedarwood and are probably no more recent than the 13th century. Inside, the unique plan of the church becomes visible: it is easy to see that the nave of the 'new' (13th century) basilica took in the entire 11th century church. It is large, and plain, and impressive from its size and simplicity. Pilgrimages brought men and women of all nations to pray in Notre-Dame-du-Puy all through the Middle Ages. The 'Black

Virgin' of Le Puy, like so many others, was destroyed during the Revolution; the one now to be seen was a copy made from memory by a local artist.

I would choose the little cloister to the left of the Porte Grateloup as the most enchanting part of this imposing cathedral (one passes through this door to go down to the town). Its arches are in different colours, and above them is a polychrome stone mosaic, with a cornice of grotesque heads. The capitals are well carved, and the brightly tiled roof strikes a cheerful note. Altogether these cloisters are really charming.

Nothing compels you to climb up to the top of the Rocher Corneille for a nearer view of the colossal statue, but in fact it can be done with relative ease by means of steps which rise from the Place du Breuil below. There is a further staircase from the platform to the head of the statue but (from a guide book and not from personal experience) it appears that 'the view from the platform is just as good'.

Local inhabitants have a very high regard for the statue and it is as well not to criticize it too loudly in their presence. This is what a local writer has had to say about it:

> The proportions of its natural rock pedestal, the sweetness of the faces, the easy movement of the Infant's hand, the discreet flow of the drapery, are such that one is more touched by the beauty of this monument than by its dimensions . . . The subject is treated with a full sense of theological implications. The sculptor, Bonassieux, has here brought together the three Catholic conceptions of the Virgin. She is Queen, wearing regal crown and mantle. She is the Holy Mother of God, holding the Child on her right arm. She is also, by a devotion which dates the statue, the Immaculate Conception treading underfoot the serpent of Sin.

Beauty is in the eye of the beholder, and one is permitted to doubt that the statue is a work of art, but one cannot doubt the sincerity and piety of those who decided to erect it.

Perhaps the greatest asset of Le Puy is that the whole is even more agreeable than the parts. It is a real pleasure to wander up and down (though, as with most hilly towns, it is extraordinary how much more one seems to go up than one ever comes down) quietly taking in its multitude of old buildings, none of which perhaps is outstanding in its own right, but which in the course of many centuries they have grown into a most harmonious whole.

One certainly worth an individual visit is the church of Saint Laurent. The Dominicans were called to Le Puy in the first quarter of the 13th century and the Chapter presented them with this church and the hospital attached to it, near the little river. The monastery flourished and in 1340 the original, rather exiguous, church was replaced by the spacious building one can still visit, for the hand of man has largely spared it. Incidentally, the date of the building is to be found, upside down, at the base of one of the pillars. It is vast, but very low for a Gothic church; it is also very dark, darker even than many of the southern Romanesque churches, for it is lit only from apse and south aisle and is cluttered with heavy pillars. On the other hand, this is a fitting church for an austere religious Order in a region of mountains.

It is over 200 feet in length, and 72 in width, and has three naves and five aisles. The square pillars are heavy, and unrelieved by tracery. And in front of the choir a wide, bare stone slab marks the place where the vicomtes de Polignac were interred. This powerful family, for ever at loggerheads with the bishop unless the bishop happened to be a Polignac brother or cousin, did much to condemn the entire region to devastation and backwardness.

The apse is lighter than the rest, which enables one to see enough of the shell-patterned carved 18th-century woodwork, and the main doorway, of which only the upper part has been preserved intact, is carved with carefully executed flower designs. And most unexpectedly, one comes across the tomb of Bertrand Duguesclin. The British, who know their Brittany, will remember with amazement that they have already seen his tomb in Dinan. The French visitor from Paris may remember that he too has seen a Duguesclin tomb, in the Royal Chapel at Saint-Denis, amongst those of the kings and queens of France!

There is at least one historical parallel. Roland and all his Peers are buried at Roncesvalles, in Spain. They are also buried at Blaye, near Bordeaux. They are buried, too, at Les Alyscamps in Arles. These burials are more legendary than historical, but the triple burial of one of the last, and perhaps the greatest, of medieval military leaders, is well-substantiated. This is how it came about.

If one accepts the date of 1320 for his birth, which is probable but not certain, he was nineteen when he first saw service for the king of France. He was taken prisoner that year by the English, but being young and as yet unknown escaped with a nominal ransom. When he was taken prisoner again after another five years of hard battling, his stature was such that his ransom was fixed at the enormous sum of 100,000 *livres*. Arch-opponent of the Black Prince who was supporting Pedro of Castile against Henry of Trastamare and Charles V of France, Duguesclin was again taken prisoner at the battle of Nájera, and this time his ransom was 100,000 gold doubloons, or very nearly three times the value of the previous one. The king paid, and his money was well spent, for Bertrand was chiefly responsible for the long series of defeats of the English which left them with no more than a handful of fortified towns.

Then Charles V took a hand in the wars for the duchy of Brittany, and Duguesclin refused to serve him against what he considered the best interests of his native country. However, the King was unwilling to let him go, but offered him a commission to clear the English and the Free Companies from Auvergne and Languedoc rather than to fight in Brittany. In May 1380, Bertrand set out with a strong force of men at arms and, on his way to the plains of Languedoc, laid siege to Châteauneuf-de-Randon on the road from Le Puy to Mende, a stronghold held by the Sire de Roos and a Free Company.

Help that the Sire de Roos expected from regular English forces did not come and at the end of June he agreed with the French that if it had not arrived in a fortnight's time he would surrender the fortress. Just before the fortnight expired, Bertrand caught a fatal fever, and died on 13 July, 1380. Next day the Sire de Roos came in state, with a page carrying the keys of the stronghold. He was shown to the tent where the body of Bertrand was laid out, and himself put the keys into the cold hands. 'To Bertrand alone,' said de Roos, 'I promised to deliver the fortress. There is no other man in France to whom I would have ceded it'.

Then came the squabble as to where Bertrand was to be buried. The king sent word that the body was to be interred amidst the kings of France at Saint-Denis. His Breton relatives and friends insisted that his native Brittany must have his tomb. The powerful bishop of Le Puy, only 20 miles away, insisted that his town should be the last resting place of the greatest warrior in Europe. The final solution was a compromise: the body would be embalmed and carried to Saint-Denis, the heart enclosed in an urn and taken to Dinan for safe keeping in the church Bertrand loved, Saint-Sauveur, and the entrails should go to Le Puy for interment in a suitable church there.

Thus, having seen already two genuine tombs in Paris and in Dinan, one finds a third equally genuine one in a recess in the west wall of the chapel which ends the aisle to the right of the choir. Despite so much destruction of and in churches during the Wars of Religion, this rather lovely early Gothic tomb with a recumbent figure of Duguesclin survived; though the Protestants removed the decorative bronzes and mutilated some of the carved religious emblems, they respected the figure. The Gothic tracery is simple but well executed, and the carving of the figure is the work of an artist of merit. The relief of the head with its soldier's beard is full of strength. There is the usual epitaph, but this one is even further from the truth than most: 'Here lies the very noble and very valiant Messire Bertrand Claiken, Count of Longueville, formerly Constable of France, who passed away in the year MCCCLXXX, XIII of July.' As we have seen, only his entrails were once contained in the tomb (it is very doubtful if they are still there today) and the epitaph borders on the deliberate lie.

A more truthful epitaph for him would be: 'Feared by many, respected by all, loved by none'. He was twice married, and saw little enough of either of his wives. The first, the Lady Tiphaïne was an invaluable help to him in his career, managing his estates, raising money for his ransoms, keeping his head financially just above the water. He hardly ever bothered to go back home to see her. Much less is known of the second wife, Jeanne de Laval, but he saw no more of Jeanne than he did of Tiphaïne, and died heavily in debt, in part apparently due to her extravagance.

For nearly all his life he knew the loneliness of command. He knew disaster and he knew the joy of victory, and the only abiding interest in his life was fighting. And in the end he knew the supreme bitterness of the warrior who finds himself dying in his own bed.

A visit to the Musée Crozatier will show how much in the past it depended upon its own industry, the making of lace. There is little or no hand-made, genuine Le Puy lace sold today. The picturesque lace-makers one sees are there to be photographed and be paid for posing, not to make lace. Le Puy depends almost entirely upon *le tourisme* for its living, and this is not a good thing for any town. The combination of rubber-necked tourists and vendors of local souvenirs and objects of religiosity with a sharp commercial spirit can, in the height of summer, come near to putting one off Le Puy for ever. This would be a pity, for there are few more picturesque and interesting little towns anywhere in France.

It is a good centre for short distance excursions. There is, close at hand, the 15th century rectangular fortress of Saint-Vidal, with wide round towers, which commands the narrow Borne valley. To some extent it suffers from 17th century interference, for to make the grim fortress more habitable in that enlightened age, a considerable number of quite disparate windows were opened in the old walls. Inside, under quaint Gothic vaulting, is the very impressive Great Hall. Other rooms have chimney-pieces of the 15th century, and there is a splendid main door to the hall surrounded with Doric ornament.

A little farther, between Coubon and Brives, on the top of a hill rising far above the Loire, are the remains of the once formidable castle of Bouzols which must in its day have been well nigh impregnable. It stands nearly a thousand feet above the river. The enormous keep probably dates from the 11th century. There are lesser cylindrical towers at the angles of the outer walls. It is a castle more impressive from the outside than from within, for though the living quarters may be presumed to date from the 13th century, the restoration which has taken place in more recent times is all too apparent, but the more distant views of the exterior are completely satisfying.

It was the home of many families whose names are part of the history of France: Polignac, La Tour-d'Auvergne and de Beaufort were the greatest. If the first-named produced a cardinal, the last-named gave the world a pope, Gregory XI. It is a pertinent comment on the state of the world of their times that these great noblemen felt safe only behind basalt walls 10 feet thick.

The village from which the Polignac family took its name is only 3 miles from Le Puy, and here are the remains of the castle which was for long the residence of the quarrelsome and powerful princes who bore its name, who considered themselves the equals of kings and hardly inferior to God. Indeed, for long they fought with His church for the right to govern the region of Le Velay. In due course they became less the robber baron and more the courtier, with dire consequences to France.

Jules de Polignac and his wife Iolanthe Martine Gabrielle de Polastron were the appallingly unwise councillors of Queen Marie-Antoinette. From her and from the king they obtained vast sums of money and played a considerable part in promoting the reckless extravagance of the court. Hated by the people and unwilling to face the results of their own foolish behaviour, they were amongst the first to emigrate. Catherine of Russia gave Duke Jules an estate in the Ukraine and he did not return at the Restoration. His son Auguste-Jules did, as the principal companion and friend of the comte d'Artois, brother of Louis XVIII. When the count became king in his turn, as Charles X, de Polignac was first appointed ambassador in London, then, in 1829, headed the last Bourbon ministry, where his sheer incompetence and stupidity cost Charles X his throne. Indeed, two such arrogant and stupid people can seldom have been in supreme control of the destinies of a great country. After that disaster the de Polignacs seem to have taken a distaste for politics. Today the name is more readily associated with the wine trade.

The castle stands on a flat basalt rock table, around which the red-roofed houses of the village are grouped. There remain a huge square keep and some broken-down walls. In its heyday it was a place of almost incredible strength: vertical fracturing of the basalt left unclimbable cliffs and the château could only be reached by means of a spiral path which led up to the north through six successive fortified gates. The fourth of the six still remains, heavy and strong in the military style of the 13th century and, like the square keep, devoid of all grace. Grain being easier to store than flour, the garrison ground their own and the foundations of their own windmill are still extant. There is a deep well to ensure the water supply, but whether it really is as deep as the two to three hundred feet claimed for it is doubtful. The keep seems a little younger than the other remains, 14th century probably in the lower part whilst the upper was completely rebuilt at the end of the nineteenth. If there is such a thing as a good pastiche, this is it.

The château of Chavaniac-Lafayette lies between the Loire and its great tributary the Allier. Chavaniac itself is hardly worth a visit, but Americans with a taste for the fairy story legend might wish to visit the birthplace of a man America honours more than he deserves. Why he should be so highly thought of is difficult to understand: he was a man it was better to have as an enemy than as a friend. He was without doubt brave, but remarkably unintelligent even for a soldier. As a man he was consumed by vanity and brought upon the monarchs he claimed to be serving literally fatal troubles. He loved the picture of himself, mounted on a white horse, earning the eternal gratitude of the king and queen as their saviour. In fact his passion for being seen mounted on a white horse and dashing here and there for no very discoverable reason reminds one strongly of Mussolini.

The little château is well sited and, through American gifts, has been turned into a memorial nursing home. It includes a small War Museum (first world war) and another dedicated to Lafayette, which brings to mind even more strongly the ineffectiveness of this foolish, brave, vain man. 'Lafayette,' wrote Carlyle, 'thin constitutional pedant, clear, thin, inflexible, as water turned to ice'. The gardens of the château are beautifully laid out, and reward for the journey.

Whilst at Le Puy, one must go to the little suburb of Espaly to see the strange basalt formations, taking on the appearance of a vast organ with innumerable pipes. If this gives you a taste for this kind of natural sculpture, Bort-les-Orgues on the other side of the *Massif Central*, on the Dordogne, has even more spectacular formations to show.

Here perhaps is the place to insert a little sightseeing note which was left out in order to speed the journey between Paray-le-Monial and Le Puy. After Iguerande the river can be crossed near Pouilly-sous-Charlieu (which itself has a quite interesting château) and a short run brings one to La Bénissons-Dieu. Here are the remains of a once important abbey, now consisting of the 12th century nave of the abbey church and a 15th century bell tower. Is it worth the journey to see so little? In itself, perhaps not, though the ruins are fine ones, but how often does one get the opportunity to visit a place called The 'Let us bless the Lord'?

Coming farther down towards Le Puy, Lavoûte-sur-Loire really demands a short stop. Here is a true fortress, high above the river, dating from the 13th and rebuilt in the early 17th century: in the gardens are scattered remains of a still earlier one, built in 1267. The first one belonged to the bishops of Le Puy, but was taken from them by their Polignac enemies in 1272. It remained with the family until the Revolution, when it was sold as a national property. In 1815 the de Polignac family recovered it. It was sold in 1862, but re-bought by the de Polignacs in 1888. At that time all that remained was a single two-storey building and the lower part of two round towers.

It has since been rebuilt with considerable taste and impeccable accuracy. The old chimney-pieces were brought from another de Polignac castle. The reconstruction has been so admirably done that it is a most satisfying place to visit. There are some magnificent portraits of the Polignac family, including cardinal de Polignac (the best of them all), the countess who was the deadly friend of Marie-Antoinette, and the last of the political Polignacs who brought ruin to his royal master. An excellent *son-et-lumière* is given here, but seeing who owns the castle you must not be surprised if it paints a slightly more flattering picture of past Polignacs than the dispassionate student of history would care to admit.

It is soon after Lavoûte-sur-Loire that the river runs into the tightest of the gorges, the Peyredeyre. The road follows the turns of the river very closely indeed and there are many places from whence one can obtain magnificent views and impressive photographs. The best time for seeing them is probably towards sunset, when the flat rays of the setting sun reflect off the grey-black basalt to give fascinating colour effects on to the water in the deep crevasse below.

Onwards again now, away from Le Puy on the last stage of the long road to the source of the Loire. Out past Bouzols for 13 miles

The handsome château de Beauregard with portraits, real and imaginary, of 363 of France's notabilities of the 15th and 16th centuries, shown in the impressive Salle d'Honneur.

Gien is an agreeable town and, seen from its hump-backed bridge, a handsome one, largely rebuilt after the 1939–1945 war. The unusual château (1484) is now a Hunt Museum.

The Porte du Croux at
Nevers, a fortified town
gate of 1398.

Paray-le-Monial, where
the devotion of the
Sacred Heart of Jesus
originated, has a
Burgundian Romanesque
church of real splendour,
built in the 12th century,
with the influence of
Cluny predominating.

along N535, with steep climbs and hairpin bends, to Le Monastier-sur-Gazeille. The Gazeille is a very charming little affluent of the Loire whose name distinguishes this Le Monastier from the other one, Le Monastier-en-Gévaudan, not very far away. It is very small, our Le Monastier, and very compact, and can seem either very sad or very stern, but those feelings are probably entirely subjective. And if the name seems faintly familiar to you, then let me refresh your memory. It was from here that Robert Louis Stevenson set out with Modestine the donkey:

> Monastier is notable for the making of lace, for drunkenness, for freedom of language and for unparallelled political discussion. There are adherents of each one of the four French parties – Legitimists, Orléanists, Imperialists and Republicans – in this little mountain town; and they all hate, loathe, decry and calumniate each other. Except for business purposes, or to give each other the lie in a tavern brawl, they have laid aside even the civility of speech.

He had had time to get to know them, for, he explained, 'in a little place called Le *Monastier*, in a pleasant highland valley fifteen miles from Le Puy, I spent about a month of fine days.'

Just on thirty years later, in 1907, the Reverend Sabine Baring-Gould, a prolific author and professional travel writer, commented on Stevenson's account of Le Monastier, saying that 'the book was published in 1879. Since then Legitimists, Orléanists and Imperialists are no more such. They have acquiesced in being good Republicans.' Such touching faith in the perfectibility of human nature is most suitable to a minister of religion, but to those who have lived in France for any length of time, even this perfectibility, if it existed, would be little likely to cover politics.

Fierce still are the political arguments in these isolated townships of Auvergne and the Vivarais. In declining towns as cut-off as Le Monastier-sur-Gazeille all beliefs and prejudices linger on long after the rest of the world has forgotten them. Since the peaceful days prior to World War I the population has declined to very little more than one half of what it was then. It seems a moderately happy place: the lot of the inhabitants is probably all the better from being as

x

Alexander Pope's blameless vestal, in the restful state of 'the world forgetting, by the world forgot'.

Up narrow streets, past ageless grey stone houses with sun-bleached roofs of once-red Roman tiles, is the way to the 11th century Romanesque church with a polychrome façade. The monastery which

Le Monastier-sur-Gazeille

gave the townlet its name was founded by Saint Calminius in the 7th century. Battered by the Saracens, ravaged by the unemployed mercenaries at the end of the Hundred Years War and, despite the protection of the powerful de Polignac clan, utterly ruined during the Wars of Religion, the vast abbey slowly disappeared, leaving as its only record the Byzantine church, the present *Mairie* which occupies one of the old abbey buildings, and the black Château de Beaufort where once the abbot lived and which now serves as a school.

From Le Monastier three ways lead more or less directly to the source of the Loire, the most direct being the most northerly, along that same N535 which leads to the little town from Le Puy, then, leaving it to the right, D3A to Les Estables and Mont Mézenc. Les Estables, which now has three modest hotels with 26 bedrooms between them, no longer justifies the turn-of-the-century description of 'a poor, dirty place where the natives shiver through half the year'. Poor, yes; it is still that. Dirty, no, but the lava used for building never looks anything but dirty, even in the handsome towns of Auvergne, such as Riom. Shivering with cold through half the year? That, yes, too. Travellers should be well prepared for cold on these bare slopes. And for astonishing heat also, high up under the sun, with only the thin mountain air to screen its rays.

Above Les Estables, Mont Mézenc rears its head. It is, at 5,755 feet, the highest peak in these ranges, if anything so rounded at the top as this extinct volcano could possibly be called a peak. In fact it is more of an inverted bowl and of all the mountains of the range perhaps the most perfectly volcanic in form. Despite its height, it does not tower overmuch above Les Estables, for the little village is itself 4,400 feet up. To reach the summit is not a piece of mountaineering, but a pleasant uphill saunter.

From the summit, given a cloudless sky, which happens often enough, the almost infinite panoramic view is as varied as any in Europe. The rounded *puys* of northern Auvergne, with Le Mont-Dore and the Puy-de-Dôme easily distinguishable, take on ever deeper tones of blue with increasing distance, until the farthest melts into the blue of the sky and only an occasional play of light gives it a shape. To the east, the serried ranks of the needles of the Alpine chain stand out against the sky in a kind of false perspective, as if they incised into the blue stuff of the heavens. Here and there a little gleam of light tells of the eternal snows. The long, tall Alpine chain ends with Mont-Ventoux, almost on the Rhône as their most western outpost. Nearer at hand, the view is striking in a drab sort of way, made all the less dramatic by the splendour of the more distant views. In the foreground is all the lava which this great, dead giant of a volcano spewed out over the millennia, which has built up in solid masses towards Le Puy, and indeed in all the approaches to the region of Le Velay.

If, instead of continuing straight on to the source of the Loire you come southwards on D36, you will soon reach the poor remains of the once rich and proud Chartreuse de Bonnefoi. Like so many others, it is credited with having originally been a monastery founded in the early years of Christianity in France, but in a land where so much was destroyed and burned during the long civil and religious wars, there is no documentary evidence left to substantiate these early beginnings. The existing ruins are of the 12th and 13th century. Of this period of its history little is known. Certainly there was a thriving monastery in the midst of the forest which bears its name when the Wars of Religion broke out to make enemies of friends, murderers out of once decent men, and narrow-visioned fanatics out of the most normal and agreeable men and women.

One day the Protestants took the charterhouse by armed assault, killing nine of the Brothers and expelling the rest. They left a garrison to defend it (sixteen strong by one account, twenty-four by another) and the rest moved on to commit further aggressions.

Word of the happenings reached Le Puy. An armed band, 200 strong or 500 strong according to which chronicler you believe, set out from Le Puy and laid siege to the Protestant-held monastery. There was a parley. Terms of surrender were agreed and the safety of the garrison was guaranteed if they would march out with their arms, under oath never to return. Their safety secured, as they thought, by the most solemn oaths Christians can take, they marched out and all, sixteen or twenty-four, were murdered in cold blood. This single episode, one amongst an incalculable number, shall be typical of them all, for book upon book would be filled if one attempted to record all the horrors which war and civil war brought to this dark region in the darker days of its grim history.

Continuing south-westwards down D 37 after leaving Bonnefoi, one reaches N 5 3 5 again about 5 miles from Saint Eulalie, which can thus be reached much more directly than via Les Estables. This charming little hamlet is only 3 miles below the source, and is just off the main road. It is famous locally for the most attractive of fairs held on the Sunday following July 12, *La Foire aux Violettes*. You may well wonder what violets are doing so late in the year, and where they come from, and where medicinal plants are found to complement the violets at the fair. The unexpected answer is that aromatic herbs proliferate on volcanic soil, and by far the greatest proportion of herbs and flowers alike come from the dull and un-romantic Mont Mézenc.

In the spring the grey and ugly soil is covered in patches with an almost purple spread of violets. Not just violets, but according to local belief the finest violets in the world. They are deeper in colour than their rival, the Alpine violet, have a fine and richer perfume, last longer and are worth much more.

Then, again, it appears that the herbs which flourish on this un-grateful soil have a scent so rich, so penetrating, so refreshing that it is impossible after one has once experienced it ever to smell thyme, for example, without being reminded of the rich scents of these dull mountains.

The herbs and the violets are set to dry, and by July are ready to be sold to the pharmaceutical and perfume trades respectively. Sainte-Eulalie lives for the Fair, and then drops back into a delicious somnolence from which only the spring harvesting of its two products will awaken it.

Another way of leaving Le Monastier is to take N500 as far as Salettes, and then face the hilly detour to reach Arlempdes by going east, south-west and north-west. Such are the burdens that mountain roads impose. A helicopter would cover only one tenth of the distance to get from the one to the other.

Once there, you see the most romantic view in all these mountains. The mountains around, the richly green and fertile valley, and the stern ruins of the ancient castle perched on an overhanging rock make a picture in the true Gothic manner. Sickening tales are told of the castle and its robber-baron owners, secure from all but a king's army in their towers and behind their thick battlemented walls, but the one I remember best is not the usual history of cruelty, murder and rapine but a totally ridiculous fairy story which illustrates a French peculiarity.

There is in France very little of the British passion for identifying birds, studying their habits and observing their least comings and goings. In the deep countryside there is least of all. A bird is a bird. If it can be shot and is considered good to eat, it has a name. If it isn't it hasn't. If it is a small bird it will be called a *moineau*, a sparrow. If it is a big bird, it will be called a *buse*, a buzzard.

In the second quarter of the 14th century, the owner of this castle which stood so romantically on a great basalt slab was one Count Armand. Unlike his predecessors and successors, he was a good son of the Church, a friend to the poor, the needy and the sick. Until then, the Devil had known nothing at Arlempdes but popularity and success, he now found vigorous antagonism. Something had to be done about it. Armand must have some weakness, and to find out what it was the Devil took the disguise of a blind and aged beggar, sat for weeks chatting to all who came and went through the castle gates, until he learned of Armand's one failing, his love of dancing. Every night the minstrels played, Count Armand took his place on the floor of the great hall and danced until there were no partners left for him to dance with. One by one the ladies collapsed from fatigue, but Armand remained still untired and longing to continue.

One night, when the last of the ladies had fallen unconscious to the floor, Armand was in despair. Very incautiously he said aloud, 'I would give anything for a partner with whom to go on with the dance.' There was a fluttering in the wide chimney and a great white bird came spinning out. Afterwards, men remembered how strange it was that its long, white feathers were unspotted with soot or ash from the fireplace, but at the time nobody remarked on it, so surprised were they all to hear this most tall and elegant bird speak to Armand in a highly refined manner. Her way of speaking in the *langue d'oc* was that of the Court of King James II of Majorca in Perpignan, which, as everybody knew, was by far the most civilized in Europe. As for her dancing, from the moment she first extended one of the tips of her wide, white wings for Armand to touch as he led her into the dance, from the moment that her long and graceful legs started to move to the measure of the dance, she became the very poetry of motion.

The dance, of course, was the saraband in three-four time, with its curious accent on the second crochet of each measure. When this Moorish dance came to an end, Armand bowed and the bird curtsied. 'Madame,' he said, 'ask what you will of me,' but the bird preferred to wait until the dancing was over before asking him for any kind of reward. The saraband was described by Father Mariana as 'having worked more mischief than the plague', but by comparison with the one that followed it was the most restrained and innocent imaginable. For this second dance, the bird herself instructed the musicians in the air and the tempo. Armand was in ecstasy. Never before had he known a partner so light on her feet, so impeccable in her timing, so graceful in motion.

Again at the end of that dance he told her to ask for what she would from him, and again she put off asking. The third dance was even more fierce and fast and of a kind Armand had never danced before. It filled him with a delirious joy. When it ended he was all but breathless, and hot, and ecstatic. He insisted that the bird (herself unruffled, cool and still supremely elegant) should ask him for a reward. 'Whatever you desire,' he said, 'and which is mine to give you shall have'. Very calmly she replied, 'this time I will take something . . . something which is yours to give. I shall take you, and your soul!' Immediately the bird turned into the Devil in person. He caught up Armand, and before a wandering friar who was present could make the sign of the Cross, disappeared with him in a clap of thunder and a very strong smell of brimstone. Armand was never seen again but often thereafter his moaning ghost walked the battlements.

When the gentleman who was so kindly remembering oddments of folklore for me had completed this tale and I had thanked him, I asked from curiosity what kind of bird this tall, elegant, white creature could have been. The wonderfully incongruous answer I got is one that I might have expected, but it threw me completely off balance. He thought for a moment and then said, decisively, 'it must have been a *buse*'. The brown and whitish-brown short-legged bird of prey with its untidy wing-tips is as far as anything could possibly be from the bird of the legend and poor Armand would have had to bend almost double to touch its wing-tips as it walked.

You would need to continue north-westwards from here and cross N 102 to find the wild route Robert Louis Stevenson took from Le Monastier to Alès. I have indicated on the map where I think it lay, but it is very difficult to be certain about it, as the roads which now serve the Lac du Bouchet did not exist in his day and his own account of where he had been is both confused and no longer descriptive of things as they are. Nevertheless, in general terms his descriptions hold good to this very day, except for campers round the lake, and the man-prepared *baignade* which makes bathing in it safe. Once across N 102 Stevenson's way is the opposite to the way to the source of the Loire.

This N 102 is the fastest road but makes the longest distance to the sources. It sweeps round a great curve, with fairly gentle hills only to surmount, as far as N 500 from Le Monastier just by Pradelles, then continues as N 102a. At Pont-de-Labaume it joins N 536, which winds its way round to Rieutord, from which D 116 takes a not too devious way north to Saint-Eulalie.

Just about 5 miles after leaving Pradelles from whence it continues N 102, an inn stands high at the junction of an unimportant south-running mountain road and the main road. Both roads existed at the time of the Roman occupation and possibly some kind of shelter or inn stood there even at that time. The present dark and forbidding stone-and-mortar single-storey and largely windowless structure, like so many of the peasant buildings of the region, is ageless, for it has been patched and rebuilt generation by generation, and has nothing by which it could be accurately dated.

The first mention of this Auberge de Peyrebeilhe seems to have been made by Faujas de Saint-Fond, pioneer of agricultural research in France and the first scientific investigator of this volcanic region. He described, in 1770, how 'there is no habitation so isolated as this inn and not a year passes that solitary travellers do not find their safety in this haven'. It is true that the inn, 4,000 feet up, must in those days have been cut off from the external world for days and even weeks in winter.

In 1807 or 1808, Pierre Martin bought the already ancient inn and put it into some kind of repair. It was probably he who added the substantial stabling with a loft over it lit by a single window.

The main building was no better lit than the stable. The front door gave on to the kitchen and when it was closed the only daylight the kitchen received was from a single, small oblong window. On one side of the kitchen was a door leading to the dining room, which had two small windows. On the other side of the kitchen was the huge fireplace and the staircase to the bedrooms above. Beyond the kitchen was the wash-house which contained a very large oven, despite the ample cooking facilities which already existed in the kitchen itself. Behind, were the private rooms of Pierre Martin, his wife Marie, daughters Jeanne (then aged eight) and Marguerite (then aged three), and the servant Jean Rochette, a gentle-seeming young man.

The new inn prospered, but not entirely by legitimate means. The first crime to be traced to the family dates to the year 1808, the very year on which work to the inn was completed. In these Napoleonic days the empty spaces of France provided shelter for a very large number of objectors to military service, who fled to the wildernesses rather than be conscripted and be made liable to shed their blood on some distant field of Europe for a cause never explained in a region whose very name they had never heard. Such a one was Claude Béraud, who arrived at the inn in a snowstorm and talked too readily about the money he carried in the pouches of a leather belt worn next to the skin. In the heat of the kitchen, and after being plied with mulled wine, he fell asleep at the table.

When they were satisfied he was not likely to wake, Pierre Martin tipped him off his chair. Rochette then slipped a noose round his neck and tightened it. All the money was taken from his belt. Rochette appropriated the unusually ornate knife the boy wore, as well as his watch, from which hung a disc of semi-precious stone. In this, he was unwise. They left a small sum of money in his pocket, then took his body and flung it into a snow-filled ditch.

There, in the Spring, the gendarmes found him. No identification was possible. As they found money in his pockets, robbery leading to murder was not suspected. The verdict was accidental death. It is believed that during the quarter of a century which elapsed between the death of young Béraud and the arrest of his assassins some sixty other victims lost their lives at their hands. It was clearly impossible to count on snow-filled ditches in the height of summer, and too dangerous to risk more corpses being found in the immediate neighbourhood: hence, it was supposed, the oven in the wash house. As the years went by the little girls became young women and took their part, laughing and joking about it, in the murders. Eventually they both got married and left home. They married well, for their father could afford a fine *dot* for each. Both went to live far from the inn and never faced trial for their part as accessories, a charge which it would have been difficult for them to deny, nor were they called as witnesses.

At long last Pierre and Marie Martin, with Rochette, went to the guillotine which was specially set up in the neighbourhood for the purpose. Rochette, with an air of the deepest resentment, proclaimed himself penitent. Pierre Martin, clamouring to high heaven to the very end, made a great show of repentance and sorrow.

As for Marie Martin, she was supremely disdainful of the comforts of religion and made history as the only woman ever to kick the prison chaplain out of the tumbril on the way to the guillotine. More than anything else what sent them to the gallows were the watch taken from Claude Béraud, and the cornelian disc hanging from it, and his ornate knife, which Rochette was still using. From them the now aged parents learned at last of the certain death of their son.

This tale sheds light upon the region. For sixty people to be murdered before justice caught up with the criminals twenty years later, and then on account of the very first crime of all, tells you much of the region's remoteness. Typical of the people as they were then, and in all probability in many cases are still, is that those living round about were so unwilling to bear witness, even in such a shocking case, that it was three years after their arrest before a sufficiently documented case could be made out against the murderers.

The hard facts of climate and geography, the isolation of villages and even towns, the poverty and the clannishness of this extension of Auvergne, make it a part of France like no other. As in Auvergne, ambition and avarice are the fruits of circumstances: Auvergne may not yet have produced its last Pierre Laval.

Yet to the traveller they are kindly within their means, often forthcoming, and sell their goods and their services at honest prices. In fact, they have the virtues and they have the vices of other peoples living in similar very remote mountain areas.

The End of the Journey

Mont Gerbier-de-Jonc – Le Béage – Lac d'Issarlès – The Veyradeyre – Montpezat-sous-Bauzon – The Fontaulière – The Ardèche – Veyradeyre dam – La Palisse – Gage dam and river – Rieutord – Suc de Bauzon – Saint-Martial – Saint-Martin-de-Valamas – Eyrieux gorges – the narrow-gauge railway – Le Cheylard – Le Chambon – Saint-Sauveur-de-Montagut – Saint-Laurent-du-Pape – Beauchastel – La Voulte-sur-Rhône.

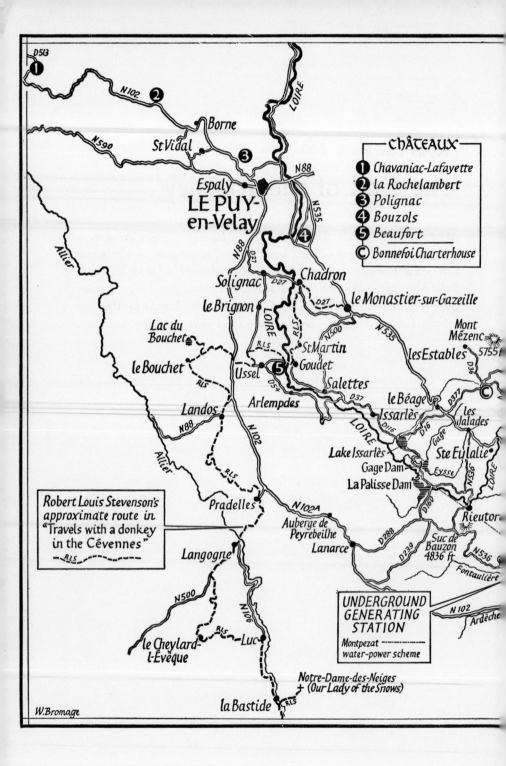

CHÂTEAUX

1 Chavaniac-Lafayette
2 la Rochelambert
3 Polignac
4 Bouzols
5 Beaufort
C Bonnefoi Charterhouse

Robert Louis Stevenson's
approximate route in
"Travels with a donkey
in the Cévennes"
--- RLS ---

UNDERGROUND
GENERATING
STATION
Montpezat ---
water-power scheme

W.Bromage

D 513
N 102
Borne
N 590
St Vidal
Espaly
LE PUY-
en-Velay
N 88
Solignac
le Brignon
Lac du
Bouchet
le Bouchet
Ussel
Landos
N 88
Arlempdes
Allier
Allier
Pradelles
Langogne
N 500
le Cheylard-
l'Évèque
Luc
N 602
la Bastide
RLS
LOIRE
Chadron
le Monastier-sur-Gazeille
D 27
D 27
RLS
N 500
St Martin
Goudet
Salettes
N 535
Mont
Mézenc
5755 f
les Estables
D 36
D 54
D 37
le Béage
Issarlès
D 116
D 16
les
Jalades
Sainte Eulalie
Ste Eulalie
Gage
Lake Issarlès
Gage Dam
La Palisse Dam
D 377
C
N 536
LOIRE
Eysse
D 160
Rieutor
N 102A
Auberge de
Peyrebeilhe
Lanarce
D 288
D 239
Suc de
Bauzon
4836 ft
N 536
Fontaulière
N 102
Ardèche
Notre-Dame-des-Neiges
+ (Our Lady of the Snows)

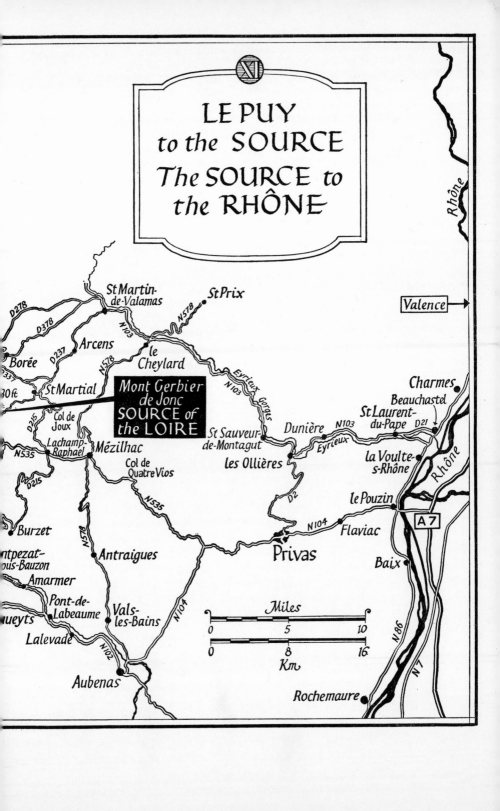

XI

LE PUY
to the SOURCE
The SOURCE to
the RHÔNE

Rhône

Valence →

St Martin-de-Valamas   St Prix

D278

D378   Arcens   le Cheylard

N578   N103   N103   Eyrieux Gorges   Charmes

Borée   D237

N578   Beauchastel

St Martial   St Laurent-du-Pape   D21

Mont Gerbier de Jonc SOURCE of the LOIRE

Col de Joux   D215

St Sauveur-de-Montagut   Dunière   N103

Eyrieux

Lachamp-Raphael   Mézilhac   les Ollières   la Voulte-s-Rhône

N535

Col de Quatre Vios   Rhône

D215   N535   D2

Burzet   le Pouzin

ntpezat-ous-Bauzon   N578   N104   Privas   Flaviac   A7

Amarmer   Antraigues   Baix

Pont-de-Labeaume   Vals-les-Bains

ueyts   N104   N86

Lalevade   N102

Aubenas   N7

Miles

0   5   10

0   8   16

Km

Rochemaure

Chapter Eleven

The End of the Journey

The nominal end of the journey is almost in sight. Only a few miles separate us from Mont Gerbier-de-Jonc (or des Joncs; there is no agreement as to which is right), from whose flanks spring the infinitesimal rivulets, one of which has to be considered *the* source of the mighty Loire. I have left to the very last my own ideal way of reaching it, which has an inherent interest the others lack.

Coming from Le Puy, I would choose N 535 and keep to it as far as Le Monastier-sur-Gazeille, continue down it to Le Béage, turn right on D 16 (the same inconspicuous mountain road which ends on N 102a at the Auberge de Peyrebeilhe), and follow it round the Lac d'Issarlès. This is a natural lake at an altitude of 3,300 feet. In the course of millennia it has been formed in the crater of an extinct volcano and has a depth of over 350 feet. It is pleasant in itself, though its waters can be very cold, as is the case with all the volcanic lakes of this region, but it has much more interest than just in being a volcanic lake. It is the key to the whole fantastic scheme of diverting the waters of the Loire into a direction which is the exact opposite of their natural flow. Strangely enough, the Loire is never less than half a mile from it, and it is visibly fed by no other stream than the tiny Veyradeyre, controlled by a dam just below Le Béage, but off the road. 'Fantastic' is not too big a word for this scheme, which is more like an engineer's pipe dream than a working reality.

Ten miles south of the source of the Loire is the village of Montpezat-sous-Bauzon, on the little river Fontaulière, which feeds the bigger and better known river Ardèche. Two hundred feet below the bed of the Fontaulière at Montpezat-sous-Bauzan is an underground turbine house and generating plant, producing some 300 million KWH each year. The Lac d'Issarlès is connected to it by means of a subterranean gallery over 11 miles long: other galleries run from the Veyradeyre dam, the dam at La Palisse which forms a new lake to the south-east of Issarlès, and from the Gage dam which has created a third little lake on the river Gage immediately north of La Palisse, into lake d'Issarlès.

Thus the Lac d'Issarlès is supplied with water from the Loire itself and from two of its tiny tributaries, Veyradeyre and Gage, and sends it cascading down the gallery to turn the invisible turbine 11 miles away. Then it flows down the Fontaulière into the Ardèche, and in due course from the Ardèche into the Rhône, and from the Rhône into the warm blue waters of the Mediterranean. The waters of the Loire which are not taken flow on in a diametrically opposite direction to end in the Atlantic.

This richly imaginative scheme employed many examples of modern engineering, including one which strikes my imagination more than all the others, though engineers might think my priorities are all wrong. This is that an outlet was created for the Issarlès waters from a point 130 feet below the bottom of the lake and the formidable task was accomplished without first emptying the lake. A gallery was driven up from that point to within 10 feet or so of the level of the lake bottom. The operation was so wonderfully planned that though the remaining thickness was holed by what is generally considered the rather uncertain method of using explosives, the water immediately flowed gently away in the volume calculated beforehand by the engineers.

The actual watershed comes just below the little village of Rieutord, 4 miles below Saint-Eulalie. It is marked by three simple signs. The biggest reads:

Ligne de partage des eaux Atlantique-Méditerranée

(dividing of the waters to Atlantic and Mediterranean) whilst below it are two pointers inscribed *Méditerranée* in one direction and *Atlantique* in the opposite one. The engineering feat deserves a memorial more impressive than these boards.

Rieutord marks the dividing of the waters by man's hand. It also marks the turning of the waters by Nature's hand. It is on the edge of a mountain, the Suc de Bauzon. From the source to here, the Loire

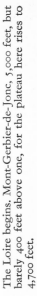

The Loire begins. Mont-Gerbier-de-Jonc, 5,000 feet, but barely 400 feet above one, for the plateau here rises to 4,700 feet.

The Rocher-d'Aiguille, a nearly 300-foot high straight-up pinnacle of rock on which stands an old and beautiful oratory, is only one of the marvels of Le Puy-en-Velay.

The Rhône (at
Valence) and
journey's end. As
you cross it into
Provence, you
cross a frontier.

had flowed southwards, but unable to force a way through the very solid rock of the Suc de Bauzon, turns round at its base and flows north-west. And that is why the Loire does not run into the Mediterranean. One mountain has diverted it to an extra length of some 500 miles.

Following it upstream from Rieutord on D116, which crosses it twice in just over 4 miles, one comes to Saint-Eulalie and the mountain meadows. Another 3 miles up through gentle pastures, and D116 brings one to the source, or sources, overhung by Mont-Gerbier-de-Jonc.

This is journey's end in a shattering anti-climax.

One's first reaction is of complete disbelief. Can this be the majestic, 5,000-feet Mont-Gerbier-de-Jonc? This puny, round-topped outcrop barely 400 feet above one, which one may climb in twenty minutes if energetic? Its absurd shape makes matters even worse. From some angles it is just a human thumb, held erect, with the natural slightly backward curve of a thumb.

It takes some time for the truth to penetrate. What has happened to the remaining 4,600 feet or so? Why, one is standing on it, or them. Where the little chalet-hotel of Le Gerbier-de-Jonc has been built, the plateau reaches nearly 4,700 feet, so that the summit (5,089 feet) is ridiculously foreshortened to about 400 feet above one.

The easy climb should be made, though on the top there is nothing but a marshy flat on which clumps of reeds grow, the whole being as dank as the unexpectedly humid tops of some Scottish hills. 'The reed-topped mountain shaped like a shock of corn' is no more impressive in itself at the summit than it is from the plateau below. One goes not for the sight of an impressive mountain top but for the view of endless ranges of volcanic hills and mountains which can justifiably be described as stupendous. In really good conditions it is of a size almost beyond belief, stretching round in a semi-circle of titanic proportions.

For a century or two the people in the farmstead about 500 yards down from Mont-Gerbier-de-Jonc have proudly shown the nascent Loire flowing from the wall of rock on which their modest dwelling abuts, and have earned many an honest penny by allowing the curious to see this uninspiring beginning to so great a river, 'born in a

Y

wilderness in a site without grandeur'. In 1825, Touchard-Lafosse, an old soldier of the Imperial armies, set out on his travels along the entire course of the Loire. He decided that the river really began in a meadow some way from the farmhouse. It is difficult today to trace which particular spring and stream he had in mind, for there are many in these wet grazing-lands which eventually run together in the valley of Saint-Eulalie below and, joining together, between them make the Loire. There is there nothing official about the farmhouse-spring marking the very beginning, and the farmhouse has a more modern rival.

The queen of French rivers is born unheralded, but as it takes form and pours itself down the damp pastures to the valley of Sainte-Eulalie it is difficult not to think of it with some emotion, as one would of the remote and insignificant cottage in which, in humble circumstances was born a child destined to take a high place in the history of the world.

Perhaps there my book should end, but it goes against all nature to leave the reader 4,000 feet up in the air on a dull table-land. There is a more fitting end, about 35 miles by road amidst scenery more exciting by far than this rather dreary spot.

First continue north-eastwards round Mont Gerbier-de-Jonc, along a very twisting D237, through Saint-Martial, round a marvellous hairpin bend and away to Saint-Martin-de-Valamas, with a right turn on to N103 and along the Eyrieux gorges, on a much smaller scale but to my mind far more impressive than any of the Loire gorges.

For a time you will be accompanied by a narrow-gauge railway. This last survivor of a past age is worthy of your respect. This is the 39-inch gauge *Chemin de fer départemental, réseau du Vivarais* and is a wonderful way of visiting remote places – provided, of course that the great god Efficiency has not done away with it by the time this book appears. If you ever do take it, make your stopping-place one where there is a known hotel, for the return to one's starting point on the same day, or even the next day, can be problematical. Here we are in a poor, unfruitful and backward region, far from the places where sightseers and holidaymakers gather and its hotels are the outward expression of its inward life. They average nine or ten bedrooms, not more, and sometimes less. Accommodation will generally be old-fashioned. Toilet facilities will range from the tolerably modern to the intolerably old. You will be made very welcome if you are willing to share what they have to offer. If your standards are those of medium grade hotels in the rest of France, these little inns of the *département de l'Ardèche* are not for you, unless they are Logis de France.

For the rest, the experience is quite admirable. The narrow railcars go shooting away up hill and down dale, linking together a whole list of places hardly known in France and unknown anywhere else. The run which begins at Tournon on the Rhône goes over the mountains to Lamastre, Le Cheylard, Saint-Agrève, le Chambon, Tence and Dunière, but there many other stops not listed in the Chaix timetable, some of which are along this riverside road. The actual timetable of the trains is quite remarkable: some, it appears, run only on the day after a public holiday. Others are marked as running only during term-time and on Fridays. Saint-Sauveur-de-Montagut, one learns, has a *correspondence par service libre* as there is no railway station there. This one gathers, does not mean a free ride but that a connecting bus to the nearest station is operated by a local firm not part of the French Railways system.

As one continues along the gorge road towards Saint-Sauveur-de Montagut, the scene gradually closes in. There are no villages, and the few hamlets stand well back from the river gorge. The quite good but constantly winding road demands a good deal of attention from the driver; so do the views to the south, so passengers have the best of the run. There is a constant fall towards the east as the little river pours down between its rock walls. Saint-Sauveur-de-Montagut is a town of 1,500 inhabitants, which is big for this region, and even has a miniature hotel used by fishermen, a race in my experience notoriously uninterested in what the French call *le confort moderne*.

The last little place until we emerge into better known surroundings is Saint-Laurent-du-Pape, whose name is a reminder that Avignon and the territories of the medieval Popes-in-exile is not all that far down the Rhône from here, and that the arms of the Avignon anti-Popes though not as long as those of the Pope in Rome, none the less had a good reach.

It is open countryside again, and the Rhône valley is before one. We end up on N86 at Beauchastel, or take N103 to the right and in La Voulte-sur-Rhône turn eastwards on the bridge to have your look at that other mighty and historic river of France, the Rhône.

The civilization which we have seen flowering in the lands of Loire began on this river. Early days, with which the Loire was but little concerned, belong to this river. The Phoenicians came up it, and the Greeks. The Romans came, and it was the broad highway of their new conquest, Provincia, *The* Province, Provence. And the missionaries brought Christianity to France up this highway, the first of them perhaps still within the lifetime of some of the Apostles. Their religion travelled northwards with them, across the Channel, up into Scotland, over to Ireland, out to Wales and to Cornwall. And from the Celtic lands it came flowing back to Brittany, and the mouth of the Loire, where it joined with the indigenous Latin church. Up this river came the stone masons and sculptors whose end product was the glorious Romanesque art of the *Massif Central* and of Anjou and the valley of the Loire and its affluents.

And as you cross the Rhône you have crossed a frontier. Behind you is the country the Loire has so profoundly affected, ahead of you a totally different concept of civilization. That they have remained united as parts of another and greater concept. France, is one of the wonders of history.

Kings and Queens of France

The Capet Dynasty

HUGUES CAPET, born 938 (?), came to throne 987, married
Adelaide d'Aquitaine (i) and Constance de Provence (ii),
died 996: relationship to predecessor, nil (elected).

ROBERT II (the Pious), born (?), came to throne 996, married
Rozala of Flanders, died 1031: relationship to predecessor,
son.

HENRI I, born 1008 (?), came to throne 1031, married Anne
of Kiev, died 1060: relationship to predecessor, son.

PHILIPPE I, born 1052, came to throne 1060, married Bertha of
Holland, died 1108: relationship to predecessor, son.

LOUIS VI (the Fat), born 1081, came to throne 1108, married
Lucienne de Rochefort (i) and Adelaide de Savoie (ii),
died 1137, relationship to predecessor, son.

LOUIS VII (the Young), born 1119, came to throne 1137, married
Eleanor of Aquitaine (i) and Adèle de Champagne (ii), died
1180: relationship to predecessor, son.

PHILIPPE II (Philippe-Auguste), born 1165, came to throne 1180,
married Ingeborg of Denmark (i) and Agnès de Méranie (ii),
died 1223: relationship to predecessor, son.

LOUIS VIII (the Lion), born 1187, came to throne 1223, married
Blanche de Castile, died 1226, relationship to predecessor, son.

LOUIS IX (Saint Louis), born 1215, came to throne 1226, married
Marguerite de Provence, died 1270: relationship to predecessor,
son.

PHILIPPE III (the Bold), born 1245, came to throne 1270,
married Isabela de Aragón, died 1285: relationship to
predecessor, son.

PHILIPPE IV (the Handsome), born 1268, came to throne 1285, married Jeanne de Navarre, died 1314: relationship to predecessor, son.

LOUIS X (the Battler), born 1289, came to throne 1314, married Marguerite de Bourgogne, died 1316: relationship to predecessor, son.

JEAN I (posthumous), born 1316, came to throne 1316, died 1316: relationship to predecessor, son.

PHILIPPE V (the Tall), born 1294, came to throne 1316, married Jeanne de Bourgogne, 1322, relationship to predecessor, uncle.

CHARLES IV (the Handsome), born 1294, came to throne 1322, married Blanche de Bourgogne (i) and Marie de Luxembourg (ii), died 1328: relationship to predecessor, brother.

The Valois Dynasty

PHILIPPE VI (Philippe de Valois), born 1293, came to throne 1328, married Jeanne de Bourgogne, died 1350: relationship to predecessor, remote (nephew of Philippe IV).

JEAN II (the Courageous), born 1319, came to throne 1350, married Bonne de Luxembourg, died 1364: relationship to predecessor, son.

CHARLES V (the Wise), born 1337, came to throne 1364, married Jeanne de Bourbon, died 1380, relationship to predecessor, son.

CHARLES VI (the Mad, or the Well-beloved), born 1368, came to throne 1380, married Isabeau of Bavaria, died 1422: relationship to predecessor, son.

CHARLES VII (the King of Bourges), born 1403, came to throne 1422, married Marie d'Anjou, died 1461: relationship to predecessor, son.

LOUIS XI, born 1423, came to throne 1461, married Charlotte de Savoie, died 1483: relationship to predecessor, son.

CHARLES VIII, born 1470, came to throne 1483, married Anne of Brittany, died 1498: relationship to predecessor, son.

The Valois-Orléans Dynasty

LOUIS XII (the Father of the People), born 1462, came to throne 1498, married Jeanne de France (i), Anne of Brittany (ii) and

Mary of England (iii), died 1515: relationship to predecessor, remote, descended from 1st son of Louis d'Orléans, brother of Charles VI.

The Orléans-Angoulème Dynasty

FRANCOIS I, born 1494, came to throne 1515, married Claude de France, died 1547: relationship to predecessor, remote, descended from 3rd son of Charles d'Orléans, brother of Charles VI.

HENRI II, born 1519, came to throne 1547, married Catherine de Médicis, died 1559: relationship to predecessor, son.

FRANCOIS II, born 1544, came to throne 1559, married Mary Queen of Scots, died 1560: relationship to predecessor, son.

CHARLES IX, born 1550, came to throne 1560, married Elizabeth of Austria, died 1574: relationship to predecessor, brother.

HENRI III, born 1551, came to throne 1574, married Louise de Vaudement, died 1589, relationship to predecessor, brother.

The Bourbon Dynasty

HENRI IV (Henry of Navarre), born 1553, came to throne 1589, married Marguerite de Valois (i) and Marie de Médicis (ii), died 1610: relationship to predecessor, remote, descended from the 6th son of Louis IX.

LOUIS XIII, born 1601, came to throne 1619, married Anne of Austria, died 1643, relationship to predecessor, son.

LOUIS XIV (the Sun King), born 1638, came to throne 1643, married the Infanta Maria Teresa, died 1715, relationship to predecessor, son.

LOUIS XV, born 1710, came to throne 1715, married Marie Leczinska, died 1774, relationship to predecessor, great grandson

LOUIS XVI, born 1754, came to throne 1774, married Marie Antoinette of Austria, died 1793: relationship to predecessor, grandson.

Republic and Empire until 1815

LOUIS XVIII, born 1755, came to throne 1815, married Marie-Joséphine de Savoie, died 1824: relationship to predecessor, brother.

CHARLES IX, born 1757, came to throne 1824, married
Marie-Thérèse de Savoie, died 1836: relationship to predecessor,
brother.

The Bourbon-Orléans Dynasty

LOUIS-PHILIPPE, born 1773, came to throne 1830, married
Maria Amelia of The Two Sicilies, died 1850: relationship to
predecessor, remote, descended from Philippe d'Orléans,
brother of Louis XIV.

Index

A typical entry for a place-name reads:

Donges–44 (63–15–4) (Map 1) 38, 39, 55

The first figure (44) refers to the *département* in which Donges is situated. The French have now stopped using the names of *départements* in addresses, but give instead its corresponding number. It is certainly a great saving of time and space to write *Donges–44* rather than the old-fashioned *Donges (Loire–Atlantique)*.

Letters to France should now always carry the number and not the name of the *département*. An alphabetical list of *départements* with their numbers follows.

The next set of numbers (63–15–4) is a concise reference to the Michelin 1:200,000 motoring map on which Donges is to be found. These maps, which may be widely bought in France and abroad, are standard for motorists. Map 63 is entitled Vannes–Angers. The figure 15 refers to the numbered fold of map 63. There are 10 upper and 10 lower folds on all these maps, numbered from 1 to 20.

The third figure of (63–15–4) refers to one of the 20 compartments on a home-made grid which divides each fold of a Michelin map into 4 oblongs wide by 5 oblongs down. The grid is marked on a sheet of map talc or other firm transparent plastic material with a permanent-ink felt pen. The grid is a very great time saver when looking for individual châteaux or hamlets. An illustration with dimensions marked follows.

The next reference (Map 1) explains on which of the book's own maps Donges is to be found. It is not possible to get on to these maps all the place-names mentioned in the written text of the book; the maps would be quite unreadable if this were done. If the Michelin map reference is not followed by a map number, the place is not on

z

any of the book's maps. On the other hand, some places useful for route-finding are marked on a book map, even though they are not named in the text: for these, obviously, no page number can be indicated.

The final figures (38, 39, 55) are the numbers of the pages on which Donges figures.

French place-names are subject to variations in spelling and you may well find variations in spelling between the Michelin map and this book. On the whole I have preferred the spelling adopted by the *Annuaire Officiel des Syndicats d'Initiative* where the two sources are not in agreement, as it can be expected that the *Annuaire* will give the locally preferred spelling.

Eight of these Michelin maps cover the course of the Loire: 63, 64, 65, 67, 68, 69, 73, 76.

Postal address numbers and car registration numbers of French *départements*

Ain	01	Ille-et-Vilaine	35
Aisne	02	Indre	36
Allier	03	Indre-et-Loire	37
Alpes (Basses-)	04	Isère	38
Alpes (Hautes-)	05	Jura	39
Alpes-Maritimes	06	Landes	40
Ardèche	07	Loir-et-Cher	41
Ardennes	08	Loire	42
Ariège	09	Loire (Haute-)	43
Aube	10	Loire-Atlantique	44
Aude	11	Loiret	45
Aveyron	12	Lot	46
Bouches-du-Rhône	13	Lot-et-Garonne	47
Calvados	14	Lozère	48
Cantal	15	Maine-et-Loire	49
Charente	16	Manche	50
Charente-Maritime	17	Marne	51
Cher	18	Marne (Haute-)	52
Corrèze	19	Mayenne	53
Corse	20	Meurthe-et-Moselle	54
Côtes-d'Or	21	Meuse	55
Côtes-du-Nord	22	Morbihan	56
Creuse	23	Moselle	57
Dordogne	24	Nièvre	58
Doubs	25	Nord	59
Drôme	26	Oise	60
Eure	27	Orne	61
Eure-et-Loir	28	Pas-de-Calais	62
Finistère	29	Puy-de-Dôme	63
Gard	30	Pyrénées (Basses-)	64
Garonne (Haute-)	31	Pyrénées (Hautes-)	65
Gers	32	Pyrénées-Orientales	66
Gironde	33	Rhin (Bas-)	67
Hérault	34	Rhin (Haut-)	68

Grid to fit the numbered fold of a Michelin
1 : 200,000 motoring map. Scale = 3 miles per inch approximately.

Index

9/70